STRINDBERG

AND THE HISTORICAL DRAMA

By

Walter Johnson

SEATTLE : 1963

University of Washington Press

This book is published with the assistance of grants from the
Ford Foundation and the Agnes H. Anderson Fund, University of
Washington.

Preface

STRINDBERG's place as one of the major figures in world literature is secure even though it depends primarily on only some of his dramas and autobiographical volumes. His reputation as a dramatist rests, internationally, on such so-called naturalistic plays as *The Father, Lady Julie, Creditors, The Stronger,* and *The Bond;* the transitional companion plays, *The Dance of Death,* I and II; and such expressionistic plays as *To Damascus, A Dream Play, The Ghost Sonata,* and, possibly, *The Great Highway.* In English-speaking countries there seems to be a general impression that Strindberg wrote other plays, historical and nonhistorical. There seems, moreover, to be some idea among students of the drama that the "strange" and "bedevilled viking" wrote a great many other works, the autobiographical elements of which have particularly fascinated psychologists and psychiatrists. The facts are, of course, that he wrote some seventy plays, many of which are among the best in world drama, and that he was also a major poet and an exceedingly important writer of prose fiction as well as a contributor to many another field.

In an English-speaking society in which those interested in theater and in dramatic literature frequently lament a dearth of good plays, it is strange that one of Strindberg's major contributions to drama and the theater has been almost wholly neglected and disregarded. Approximately one of every three of his plays is a historical drama, and at least a dozen of them merit serious consideration by anyone who wants a fairly thorough knowledge of modern drama. At least seven of them—*Master Olof, The Saga of the Folkungs, Gustav Vasa, Erik XIV, Queen Christina, Charles XII,* and *Gustav III*—have stood the crucial test of frequent production in Sweden, a country equal to any other of our century in interest in the theater, in theatrical standards, in the refinement of dramatic taste of many patrons of the theater, and in severity of criticism.

Even in Sweden much remains to be done with the historical dramas. Aside from *Master Olof,* none of the historical plays has been exposed to the close scholarly scrutiny that major literary works deserve, and most of what has been done by Swedish scholars on Strindberg's other works has resulted in remarkably thorough scholarly volumes that emphasize such matters as the autobiographical elements, influences, and deviations from accuracy. Professor Martin Lamm's impressive two-volume *Strindbergs dramer* (1924-26) has apparently set the pattern for later research. There has been amazingly little concentrated attention given to the historical plays, for example, as theater and as literature.

That Lamm and others have been highly interested in Strindberg's works as reflections of Strindberg's personality and of his thinking and feeling at the time he composed any and every one of his works is understandable. The temptation to consider the characters in the historical dramas as revelations of Strindberg himself, and the ideational content of each of the plays as expressions of his own ideas and prejudices, is almost overwhelming. Strindberg admitted, in *Open Letters to the Intimate Theater (Öppna brev till Intima teatern),* that he made his major characters live by taking blood and nerves out of his own life. In doing so, Strindberg believed that he was doing what every writer of serious historical drama must do and in fact what every artist and every gifted historian does. The extent to which Strindberg did so was at least on occasion undoubtedly greater than that to which most others go. Important as the whole question of the autobiographical elements in the plays is to the Strindberg scholar, and fascinating as its thorough treatment would be for general readers, it seems to me that Strindberg's historical dramas will have to be judged as plays, that is, as literature and theater.

In this volume, I have tried at least by way of introduction to clarify one of the most important segments of Strindberg's fantastically great literary contributions by examining his intentions and the results of his creative efforts in the area of the historical drama. The wealth of source materials, published and unpublished, has made it necessary to consider here only in passing such fascinating aspects of the subject as the plays as revelations of his personality and ideas, the sources of his historical information, the extent to which he learned from predecessors and contemporaries, the critical reception of the plays in Sweden and abroad, and the stage histories of the plays. Major studies of these aspects of the subject are needed, as there is at present no thoroughly complete or reliable treatment of any of them. In the pursuit of my study I have gathered so much material about these matters that if I had used it with even a little less discretion this volume would have expanded into several.

Take, for example, the stage history of the major plays. In spite of the excellent collection of clippings and other sources of information at the Royal Library and at other Swedish libraries and institutions, only painstaking and extended search of records throughout the country would give one a fairly complete account. Or take Strindberg's sources for historical detail. Although he freely admits that the semipopular *Berättelser ur svenska historien (Stories from Swedish History)*, by Anders Fryxell, and *Berättelser ur svenska historien*, by C. Georg Starbäck and P. O. Bäckström, were his major sources (and that admission can easily be established as a fact), they were by no means his only sources. Not only was Strindberg a member of the staff of the Royal Library for several years, but he was an insatiable reader of historical material over the years. The thorough scholarly study of his use of historical sources will be a Herculean task.

The early post-Inferno reception of Strindberg's historical dramas in Sweden is traceable, I suspect, to several factors, at least two of which still have significance in his homeland. The ultimately less important one was Strindberg's faculty for being irritated by and irritating others; as so many of his contemporaries have testified, he could be an extremely charming and delightful human being, but he could also be extremely difficult. Far more important than Strindberg's personality, it seems to me, was the failure of Strindberg's contemporaries and even of a goodly number of people since then to distinguish carefully between scholarly history and the historical drama. The latter is literature, as Strindberg knew and insisted; his historical plays were conceived and composed as works of art, not as substitutes for history with its necessarily strict scholarly standards of objectivity and accuracy. Strindberg was an artist and an intellectual very much interested in the history of his people and of the world, but he was not particularly inclined to painstaking search through every available source and to scrupulously objective judgment of each. He believed, of course, that his powers of insight were such that on occasion he could achieve an understanding of the past and of the historic dead that was distinctly superior to what a professional historian with his scientifically scholarly approach could achieve.

Swedish historians may still be disturbed by Strindberg's anachronisms, his neglect of some acceptable scholarly sources, and his intense personal and even prejudiced engagement with the persons he was re-creating and the issues with which they were involved or with which Strindberg felt they must have been involved. But the vast majority of Swedish patrons of the theater and of the general Swedish public naturally enough consists of men and women who are not professional historians but who at best have a broad but still largely general knowledge of and interest in Swedish history. It is for such people and for non-Swedes that the historical dramas have served and can serve to illuminate Swedish history through one artist's insight into the past and his gift for making it come alive. American or British readers can judge to some degree Strindberg's insight into the great figures of the Swedish past by comparing what Strindberg has to say about any one or all of them with what Dr. Ingvar Andersson, for example, has to say in *A History of Sweden*.

Swedish readers may be dismayed by Strindberg's use of family names for characters who lived at a time when very few family names existed. (Swedish aristocrats, with such rare exceptions as Sten Sture and Erik Puke, did not have surnames until the late sixteenth century. Thus, Gustav Vasa was known as Gustav Eriksson, not Vasa, and the "Eriksson" was a pure patronymic. Most commoners did not have family names until the eighteenth and more usually the nineteenth century.) For the sake of easing for foreign readers identification of many of the individual characters, it has seemed to me justifiable to maintain Strindberg's practice and to extend it to a fairly logical point of consistency. Thus, the wife of Master Olof (Olaus Petri) becomes Kristina Petri, and their son, Reginald Petri, even though Petri was not a family name. Similarly, the name Gustav Vasa has distinct meaning for many non-Swedes, while Gustav Eriksson would be confusing, if not meaningless.

Strindberg's *Öppna brev till Intima teatern (Open Letters to the Intimate Theater)* has been decidedly useful in determining his intentions in writing the major plays, even though the letters were written later than were many of the plays, during the period (1907-10) when his and August Falck's Intimate Theater added a fascinating and vital element to theater life in Stockholm. Comparison of the many manuscripts and other notes on the plays, prepared before or during their composition and available in the Royal Library, with what he says in the letters about his intentions in each of the plays leads to the conclusion that his statements in the open letters agree essentially with what his notes clearly indicate. See, for example, the chapter on *The Saga of the Folkungs*.

I am deeply grateful to the institutions and individuals who have helped make it possible for me to pursue research in such an interesting and rewarding area. A fellowship grant from the Guggenheim Foundation for 1957-58 and a sabbatical for most of that year permitted me to go to Sweden to examine unpublished source materials. There librarians at several institutions graciously gave me the fullest cooperation. Two men, Dr. Nils Afzelius and Dr. Bengt Dahlbäck, of the manuscript division at the Royal Library, went far beyond the bounds of professional courtesy in making my stay in Stockholm rewarding and delightful; they not only provided me with quarters within the division itself in which to do my research but searched out and put at my disposal manuscripts, letters and other documents, collections (among them, the Nylin), and books. Mr. Rudolf Simonis, then curator of the Bonnier Archives, was one of those who made Strindberg letters available. Two colleagues, Dr. Karl-Ivar Hildeman of the University of Stockholm and Professor Assar Janzén of the University of California, have read the manuscript critically. Very special appreciation goes to my wife, Ruth Ingeborg.

Five volumes containing my translations of what I consider Strindberg's greatest historical dramas have appeared under the imprint either of both the American-Scandinavian Foundation and the University of Washington Press or of the press alone. Readers who would like to have more complete information about the historical background of each of these plays than I could include in this book may find the introduction to and notes on each play useful. The volumes are all listed in Notes.

WALTER JOHNSON

Seattle, 1961

Contents

Strindberg and the Historical Drama

1

Strindberg's Interest in History

After Fagervik I understood that there had to be a pause in my writing, and as a means of killing time I read right through world history. This strange story, which has always seemed like a picaresque novel, revealed itself as a creation of a Conscious Will, and I discovered logic in its antinomies, a result of its conflicting components. Thus I found at the very beginning the world spirit revealed itself concurrently in several places on the earth without these places having any contact with each other. For example: at the very time the Mosaic Law [was handed down] on Sinai (1300 B.C.) India got Rigveda, Greece Orpheus . . . and China Schi-King. This is not chance! . . . My investigations were continued synchronically and the "Conscious Will" in history was proved.[1]

At no time in his years as a writer did history fail to interest August Strindberg. The innumerable statements in his letters and in his other works suggest that his reading in history was extensive and at times intensive even though it rarely approached scholarly research. The literary results of his reading are by no means limited to the historical dramas considered in this volume; they include as well, aside from essays and newspaper articles, volumes such as *Gamla Stockholm* (*Old Stockholm*, in collaboration with Claes Lundin), 1880-82; *Det nya riket* (*The New Kingdom*), 1882; *Svenska öden och äventyr* (*Swedish Destinies and Adventures*), 1882-92; *Historiska miniatyrer*

3

(Historical Miniatures), 1905; and *Hövdingaminnen (In Memory of Chieftains)*, 1906. Remarkable achievements in themselves, they range all the way from fascinating though not, in detail, always accurate cultural histories of his people and of his native city to highly illuminating studies of episodes out of the Swedish past.

In all these works, including the historical dramas, there is direct testimony as to the nature of his interest in history. There was, as he says in his letter to Emil Schering, a fascination in history that was like that in a picaresque novel: human history was not pretty, and the behavior down through the ages of human beings, individually and in the group, cast light on the nature of man for Strindberg, who was always intensely interested in himself and his fellows, past and present.

As important as his interest in human nature was Strindberg's concern with the nature of the world and of the force that might have set it and man going. For Strindberg, the world was chaotic and complex just as man himself was chaotic and complex. Throughout his life he searched for some meaning in life itself; for him, history seemed likely at least to offer clues to the whole set of enigmas men label God, man, and the universe.

Since Strindberg has provided ample documentation for his interest in history and for his speculations about its meaning, future scholars will find rewarding subjects for research in the development of Strindberg's thinking about the significance of history and in the theory he evolved. There is, however, one relatively short essay which anyone who studies these matters will have to accept as the central core of the results of his thinking—*Världshistoriens mystik (The Mysticism of World History)*, published in *Svenska Dagbladet* of Stockholm in 1903 and included in Volume LIV (pp. 330-401) of Landquist's edition of Strindberg's collected works.[2]

Strindberg himself modestly disclaims any notion on his part that the essay is a complete and finished presentation of his philosophy of history: "These articles which now are in print are the plan for a book, put together in haste so that the general unifying element and the broad views should not be lost in the study of details. I have included many errors, of course, but they will eventually be removed" (p. 401). Strindberg never completed such a book, and the scholar who will write a sound monograph on Strindberg's interest in and conclusions about history will have to do painstaking and extensive research in Strindberg's whole literary production.[3]

The essay is highly important in that it states clearly what Strindberg's broad conclusions were. That is particularly helpful because those conclusions were essentially applicable throughout the post-Inferno years when he was writing most of the historical plays about great figures from the Swedish past. The conclusions in the essay also reveal plainly why he wrote the series of plays about great figures from the non-Swedish past. In the early years devoted to *Master Olof,* he accepted the key implications of the Christian doctrines about God, man, and the universe.

In his examination of world history, Strindberg found that there were periods when world-shaking events occurred here and there throughout the world, parallel and apparently not connected with each other but roughly similar in nature and in effects. He cites examples for what he considers the times of greatest change, running all the way from the exodus of the Hebrews from Egypt (which he relates to events in Greece, India, and China) up to his own day. For present purposes, the details are relatively unimportant; the conclusions are not. Note, for example:

It would seem as if the whole then civilized world had at the same time awakened to a consciousness of humanity's great common goals and duties, or as if the world soul had forced its way simultaneously into the consciousness of the masses, revealed itself and transformed itself according to each people's ability to grasp and express. How this happened we do not know, but thinking men have tried to explain it in two different ways. Some believe that the will and the movement are within men and deposited in human souls from the beginning (immanence) and others that the human soul is influenced from without and created as an instrument for a will outside ourselves (transcendence), which from above guides the fates of peoples and individuals to a conscious goal which only the guide knows completely. To this latter point of view I would subscribe because in my excursions through world history I have found evidence to support it [p. 341].

Stated, referred to, and applied in several other places by Strindberg throughout the highly productive years after his Inferno period (1894-97), this idea is Strindberg's lasting statement of faith in a deity who not only was the creator but is the guide.

It is, furthermore, Strindberg's final conclusion that, irrational and beyond human understanding though it may seem, there is a definite plan: "If we, for example, consider the coming and entrance of Christianity into western culture, this world historic event reveals itself as a planned action or a well-calculated expedition which was planned in advance and executed in keeping with all the rules of tactics and strategy" (p. 341). Or, "Why, it's like a colossal chess game in which a single player, who moves both black and white, is completely impartial, takes when he should take, makes plans for both camps, is with himself and against himself, thinks through everything in advance and has only one goal: to maintain balance and justice, and to end the game with a draw!" (p. 353).

Nor does the game seem pointless. There has, Strindberg concludes, been a gradual evolution toward monotheism. The gods created by human imagination and reason have served as tremendous accumulators, out of which nations have secured strength, and have supplied humanity with civilizing ideas. According to Strindberg, the central idea of Christianity—atonement—is not a new idea but an old idea more fully developed. The deities produced by human minds have in the thinking of men become personal beings and have been so treated; these have in turn become the objects of human doubt, been rejected, and been replaced. Difficult as Strindberg found it to interpret the events in history, he nevertheless felt that a development had been and was taking place toward monotheism and human enlightenment.

There are other closely related ideas in the essay. Strindberg felt that historical evidence indicated that both nations and great men have definite roles assigned to them—in the chess game. Having discussed the roughly concurrent appearance of several great men in the late middle ages, and having pointed out what Columbus had achieved in discovering America, Strindberg adds:

Columbus died without knowing what he had done; another illustration of how human beings do not know what they are doing when they are sent with sealed orders on the missions of the Conscious Will. . . . The new land, a new world, which had been in reserve for future needs, did not dream of its purpose, which in our times has demonstrated its real nature: to gather and mix all nations, to tolerate all religions and all languages within one state, all kinds of customs and manners, where all men can recall the apostle's words: "Ye are dearly bought; be ye slaves of no one!" [pp. 360-61].

Although what he has to say about Martin Luther in the essay is of particular importance to the understanding of *The Nightingale of Wittenberg* (1903), the most impressive play in the series centering in non-Swedish world history, Strindberg's idea of the role great men have to play in history can be further clarified by these quotations:

It was a doctor of theology in Wittenberg who wanted to reform the faith, and who died believing he actually had done so, who became the cause of the fall of Roman Power, spiritual and worldly—that was Luther's assignment. . . . A man of Providence, a man in the ranks who goes blindly ahead without knowing the commander's intentions, a great instrument, a symbol of contradiction and a rock of irritation, a human being filled with pride and humility, with sound ideas and obscure purposes—that was Luther [pp. 363, 365].

Just as individual men have their roles to play, so do nations, including Sweden, for example.

History has much to teach men, Strindberg believed:

The study of ancient history should teach us, first, a certain regard for the future, when we see how it marches on toward a destined goal; and then tolerance, when we have seen how many mansions there are in the vineyards of the Lord, how the one child is not rejected for the other, or what amounts to the same thing, how just it is when no nation, no religion can be said to have the favor of the great teacher [p. 385].

A summarizing paragraph is exceedingly important to an understanding of the historical plays:

People have undoubtedly for a long time thought they could detect laws governing the march of history resembling those which control nature. In history men have detected traces of the physical law of balance (European balance), the power of attraction (larger nations' inclination to assimilate smaller ones), elective affinity, substitution and so on. And from the organic world men have borrowed the concepts of the splitting of cells, segmentation, struggle and selection and the like. But the march of history shows such a union of freedom and necessity that on the one hand *one has to admit freedom of the human will to a certain degree,* on the other *admit the existence of a necessity, which in keeping with circumstances limits the efforts of the individual and brings about the synthesis.* The great synthesist who unites antitheses, resolves incompatibles, maintains the balance, is no human being and can be no one but the invisible lawgiver, who in freedom changes the laws according to changed conditions: the creator, the solver, and the preserver he may then be called—whatever you like [p. 398].

Most important for present purposes is Strindberg's conclusion that there is a degree of freedom of the human will. What he has to say about that in the essay is decidedly reminiscent of what he had said long before in *Creditors (Fordringsägare,* 1888), for example. The margin of individual responsibility and the measure of freedom of the individual permit Strindberg to present his figures from the past as beings far removed from mere puppets.

Any introductory discussion should not disregard Strindberg's other major conclusions about history. All of them are either touched upon or implied in the essay, and all of them are sufficiently important to an understanding of the historical plays to be restated here. There are such matters as his belief that events and situations recur again and again, with modifications to be sure *(allt går igen,* everything repeats itself); his conviction that history is a series of alternating disintegration and integration (extreme nationalism alternating with internationalism, for example); his belief that a process of unification both "racially" and culturally is advancing; and his belief that truth *is* relative.

It is highly significant that the man who gave his country the most impressive plays about its past should also have been one of its severest critics. Anyone who reads the many essays, articles, dramas, and other works in which Sweden or Swedes are the subject might easily get the impression that Strindberg did not love his country or his people. But that is simply not true. While Strindberg was no chauvinist, he was a loyal Swede. His objection to what he considered weaknesses in the Sweden of his own time undoubtedly stemmed from his conviction that it was his duty to help get rid of such weaknesses even though his criticism might be considered unpatriotic by ultranationalists. In the same way his interpretation of great Swedes of the past and the periods in which they lived distressed his fellow countrymen who insisted on preserving the traditional views of great Swedes as on the whole flawless heroes and the past as one of nearly unalloyed greatness.

But Strindberg had the conviction that Sweden, like any other country, fitted into the western world as an integral part of that world, that it had received much of its culture from abroad, that it had played its role internationally on occasion (during the Thirty Years' War, for example) and had made its contributions to world culture (through such men as Linné and Berzelius), and that under no circumstances could Sweden be considered socially, politically, or religiously radically different in any basic sense from other European countries. Yet Sweden and its history fascinated him from his childhood to his death. The land itself was home for Strindberg, and his works contain innumerable bits of evidence of his deep love for and appreciation of it. Its history was as interesting to him as any picaresque novel could be, but he did not think of it as a source for chauvinistic satisfactions. Its people had his sympathetic understanding, and its leaders in the past were—as the objects of his searching scrutiny—people as human as himself and therefore as complex and dynamic and as little heroic in the traditional sense as he.

2

Plans and Fulfillment

THE historical plays break into four groups: (1) the three early apprenticeship dramas, *Hermione, I Rom (In Rome),* and *Den fredlöse (The Outlaw);* (2) the plays written in the early 1880's, at least partly to provide Siri von Essen with rewarding roles, *Gillets hemlighet (The Secret of the Guild,* 1880) and *Herr Bengts hustru (Lord Bengt's Wife,* 1882); (3) the twelve plays about leading figures of the Swedish past; and (4) the four plays having to do with world history, *The Nightingale of Wittenberg, Through Wilderness to Promised Land, Hellas,* and *The Lamb and the Wild Beast*—all of them from 1903. The four groups differ from each other very much both in purpose and quality, although, as we shall see, they have much in common.

Scattered throughout Strindberg's almost overwhelming correspondence and literary production and the unpublished materials preserved at the Royal Library in Stockholm are many details about his plans for writing historical plays, a few of which, like *Blotsven* and an early *Erik XIV,* were actually written but then destroyed, and many of which remained ideas or outlines or fragments. A study of all the available material can lead to certain conclusions about each of the four groups of plays that were published and are parts of the Strindberg canon.

Hermione, In Rome, and *The Outlaw* were obviously attempts on Strindberg's part to demonstrate to himself and to others that he could compose historical or semihistorical plays of the three types then popular in Sweden—the rhetorical tragedy, the historical proverb, and the historical drama about a theme from early or Viking Scandinavian history. The plays are in no sense units of a historical cycle. *Hermione* concerns the Greece of the fourth century B.C.; *In Rome* deals with an episode in the life of the nineteenth-century Icelandic-Danish sculptor Thorwaldsen; and *The Outlaw* has a late Viking setting in Iceland. It is significant, however, that the best of the three plays, *The Outlaw,* really concerns Swedes and that many of its most moving passages concern Sweden.

The Secret of the Guild and *Lord Bengt's Wife* have in common a medieval Swedish setting, reflect contemporary interest in the discussion of problems, and were deliberately composed, with what was a rare indulgence for Strindberg, to provide roles for a specific actress.

But the twelve plays about the great figures of Sweden's history represent a far greater certainty of purpose, a far clearer plan, and a far greater achievement. If one considers, as Strindberg did, the eleven plays from *The Saga of the Folkungs* (1899) to *Earl Birger of Bjälbo* (1908) as logical parts of a cycle begun in the prose *Master Olof* (1872) and continued in its various versions (especially the verse-prose *Master Olof* of 1876 and *The Epilogue* of 1877), it will be clear that Strindberg planned a cycle of plays treating Swedish history from St. Erik (king, *ca.* 1150-60) to Gustav IV Adolf (king, 1792-1809). That Strindberg varied his plans for this cycle from time to time is clear from Strindberg's manuscript and other notes at the Royal Library and from the available letters that concern the historical plays.

Interesting as the various notes, outlines, and fragments are, they are far less significant to this study than what Strindberg actually completed. A consideration of the following table of the twelve plays, arranged according to historical time rather than to the chronological time of composition, will indicate how far Strindberg succeeded in writing a cycle of plays concerning the history of Sweden from the twelfth to the nineteenth century:

PLAY	ENGLISH TITLE	TIME	WRITTEN
1. *Bjälbo-jarlen*	*Earl Birger of Bjälbo*	late 1200's	1908
	Earl Birger, regent, 1250-66		
	Valdemar I, king, 1250-75		
	Magnus Barnlock, king, 1275-90		
	Birger Magnusson, king, 1290-1318 (Torgils Knutsson, regent, 1290-98)		
2. *Folkungasagan*	*The Saga of the Folkungs*	middle 1300's	1899
	Magnus Eriksson, king, 1319-64		
	Erik XII, co-king, 1357-59		
	Håkon, king, 1362-71		
	Albrekt of Mecklenburg, king, 1364-89		
3. *Engelbrekt*	*Engelbrekt*	1430's	1901
	Margaret, regent, 1389-1412		
	Erik XIII of Pomerania, king, 1396-1439		
	Engelbrekt, folk leader, 1435-36		
4. *Siste riddaren*	*The Last of the Knights*	1512-20	1908
	Karl Knutsson Bonde, regent, 1436-40; king, 1448-57, 1464-65, 1467-70		
	Christopher, king, 1440-48		
	Christian I, king, 1457-64		
	Sten Sture the Elder, regent, 1470-97; 1501-3		
	Hans, king, 1497-1501		
	Svante Sture, regent, 1504-12		
	Sten Sture the Younger, regent, 1512-20		
	Christian II, king, 1520-21		

PLAY	ENGLISH TITLE	TIME	WRITTEN
5. *Riksföreståndaren*	*The Regent*	early 1520's	1908
	Gustav Vasa, regent, 1521-23		
	king, 1523-60		
6. *Mäster Olof*	*Master Olof*	1520's-40's	1872
	The Lutheran Reformation		
7. *Gustav Vasa*	*Gustav Vasa*	1540's	1899
8. *Erik XIV*	*Erik XIV*	1560's	1899
	Erik, king, 1560-68		
	John III, king, 1568-92		
	Sigismund, king, 1592-99		
	Charles IX, regent, 1599-1604		
	king, 1604-11		
9. *Gustav Adolf*	*Gustav Adolf*	1630-32	1900
	Gustav II Adolf, king, 1611-32		
10. *Kristina*	*Queen Christina*	1654	1901
	Christina, queen, 1632-54		
	Charles X Gustav, king, 1654-60		
	Charles XI, king, 1660-97		
11. *Karl XII*	*Charles XII*	1715-18	1901
	Charles XII, king, 1697-1718		
	Ulrika Eleonora, reigning queen,		
	1718-20		
	Fredrik I, king, 1720-51		
12. *Gustav III*	*Gustav III*	1789	1902
	Adolf Fredrik, king, 1751-71		
	Gustav III, king, 1771-92		
	Gustav IV Adolf, king, 1792-1809		
	Charles XIII, king, 1809-18		

Strindberg succeeded remarkably well in putting the history of his country into dramatic form far more fully and, aside from Shakespeare, far more effectively than any other playwright anywhere.

A second examination of the table can illustrate another fact. *The Saga of the Folkungs,* for example, deals primarily with King Magnus Eriksson (1319-64), but anyone who knows the play will readily see that Strindberg by means of numerous allusions to the past and by means of King Magnus' relation of the history of his race in the last act illuminates far more than the reign of one king. The play gives an amazingly broad coverage of the whole of the Folkung period from before Birger became earl in the 1240's until Albrekt of Mecklenburg succeeded in gaining the throne in 1364. *Engelbrekt* does the same for the period between 1364 and the 1430's. Each of the twelve plays ties up naturally and economically with its predecessor and successor in terms of historical background, so that what Strindberg has done by means of these twelve plays is to give Sweden a dramatization of its history from the twelfth century (in *Earl Birger of Bjälbo*) to the late eighteenth century. It is a remarkable achievement.

Consider Shakespeare's histories for a moment. Arranged in terms of historical time, his historical plays about English history—*King John* (1199-1216), *Richard II* (1377-99), *Henry IV* (two parts, 1399-1413), *Henry V* (1413-22), *Henry VI* (three parts, 1422-61), *Richard III* (1483-85), and *Henry VIII* (1509-47)—present remarkable similarities in coverage for an obviously briefer span of time.

The last group of historical plays represents Strindberg's plan to create a cycle about crucial events in world history. The following outline—preserved in note form in the manuscript division in the Royal Library—will indicate what Strindberg had in mind:

THE SAGA OF MAN

THE FIRST TRILOGY

PROLOGUE

I	II	III
Act 1: Egypt.	1: The First Olym-	1: Brutus the Elder.
Act 2: The Argonauts.	piad, 776 B.C.	2: The Roman con-
Act 3: Solmanassar I.	The founding of	quest of Greece
Act 4: India from India	Rome. Hosea.	(Mummius at
to Brahma.	Solmanassar.	Leukopetra; Me-
China, Won		tellus at Chaer-
Ting.	2: The Persian Wars.	onea, 147 B.C.)

Act 5: The Trojan War. 3: Tarquin the Great, 3: Graecherna   [The
     Nebuchadnezzar.   509 B.C.   Gracchi].
     The Phoenicians.   Rome a republic. 4: Marius and Sulla.
     Tyres. Judges in 4: Socrates.   5: Caesar. Actium 31.
       Israel.   5: Alexander. Chaer-   (Octavian-Augustus
                    onea, 338 B.C.   over Anthony)

EPILOGUE

THE SECOND TRILOGY
PROLOGUE

I	II	III
Act 1: Christ.	1: Mohammed—632.	1: Charlemagne. The
Act 2: Nero.	2: Gregory 2. St.*—	Northmen. Ver-
Act 3: The Folk Migra-	604.	dun.
tions.	3:	2: The Crusades.
The decadence of	4:	3: Henry IV. The
Christianity.	5:	Pope.
Act 4: Christian Rome		4: Olga.
and the Rome		5: Constantinople. The
of the West.*		Turks. Granada.
Byzantine.		America.
Act 5: Rome. The Teu-		
tons.		

EPILOGUE

THE THIRD TRILOGY
PROLOGUE

I	II	III
Act 1:	1:	1:
Act 2:	2:	2:
Act 3:	3:	3:
Act 4:	4:	4:
Act 5:	5:	5:

EPILOGUE

* Handwriting obscure.

Incomplete as the outline is, the plan is clear enough. Probably in connection with his rereading of world history, his writing of the essay on the mysticism of world history, and his intense engagement with dramatic composition, Strindberg toyed with the idea of doing for world history what he was already doing effectively for Swedish history. But just as the outline is incomplete, the cycle of plays about world history is unfinished. Of all the plays he may have dreamed of creating for this cycle only one—*The Nightingale of Wittenberg* (1903)—is a fully completed play. Three others—*Through Wilderness to Promised Land, Hellas,* and *The Lamb and the Wild Beast*— are not, as we shall see in a later chapter, plays ready for the conventional stage. But these plays, centering about the periods of Moses, Socrates, and Christ, have their own peculiar interest.

3

Apprenticeship and Experiment

WHEN Strindberg began writing plays in the late 1860's, he had every reason for using the various forms of the contemporary historical drama as his points of departure. The rhetorical historical tragedy, the historical proverb, and the historical drama centered in early Scandinavian history were the accepted and popular forms of native Swedish dramas; playwrights such as August Blanche (1811-68), Johan Jolin (1818-84), Frans Hedberg (1828-1908), and Edvard Bäckström (1841-86) had made their contributions to these types and had won appreciable public approval for their efforts. An intense interest in Shakespeare's plays had fortunately set in, however, after Carl August Hagberg's justly famous translation had appeared in 1847-51. Although most of Shakespeare's best plays were performed on the Swedish stage during Strindberg's boyhood and youth, the chronicle plays and the great tragedies (several of which were nominally historical) had been most favored. The historical plays of Oehlenschläger, Schiller, Ibsen, and Björnson were widely read and on occasion successfully presented. Even the Frenchmen Dumas *fils,* Augier, and Sardou, who became popular in the 1860's, did not neglect the genre. It was, in brief, a time when the historical drama enjoyed popularity both in the study and on the stage.[1]

Sensitive even in his teens to contemporary taste, Strindberg understood well enough that he needed to demonstrate his skill at writing the kind of historical plays then in demand. The results were fivefold: two tragedies, *Erik XIV* and *Blotsven,* both of which he later destroyed because they satisfied neither himself nor his closest friends; *Hermione* (1869), a historical tragedy; *In Rome* (1870), a historical proverb or dramatic situation in one scene; and *The Outlaw* (1871), a one-act historical tragedy with an early Scandinavian theme. None of them is a masterpiece; they are little more than apprenticeship pieces that derive, both in content and form, from the plays that he was reading and the plays that were attracting audiences to the Swedish theater. They deserve attention, however, as they indicate that at a very early age Strindberg understood what others had either done or were doing and could appropriate for his own uses and in his own fashion what he understood.

No one has ever given a more effective definition of the type of tragedy popular in Sweden in the 1860's than the following, written by Strindberg years later in his *Open Letters to the Intimate Theater:*

When anyone in the 1860's and 1870's submitted a full-length play to the Royal Theater, he had to observe the following requirements if he were to get it performed. The play should preferably have five acts, each act [should be] approximately twenty-four sheets long, or, in all, $5 \times 24 = 120$ folio pages. The division into scenes was not appreciated and was considered a weakness. Every act should have a beginning, a middle, and an end. The end of an act should be the place for applause, which was aroused by an oratorical figure, and if the play was in blank verse, the last two lines should rhyme. Within the play were "numbers" for the actor which were called "scenes"; the soliloquy or monologue was permitted and frequently was the high spot or climax; a longer emotional outburst or a speech of condemnation, [and] an exposure were almost necessary; one could even relate something—a dream, an anecdote, an event. But roles were required, rewarding roles for the stars in the theater [p. 9].

How well *Hermione* fits this definition can be suggested by a fairly brief summary of the play, not yet translated into English. Written almost completely in blank verse and ending in a rhymed couplet, *Hermione* deals with the Athenians' struggle to preserve their freedom against Macedonia's King Philip's efforts to gain control over the Greek states in 338 B.C.:

Act I (symposium at Kallimakos' home in Athens): Alkinoos protests against his fellow guests' lack of faith in and respect for the gods, their immoral behavior, their lack of interest in Homer and other older literature, and their preference for the latest songs. For this decadence in Athenian taste and behavior Alkinoos blames the corrupting Macedonian plague; he leaves by way of protest. The Spartan Kallias confirms Alkinoos' charges and asserts that Sparta will not spill one drop of blood to help Athens defend itself against Philip of Macedonia, the barbarian. Kallimakos and others believe Philip is interfering in Hellenic affairs with the welfare of Hellas in mind. Kallimakos then reveals that he is engaged to marry Hermione, daughter of Kriton, priest of Ares—god of war and manly combat. A Macedonian rushes in to seek refuge with Kallimakos: The Athenians have just been stirred up against Macedonians because of Philip's siege of Olynthos, and Kriton has urged the Athenians to be worthy of their ancestors' greatness and Athenian honor and to defend their freedom against the barbarian tyrant or die in the attempt. Kriton comes, explains that the Macedonian has been in Athens to secure the support of Athenians for Philip's proposed conquest of Athens, and insists that the Macedonian be handed over as a hostage. When Kallimakos refuses to hand him over, Kriton accuses Kallimakos of decadence, frivolity, and treason, and says he will never marry Hermione.   . .

Act II (the Agora or Assembly Square in Athens): Intensely aware of the corruption of Athenian youth, Kriton appeals in vain to the demagogue Aischines to sacrifice his selfish interests and to join Demosthenes in arousing the Athenians to defend their freedom. Kriton tells Hermione that Kallimakos is a scoundrel and traitor and is not worthy of her. Demosthenes analyzes Philip's plan to become king of the Greeks and Athens' resulting danger and appeals for war against the barbarian. Aischines then presents a pro-Macedonian youth, who delivers Philip's warning that resistance would be foolish and tries to assure the Athenians that

Athens can have peace on the condition that Philip be elected its ruler. Aischines then appeals for submission to Philip, whom he calls a Greek. When the majority of the people are swayed by Aischines' argument in support of Philip's message, Kriton curses all those who will not fight to defend Athenian liberty. Demosthenes calls for the aid of all Athenian men to avert a decision for submission at the forthcoming assembly on Pnyx.

Act III (Pnyx, the Assembly Place in Athens): Kallimakos tells Hermione that only a small minority support actively the public decision to take up arms against the barbarians and urges her to flee with him. When she refuses and tries to arouse him to loyalty to Athens and to fighting for the defense of its freedom, he leaves her. Kreon, a demagogue and a weaver who resents the power and the prestige of the aristocrats, is proposed by Demosthenes for the command of the defending army. Kriton dedicates the young volunteers to immortality and to Hades. Hermione decides to save Athens by assassinating Philip.

Act IV (at Chaeronea, a city in western Beotia): Approving Hermione's decision after having consulted the priestess of Delphi, Kriton makes her swear that she will kill Philip and promise to signal the Athenians when she has done so. Philip walks nearby with his friend Parmenion; the king reveals that he admires the Greeks and their way of life but would nevertheless conquer them. After talking with Diogenes, Philip—to show that he is not a barbarian—sends Parmenion to the Greeks with another offer of peace. Just as Hermione is about to kill Philip, she is overcome by passionate love for him. She talks with him, gives up her decision to kill him, and inadvertently signals to the Athenians to attack.

Act V (a festival hall in Chaeronea): Kriton, now a prisoner, discovers that Hermione has betrayed her people because of her love for the victorious Philip. Jealous of Hermione, Queen Olympia berates her. In the presence of the traitor Kallimakos, Olympia demands that Hermione be awarded to her as a slave; Philip unwillingly grants her request. Kriton kills Hermione; Kallimakos —at last awakened to the implications of his attitudes and acts— is poisoned; and Kriton commits suicide.

It is a play written, I suspect, in deliberate imitation of the form of the typical rhetorical tragedy then in favor in Sweden. As such it fulfills admirably the requirements listed by Strindberg himself in the passage from *Open Letters to the Intimate Theater* quoted above. It has the required five acts or divisions; acts not divided into scenes; an easily discernible beginning, middle, and end in each act; an appreciable sprinkling of "numbers" or "scenes"; a liberal use of soliloquies and monologues; definite provisions for applause at the end of each act; the oratorical manner and vocabulary; and a couplet at the end of the play.

There are, for example, several soliloquies: Kallimakos' statement at the end of Act I, Kriton's lamentation over the degeneracy of Athenian youth in Act II, Hermione's decision at the end of Act III to save Athens by assassinating King Philip, and her preparation in Act IV to kill him, not to mention shorter ones. There are contrasting orations by Demosthenes, Aischines, and Kreon the demagogue. There are asides. There are emotional episodes which would provide the actor or actress or both (father and daughter, for example) with ample opportunity not only to move the audience but to evoke applause. There are emotional outbursts, speeches of condemnation, speeches of exposure, and the relation of dreams, anecdotes, and events. As an exercise in dramatic composition it is commendable. Even the blank verse—and most of it is in that form—is competent though far from brilliant.

But there is little in it to suggest that the author was within two or three years of composing a play that later generations of critics, students, and theater audiences would consider great drama and great theater. The artificial and traditional diction and form are in startling contrast to the predominantly colloquial prose and naturalness of structure of *Master Olof* (1872).

There are to be sure genuine dramatic merits in *Hermione*. The exposition, the foreshadowing or preparation, the presentation of the issues involved, and the plot structure are carefully handled. The sympathetic reader can even detect on occasion a hint of the Strindbergian powers of characterization. Not all the characters remain statically black or white. Kreon the demagogue becomes an understandable and believable rascal, and the development of Hermione's defection from her plan to save Athens has nice touches. But the model was a strait jacket for Strindberg: it did not set him free.

Who Strindberg's models were can easily be determined. The choice of subject is obviously traceable to a great historical novel, Viktor Rydberg's *The Last of the Athenians* (1859), one of the earliest and most important Swedish novels of ideas.[2] It deals in moving fashion with the struggles between paganism (Hellenism) and Christianity (Hebraism); advocates individual political, religious, and intellectual freedom; and finds the happiest solution in the combination of the best in the two conflicting principles of life. In a very definite sense Rydberg's novel is an attack on barbarism and a defense of that form of western culture which centers in the freedom of the individual and the well-rounded development of all his powers. What Strindberg's Kriton and Hermione are defending is essentially the same ideal.

Although Strindberg undoubtedly learned much from the content of Rydberg's novel, his models in structure and form were such dramatists as Oehlenschläger, Shakespeare, Schiller, Lessing, the Norwegians, and native dramatists then popular on the Swedish stage. Their influence, however, was the sort that is restricted to the crippling imitation of technical devices, on the one hand, and broad similarities of patterns of characterization rather than to slavish copying of individual passages, on the other.

Strindberg's hopes for making a place for himself on the Swedish stage as a dramatist were not realized in the least by means of *Hermione*. So far as I have been able to determine, the play has never been performed. He did have reasons for not feeling absolutely unrewarded, however. He had, of course, gained genuine rewards in the useful exercise of dramatic composition. He submitted the play to the Royal Theater in June, 1870, and, when it was rejected, submitted it in somewhat revised version to the Swedish Academy. Although it did not receive a prize, it did receive honorable mention. Strindberg had written on October 13, 1870, to Frans Hedberg, the dramatist and then director of the Royal Theater, "Hermione is

now in the hands of the eighteen wise men—God protect her! I can
at least expect criticism in any case!" [3] When C. R. L. Manderström,
secretary of the academy, made the results of the competition public
on December 20, 1870, the honorable mention was accompanied by
the verdict, ". . . a study of the world of antiquity, with good single
scenes and a vital grasp of the conditions of the time." [4] It was a
generous comment.

Det sjunkande Hellas (Greece in Decline), which Strindberg discusses in *The Son of a Servant* (Vol. II, chap. iii), is nothing but an
earlier version of *Hermione.* Written in the same verse form as the
latter, *Greece in Decline* was submitted to the Royal Theater and
understandably rejected by the authorities there. In 1960, *Bokgillet*
(the Book Society) of Uppsala published a limited edition based on
Count Birger Mörner's manuscript and edited by Erik Gamby. A
tragedy in three acts, the play tells the same story as *Hermione,* concentrates its major attention on Athenian decadence, and emphasizes
the basic importance of political freedom for a society that is not
only to sustain its cultural greatness but to retain it.

Act I has the Pnyx in Athens as its setting; Act II, the battlefield
at Chaeronea; and Act III, the festival room in Chaeronea the day
after the defeat of the Athenians and the other Greeks. Even this
brief statement should suggest that Strindberg simply expanded his
shorter play into a five-act tragedy that he thought would meet the
contemporary standards for an historical tragedy and most specifically
the preferences of the theater officials in Stockholm. To be sure, he
not only expanded the first version but revised speeches here and
there, reassigned others, and even changed the names of some of
the characters. In the earlier play, for example, Hermione was called
Antigone, and Kriton was called Bakis.

At best one can only say that *Greece in Decline* was a useful exercise but that in it there is very little to indicate that Strindberg had
succeeded in doing more than imitating fairly well the rather dis-

tressing diction and declamatory style of his Swedish predecessors and contemporaries.

In Rome was a much less ambitious project than *Hermione* and a much more rewarding one. Composed as a proverb or one-act comedy of the type then popular, and written in rhymed pentameters, *In Rome* presents an episode in the life of the great Icelandic-Danish sculptor Bertel Thorvaldsen (1770-1844), who from 1797 to 1803 struggled for artistic achievement and recognition in Rome until suddenly his first masterpiece won him fame and orders in 1803.

Strindberg's play centers its attention directly on the artist's duty to his calling as an artist:

> Convinced that his son's studies in Rome are futile, Thorvaldsen's father secures a job for him in the shipyards in Copenhagen and sends him money so he can return. The sculptor's friend Pedersen urges him not to forsake his art. Torn between the common-sense solution offered by his father and his own dedication to his art, Thorvaldsen decides to return to Copenhagen. A French patron of the arts sees the model of Jason, admires it, and leaves without offering Thorvaldsen any help. Soliloquizing about his Jason as the expression of his art, Thorvaldsen tries to muster up courage to crush the model. He explains why he must leave to Marianne, the girl he loves. The landlord prevents his leaving. A policeman is about to take both young men to the judge when the British patron Sir Hope enters, grasps the situation, gives the policeman a few gold coins, sees the model of Jason, is struck with admiration, and orders a marble statue of Jason. Thorvaldsen, Pedersen, and Marianne go out to celebrate. Thorvaldsen has been saved for his art.

It is, as the summary suggests, a dramatic episode, and it is, moreover, as any one who reads Strindberg's letters of the time will guess, a dramatization of the author's own inner conflicts under the camouflage of the lightly historical coloring of an episode from an earlier artist's life. The essence of it is the artist's duty to be faithful to his call to be an artist, a subject then receiving peak attention because of Ibsen's Kierkegaardian *Brand* (1867) and a matter of intense concern to a young man desperately engaged in making up his own mind about his future.

Strindberg wrote a great deal about *In Rome* both in his letters to friends and relatives and in the much later *Son of a Servant* (1886-87). His hopes for the little one-act comedy were evidently high, and his hopes were to be realized—within limits. On September 13, 1870, he attended the *première* of the play at the Royal Theater, suffered the agonies of perceiving weaknesses in his own work, yet humanly enough hoped for favorable reviews and financial rewards.

The play was presented eleven times, including the performance on November 19, 1870, in honor of the centennial of Thorvaldsen's birth. The audiences were not unkind. Strindberg's royalty amounted to 209 *riksdaler* and 66 *öre*. Strindberg was glad to get the money but hoped (in vain) to earn more through performances in other Scandinavian cities. The reviews and notices were not too bad. The one Strindberg quotes in a letter to Johan Oscar Strindberg in November, 1870, may have stung him a little: on November 21, *Dagens Nyheter* had summarized its opinion of *In Rome* as "a likable little thing" *("ett älskligt litet stycke")*.[5] Only the fact that Strindberg wrote it will ever justify detailed examination of it.

But the third play is something else. A student at the University of Uppsala and by then an enthusiast about Old Scandinavian (particularly Old Icelandic) languages and literature, Strindberg tried his hand at composing the third kind of historical play then popular in Sweden: a tragedy centered on an Old Scandinavian theme. The final result was the one-act *The Outlaw,* written primarily in prose:

> Gunlöd, the secretly Christian daughter of the pagan Swedish viking Thorfinn, and her mother, Valgerd, are in Iceland awaiting the arrival of Thorfinn, who plans to become earl *(jarl)* of the country. Valgerd advises Gunlöd to suffer in silence the separation from the Christian Gunnar. Gunnar suddenly arrives, urges Gunlöd to flee with him to Sweden, but leaves as Thorfinn, who

had rejected Gunnar's suit for Gunlöd's hand because Gunnar is a Christian, is about to arrive. A storm arises at sea. Valgerd, who loves her husband even though he has never shown her any affection, tries to help Thorfinn by a signal fire. Orm, "blood" brother of Thorfinn and a skald, enters, and a moment later Thorfinn arrives. All but one of his ships have been destroyed, but Thorfinn, who insists that his wife and his daughter believe in and worship the pagan deities, refuses to thank the gods for his safety and insists that he received help from himself alone. Thorfinn fails to make Gunlöd empty the mead horn in honor of Odin; admitting she is a Christian, Gunlöd pleads for her father's affection and understanding. Thorfinn is disturbed. Orm tries to convince him that he should examine his past and his thinking and should accept what a new time demands. A messenger arrives to tell Thorfinn that the Althing has declared him an outlaw and that his enemies are about to descend on him. Inspired against his will by Orm, Thorfinn considers his past and present, recognizes his human weakness, and calls upon Valgerd and a Christian slave for help. Mortally wounded in combat with his enemies, Thorfinn comes on stage, is reconciled with Gunlöd and Gunnar, whose prospective union he blesses, with Orm, and with Valgerd. He dies, having faced the truth.

For those who know Scandinavian drama as Strindberg did in 1870, even the summary will suggest echoes from Oehlenschläger, Ibsen, and Björnson, not to mention Swedish dramatists. What the primary sources of the material were Strindberg himself stated in a letter to Eugene Fahlstedt in May, 1872: "It will amaze me very much if no one will happen to mention Bjørnson as my model—if someone does, tell him to kiss my . . . and read the Icelandic sagas and he'll find out that we—Bjørnson and I (!) . . . have scooped it out of the same source." [6]

Strindberg undoubtedly meant precisely what he said: his sources for the general background, theme, setting, and story were the sagas. That he knew and learned much from the plays of his fellow Scandinavians about themes from the same general Old Icelandic sources is just as clear. But a comparison of *The Outlaw* and Oehlenschläger's

Håkon Jarl (1805), Ibsen's *The Pretenders* (1863) and *The Vikings in Helgeland* (1858), and Björnson's *Sigurd Slembe* (1862), to take a few that served Strindberg well, will find no clinching evidence of slavish imitation either of individual phrase or speech but rather a striking similarity in mood and manner of speech. Strindberg wrote an essay on Oehlenschläger at Uppsala; his interest in and knowledge of the three other Scandinavians are admitted and documented particularly in his early letters and in *The Son of a Servant*. But *The Outlaw* is not simply an imitation; it is rather a young playwright's attempt at demonstrating that he, too, could write a historical play of the kind that had won recognition for the others.

The exploiting of Old Icelandic themes was, of course, nothing new in Sweden or for that matter elsewhere in Scandinavia. Swedish poets and dramatists had dealt with such themes to such an extent that they were recognized parts of the Swedish cultural tradition. For example, Strindberg wrote to August Dörum in 1871:

Do you know Hansson [scheduled to play Thorfinn at the Royal Theater] . . . take him aside—shake him up—give him a jolt (we respect him anyway)—explain to him what it is to be the last of the vikings—ask him to read Geijer's "The Last Warrior"—but ask him to consider that the author wants to see more than a rotten, stubborn, stiffnecked old man who is crushed by women—say that I want a self-sufficient human being who is forced to acknowledge a supreme being, a Titan, a Prometheus who fights against the gods or a King Fjalar who challenges destiny —well, tell him everything you can think of—ask him to search his memory for a deep sorrow—a really deep one, if he has had the good fortune to have one—ask him to recall it when he says the single word "Gunlöd!"—when she refuses to drink.[7]

The two Swedish references are highly significant; they suggest a set of Strindberg's sources not only for much of the content of his play but also for his concept of the characters in the play. Erik Gustaf Geijer (1783-1847), one of the great romantics, was only one of the many Swedish poets who had found inspiration in the sagas and had popularized a concept of the vikings that glorified both the

Old Scandinavian heroes and their heroic ideals; Strindberg might have mentioned Geijer's "Vikingen" ("The Viking"), "Manhem," and "Den siste skalden" ("The Last Skald") to Dörum as well. The Geijer viking has a youthful zest for doing great deeds, never-failing courage, a manly self-control before fate and changes in fortune, a conviction that compromise is likely to lead to shame, an insistence on being master of his own life, an unwillingness to display affection, and a realistic appraisal of evil. Johan Ludvig Runeberg (1804-77) presented a similar hero in *Kung Fjalar* (*King Fjalar,* 1844); Runeberg's epic deals precisely with the crushing of his hero's arrogant faith in his self-sufficiency. Geijer's and particularly Runeberg's heroes do not grant women the understanding and respect many a heroic viking in the Old Icelandic sagas does.

While *The Outlaw* does deal appreciably with the conflict between Scandinavian paganism and Christianity, Strindberg places his major emphasis on characterization. As the title suggests and he himself insisted, he is primarily concerned with the tragedy of Thorfinn, the outlaw, his "last of the vikings." If one examines every bit of evidence the play has to yield about Strindberg's concept of Thorfinn, one will have to come to the conclusion that Thorfinn, like Geijer's and Runeberg's heroes, is an exceptionally able man of action, living by a harsh heroic ideal, who can say, "I have never known any other god but my own strength, and that god I believe in!" His wife, Valgerd, and his daughter, Gunlöd, are in keeping with the traditional Swedish concept of strong, self-reliant viking women. Orm, the skald and Thorfinn's brother by mutual agreement, is very much like Geijer's skald. Through his relationship with each of these three, Thorfinn is brought to self-examination, admission of the inadequacy of his dependence on himself alone, and, in effect, loss of his arrogance. He dies a humbled man.

A one-act tragedy, *The Outlaw* represents a distinct advance in writing historical dramas, thin though the historical patina may be. The concept of tragedy is the traditional one of the fall of a superior human being through his own arrogance and inner flaws. But his story is told in promising prose with a conciseness of expression and compactness of form that were distinct improvements over *Hermione.*

The Outlaw, however, did not so appreciably break with the conventions of the day that the Royal Theater could refuse it. It was in fact accepted in the spring of 1871 on the condition that it be revised a little. In August the revised form was ready, but Strindberg's own comment, made September 13 in a letter to Frans Hedberg, is revealing:

When I reread *The Outlaw* yesterday I found it unfortunately so unlike what it had been in its original form that it would have been better to have burned it in the same way as its predecessors [*Blotsven*] than to become known by everyone. All the characters have become so miserably sentimental—the icy coldness has disappeared—the Nordic stoicism is gone and the thing has a completely different color—they'll throw all that in my face, I suppose—let them! It's a good thing I'm so busy that I have little time to devote to their—the critics'—teachings—which I look forward to with gratitude, though—since one can't see one's own flaws.[8]

On October 16, 1871, the play was presented for the first time, apparently as one of four one-act plays. Its reception then and during its ten other performances was not enthusiastic. The critics were far from kind, although *Aftonbladet* on December 8, 1871, did admit that "in this play is revealed promising talent." The comment came, however, after King Charles XV had seen the play, summoned young Strindberg to the Royal Palace, and—apparently without clarifying his intentions fully—awarded Strindberg financial support for his studies at the University of Uppsala. (Both the autobiography and the various biographies treat the whole episode in some detail.) Strindberg gained a great deal from writing *The Outlaw,* however. He had made use of prose, the form in which he was to make his greatest contributions, and the prose was far less rhetorical and oratorical than that of his Swedish contemporaries. He had won a measure of self-reliance in dramatic composition. He had at last turned to Swedish characters, and his major historical plays with one possible exception—*The Nightingale of Wittenberg* (1903)— were all to deal with Swedish history, which he knew best and about which he felt most keenly.

The Outlaw was put on again in 1910 in August Falck's and August Strindberg's own Intimate Theater. Performed nine times, the play, first on the same program as *The Face of Death* and then with *The Bond (The Link)*, *The Outlaw* was received well by the audience in Stockholm, according to the newsletter published in *Göteborgs Handels-och Sjöfarts-Tidning* on April 4, 1910. On March 7, Stockholm's *Social-Demokraten* said, among other things, "But in the twenty-year-old Strindberg's concentrated depiction of the struggle of Christianity against heathendom, personified in the arrogant Thorfinn, who finally is broken and unsure, there are sparks of strength and originality, which made one follow the play with a certain excitement, no matter how schematic the characters were." [9] The critics were kind but not enthusiastic.

Hermione, In Rome, and *The Outlaw* were exercises in dramatic composition, and as such they deserve a measure of consideration. Historical only in a very loose way, they do demonstrate that Strindberg could do as well as his Swedish contemporaries in the three fields of the historical drama. They demonstrate very well, too, what was to become Strindberg's practice through the years: to give life to his figures from the past by interpreting them in terms of his own experiences and his own being. The three plays are apprenticeship pieces which glorify idealists who fight for their particular faiths. That was what Strindberg was doing when he wrote these plays.

4

Master Olof: *Achievement and Ordeal*

THE year 1872 is one of the most important dates in the history of Swedish literature. That year saw the completion of *Master Olof*, Strindberg's first great play, which in turn was the first Swedish drama that could gain attention and recognition beyond the Swedish-language barrier, that marked definitely the beginning of another era of greatness in Swedish literature, and that was to give Strindberg ultimately the full measure of confidence in his ability to compose plays that would bear comparison with the great plays in world literature. At the same time it was to be an immediate and continuing source of frustration, the results of which were never to be fully dissipated in his lifetime.

Strindberg has provided ample information about *Master Olof*, its composition, its submission to the theaters, its rejection by the startled directors who had never examined another Swedish play quite like it and who advised Strindberg to revise or rewrite it so as to meet their preferences and requirements, his doing so over a six-year period, his personal agony, and its ultimate success. Least extensive but most reliably informative are the few available letters he wrote while composing the play. The letters following the rejection of the play and the extensive account in his four-volume autobiography *Tjänstekvinnansson* (*The Son of a Servant*, 1886-87), are exceedingly important but are to a degree colored either by his own disappointments or by the effects of time on his memory.

The few references from Strindberg's letters to friends and relatives up to the submission of the manuscript to the theater officials suggest Strindberg's excitement and inner satisfaction when he was writing the play. To Johan Oscar Strindberg, for example, the author wrote in July, 1872: "I'm writing the fourth act of my five-act play, in an absolutely new style in keeping with the times." [1] Only in moments of depression was he ever to change his opinion that the play in colloquial prose was very good indeed and could have served as an officially recognized landmark in Scandinavian literature at the time he wrote it—if it had been performed or published then.

Strindberg's most considered and accurate judgments of his first *Master Olof* are probably those in the 1908-9 brochures included in *Öppna brev till Intima teatern*.[2] He was then far beyond the disappointments of the 1870's; he had written other successful historical plays; and he had become fairly well used to the uncertainties of critics' and directors' reactions.

I shall end with a confession and an admission which I have long since made. Shakespeare's manner of depicting historic persons—even heroes— intimately in *Julius Caesar* became the decisive pattern for my first big historical drama, *Master Olof,* and, with certain reservations, even for those written after 1899. This freedom from "theater" or calculated effect which I took as my guiding principle, was long held against me until Josephson at the Swedish Theater discovered *Master Olof* in 1880. But even as late as 1899 Molander did not understand that my *Erik XIV* was playable. After reading the play, he exclaimed: "Am I to put on this play? Why, it has only two scenes!" Molander was so conditioned to French technique that scene meant effect to him [p. 123].

In another significant passage in the same source Strindberg says:

Still in *Master Olof* (the first version) I tried a compromise [between the traditional technique of the 1870's and his own feeling for a less rhetorical and more realistic technique as applied in *The Outlaw*]: verse was eliminated, prose took its place, and instead of the operalike iambic drama with solos and numbers, I composed [my play] polyphonically, a symphony, in which all the voices were woven in with each other, and in which no one accompanied the soloist [p. 10].

On pages 239 and 240 of the same source he explains that he did not feel it would do to use verse for the aristocrats and prose for the commoners: "Consequently I knocked off the high heels on the aristocrats and raised the level of the lower classes a bit" (p. 240).

The Master Olof that emerged in Strindberg's mind and imagination, as he read extensively and speculated about the man who more than anyone else was responsible for the Lutheran reformation of Sweden, is neither a practical and realistic Swedish Martin Luther in behavior and manner nor a self-reliant idealist. He is instead a decidedly complex young man richly endowed by nature with the intellectual, physical, moral, religious, and social attributes essential for the exploitation of ideas that appeal to him and for their realization within the limits of his foresight. He is a young man capable of being stimulated to doing great things by others, by current ideas, and by his own convictions.

The Master Olof that the authorities at the Royal Theater met in the great prose version of 1872 must have startled them very much indeed. For unlike the major characters in earlier Swedish historical plays Strindberg's Master Olof is no apotheosis of the great historical figure. He is instead a thoroughly believable being of flesh and blood who has not been burdened by the traditional clear-cut insight, the clearness of purpose, the indomitable will to realize it, and the uncompromising forging ahead to a logical, yet idealistic goal. Strindberg's Olof is not a glorified folk hero designed to be the object of veneration and the source of inspiration for fellow Swedes of Strindberg's own and later generations.

He is instead as Strindberg conceived him and presented him a thoroughly human young man whom theater audiences and unprejudiced readers could readily accept as one sharing their own human weaknesses and one who understandably enough does not quite know what he wants to do, what—on occasion—he is doing, and what the ultimate significance of his actions is. Master Olof's limited major idea and purpose—the Lutheran reformation of Sweden—is not his own really; it is Luther's idea taken over by an enthusiastic disciple and merely extended geographically to his own country. Master Olof has not even thought through his purpose; in fact, it is only through the stimulation of others and of circumstances that he carries the idea through to its relative but appreciable realization. He is indeed no paragon, but he is, in a sense that every man and woman must recognize as valid, a complex and dynamic compound of strength and weakness.

Strindberg's problems in putting such a hero into a drama were, as he admitted in various places, considerably eased by his reading of Shakespeare. As significant as any of Strindberg's statements about this particular debt is what he wrote in *Open Letters to the Intimate Theater:* "My purpose was, as it was my teacher Shakespeare's, to depict human beings both in their greatness and their triviality, not to avoid the right word; to let history be the background and to compress historical periods to fit the demands of the theater of our time by avoiding the undramatic form of the chronicle or the narrative" (p. 240). Implicit in this statement are most of the facts about Strindberg's play of 1872 which startled the men at the Royal Theater. Strangely enough, they apparently judged *Master Olof* largely on the bases of the traditional Swedish historical plays and the conventional continental, particularly French, plays they had produced with success. Why they did not judge it partly at least in terms of equally successful Shakespeare plays—in Hagberg's admirable translations—is difficult to understand. For *Master Olof* is, technically, Strindberg's for the most part happy but not slavish adaptation of elements from both kinds of technique.

Master Olof does have five acts and on occasion makes use of the rhetorical, even oratorical, manner of the traditional historical play; on the other hand, it presents the characters as human beings, complex and, with the exception of Gert, dynamic. To a remarkable degree, the language is conversational and colloquial, not formal and oratorical; Strindberg does not shun the right word. Nor is the play a series of tableaux out of history but rather a humanized dramatization of a historical character, as he may have been in the setting of his time. It is no attempt to present a lesson in history through the observation of scholarly accuracy but rather an imaginative recreation of a person and a period. History, as Strindberg says, becomes the background but not a tyrannical master that dooms the drama to nondramatic dullness and ineffectiveness.

Examined in detail for the techniques by means of which Strindberg succeeded in bringing the Lutheran reformer alive, *Master Olof* reveals an almost incredible mastery of dramatic composition only slightly foreshadowed in his earlier plays. The broad structure can perhaps be most conveniently recalled by means of a list of acts and scenes together with brief but pertinent details about them:

Act I (in the cathedral city of Strängnäs; one scene): Young Master Olof, fairly contentedly serving as teacher in the cathedral school, is stimulated by Lars Andersson to undertake the Lutheran reformation in Sweden, refuses to be "bribed" by Catholic Bishop Brask, defies the church, is prepared by the idealist Gert for expanding his thinking, and, without careful consideration and forethought, enters the service of Gustav I as a means of achieving his goal of freeing Sweden from the Church of Rome.

Act II (in Stockholm; two scenes and an interlude).

Scene 1 (a tavern in the wall of the Great Church): Representative Swedish commoners, clerical and lay, together with a Lübecker and a Dane, appear in a richly colorful folk scene, which not only ties in Master Olof and his time with what is happening abroad but sketches clearly what is happening in Master Olof's Sweden—politically, economically, socially, and religiously; and throws light on Master Olof's most dangerous antagonist, King Gustav. Against such a background, Master Olof breaks with the Church of Rome.

Interlude (the sexton, his wife, and the drunken Captain Windrank in the deserted tavern, broadly comic in a Shakespearean way).

Scene 2 (a small room in the Great Church of Stockholm): In spite of the pleas of his devoutly Catholic mother, Master Olof preaches a Lutheran sermon and is stoned. Master Olof becomes engaged to Gert's daughter Kristina in spite of his being a monk.

Act III (in Stockholm; two scenes).

Scene 1 (a room in Stockholm Castle): Received in audience by King Gustav, who has decided to strip the church of power and possessions, Master Olof accepts the assignment to lead the attack against the church but without understanding the full implications of his assignment.

Scene 2 (Olof's study): Continued pressure from his mother does not persuade Olof to give up his pursuit of Lutheran reformation. Domestic troubles pile up. The king's decision to use the church, not to carry through the reformation as Master Olof wanted it, and to reward Master Olof for his part by an appointment as rector emphasizes the reformer's defeat in attaining his goal and prepares him to accept Gert's suggestion of opposition to the king.

Act IV (a room in Olof's mother's home; one scene): His mother dies evoking God's curse on him for not returning to the faith and service of the Church of Rome. Master Olof compromises by observing certain Catholic practices he no longer accepts.

Act V (in Stockholm; two scenes).

Scene 1 (the churchyard of St. Clara's Convent): Master Olof breaks openly with the king, having permitted Catholic practices. Master Olof agrees to the plot to assassinate the king. Kristina becomes the means by which the plot is revealed to the authorities. Olof is arrested.

Scene 2 (a part of the Great Church): Tried, condemned to death and in the pillory, Master Olof is offered mercy if he will retract what he has said and done against the king. Olof's brother Lars (now archbishop) and Sparre (representative of the king) bring pressure to bear on Olof to retract in the name of common sense and duty and in terms of his own selfish interests. Confronted by his wife, Master Olof retracts and promises to serve the king faithfully. Having denied himself, the reformer is dead—as an idealist. The point is stressed by the pupil's praise of Olof as a martyr and Gert's shout of "Renegade!" as the curtain falls.

Strindberg composed his play, as he says, polyphonically, as a symphony. If the action of the play is considered as representing basically a more or less broad struggle for power—political, social, ecclesiastical, religious, economical, and intellectual—it can be understood why Strindberg toyed with the idea of calling the play *What Is Truth?* For each of the four forces whose efforts are directed at gaining power is in its way right. The fact that interests and efforts overlap frequently is evidence for the twenty-three-year-old author's conviction that truth is relative. The idealistic and anarchistic Gert who would simply but unrealistically set the people free from all spiritual, intellectual, and political bonds is right from certain points of view, Strindberg believed. The Master Olof who would set the Swedes free from the bonds of Rome but who would substitute the Bible (and particularly the Lutheran interpretation) is right from his and many others' point of view. Bishop Brask, the most effective of the Catholics, is right, too, in a way in wanting to preserve the power of the Church of Rome and if possible to extend it. The fourth and victorious force, embodied in the practical, realistic, yet idealistic King Gustav, certainly is right, Strindberg feels, in wanting to make Sweden a strong and genuinely independent country, free from both the bonds of the church and other forms of foreign control.

Strindberg has effectively blended these four integral parts of his entire play and has demonstrated the complexity and shadings of each group's components. Consider, for example, the group or party primarily represented by Bishop Brask. The bishop himself is a brilliant intellectual who has few if any illusions about himself, his fellow men, or institutions in this world. A practical realist, not a little cynical about human affairs, the bishop nevertheless has a sincere conviction that his church has a sound purpose and function, not perfect to be sure but one very much needed in a world populated by a variety of imperfect beings. When the bishop is considered with the other characters nominally or really, consciously or unconsciously, supporting the Catholic struggle for power—the corrupt monks, the faithful nuns, the blindly believing mother of Master Olof, and the pliable Bishop Måns—Strindberg's great skill even at twenty-three in suggesting and illuminating the shadings of the human fabric becomes clear indeed. Perhaps the lack of heavy-handed and obvious emphasizing of the main elements within each of the four groups startled the theater men of the 1870's most. But Strindberg knew that in life itself the major elements in a struggle are clear only in varying degrees to the participants. He knew that even the major protagonists may at times only dimly perceive much of their purpose and many of the implications of their actions. At the same time, he knew very well that any struggle between human beings involves such matters as economic advantages, selfish ambitions, and varying degrees of insight and stupidity.

To compose a play about a young idealistic human rebel opposed to the *status quo* in his professional area and not apparently too sure of himself and his ideas, Strindberg consulted many sources, popular and scholarly; he departed from the traditional dramatic techniques of the conventional Swedish historical plays, adapted a freer form suggested by Shakespeare's *Julius Caesar,* and rejected verse for largely conversational speech as the medium, presenting an interpretation of one of Sweden's great historical figures that was in time to become the generally accepted one.

The ultimate acceptance of Strindberg's interpretation of Master Olof is due, I believe, to Strindberg's conviction that even great men and women of the past were human beings, that they were complex and dynamic, and that under no circumstances were they ever paragons who deserve blind veneration. From his reading about the reformer and from his own knowledge of the human condition, Strindberg knew that the number of interpretations of Master Olof was limited only by Olof's ambivalent concept of himself and the concepts of him held by all those who were directly concerned with him. The rebel against the Roman Church and the idealist who wanted to carry out Luther's work in Sweden is not merely a rebel and an idealist. He is also a teacher at a cathedral school, a subordinate, a colleague, a co-worker, a priest and pastor, a defender of the unfortunate, an employee, an official, a subject, a son, a brother, a man in love, a husband, an enemy, a friend, a leader, a superior, and a follower—to the people whose lives he touches and affects. He is, moreover, a product of his time and a representative of what surely must be among the best of human beings. In his skillful presentation of all these Master Olofs fused into one by means of polyphonic dramatic composition, Strindberg gives us a hero who can arouse many reactions and emotions in those who deal with him. It is easy enough for a theater audience or a reader to recognize as sound in Strindberg's *Master Olof* Mårten's hatred of a man who sees through him, the prostitute's unqualified admiration for the man who dares to help her, the mother's concern over a son who does not want to believe and behave as she would have him, Brask's grudging admiration, King Gustav's evaluation of a gifted man who can be used, Kristina's desire to have him be the kind of man she thinks she wants him to be, and, to take one more illustration, Vilhelm's blind faith in the teacher he believes is someone far above ordinary human mortals. The fact that Strindberg succeeds in making all the other characters come sufficiently alive to be believable human beings has undoubtedly helped materially in gaining acceptance of Strindberg's interpretation of Master Olof in Sweden.

Another quality that helps make *Master Olof* a decidedly moving play is the carefully subdued treatment of the tragic implications in Master Olof's career. While Master Olof is not a tragic hero in terms of the conventional and narrow concepts of high tragedy, he nevertheless is conceived and presented as a man who believes that human life is meaningful, who is keenly aware of the misery of the human condition, and who is quite capable of arousing inspiration and passion in his followers and, in his ultimate defeat, pity on the part of either audience or reader. The final "Renegade" may come as an unexpected comment from Gert who has shortly before urged Master Olof to allow himself to be reprieved, but it is nevertheless an indication of Strindberg's understanding of the tragic elements implicit in Master Olof's retraction. Consider one key speech:

The name of every new martyr will be a battle cry for a new host. Never believe that a lie has lighted a fire in a human soul; never doubt the emotions that have shaken you to the very core of your being when you have seen anyone suffer because of spiritual or physical oppression. Even if the whole world says you're wrong, believe your heart, if you have the courage. The day you deny yourself, you're dead, and eternal damnation will be a favor to the one who has committed the sin against the Holy Ghost!

The superior human being with his appreciable measure of genuine nobility and greatness but with his crippling shortcomings—his being too easily influenced and his very human failures of insight and will—gives way under emotional and intellectual pressure of appeals to his common sense and his sense of duty and retracts instead of dying for his cause. It is for an audience or a reader an entirely understandable tragic human pattern. Figuratively and idealistically speaking, the Master Olof who is released from his bonds is dead.

Impressive as *Master Olof* is, it is not a perfect play, nor has anyone, so far as I know, insisted that it is. It contains rhetorical and even oratorical speeches reminiscent of the artificial pre-Strindbergian historical plays, speeches of the kind that in the earlier plays were designed for special "numbers." There are, moreover, such matters as the static characterization of Gert and the awkwardness of the final speech. Least convincing in the whole play, perhaps, is Strindberg's treatment of the relationship between Master Olof and Kristina, both before and after their marriage. It appears to be what the author has heard or read about; it does not reflect the understanding that was to come from personal experience.

In spite of such flaws *Master Olof* was a play that was to make Swedish theater history. In 1872, however, Strindberg's interpretation of Master Olof and the prose play in which that interpretation was dramatized were not acceptable to the men at the Royal Theater. In chapter iii of *In the Red Room,* one of the volumes of the autobiography *The Son of a Servant,* Strindberg accounted for the rejection:

The next morning he [Strindberg] went to see his former instructor [Frans Hedberg, director of the Royal Theater] to find out how things stood. The latter began by praising the play and ended by criticizing it, as was just. Gustav Vasa and Olaus Petri were misrepresented and reduced in stature. Johan insisted that on the contrary they were restored to the [human] condition in which they had once most likely existed but which through patriotic and idealistic errors had gradually been distorted. That could not be helped, and the public would not accept a new interpretation until the scholars [historians] had prepared the way.

That was probably right, but the blow was crushing, although it was given as gently as possible and the author was encouraged to rewrite the play. He had once more come too early. All that he could do was to wait and to kill time. To think of rewriting the play now was not possible, for Johan [Strindberg] saw when he reread the play that it was a sound unit and that everything was in its proper place. It could not be changed unless his ideas changed, and for such a change he would have to wait.[3]

Hedberg's major objections included not only the alleged misrepresentation and reduction in stature of such great Swedes as Gustav Vasa and Olaus Petri and the interpretation of their time and roles but the unusual structure of the drama, an alleged occasional lack of motivation, and Strindberg's whole approach to his subject as represented in the last speech—"Renegade!" As Strindberg makes clear in his letters and autobiography, the elimination of that approach and that point of view toward the reformer would not only destroy his interpretation but also force him to write a new play, not to rewrite the one he felt was very good indeed.

By the summer of 1873, however, Strindberg was reconciled to the idea of the revision and rewriting of *Master Olof* in the hope that he could compose a version that would be acceptable to the men who controlled the theaters. As Per Lindberg has demonstrated in *Tillkomsten av Strindbergs "Mäster Olof"* (1915), Strindberg composed various versions of his play, the manuscript forms of which

are in the university library of Göteborg. Strindberg himself wrote
to August Lindberg, stage manager and actor at the Royal Theater,
on August 24, 1884:

> What the Royal Theater is doing to me is anything but a favor! If it
> wanted to do me a favor, it would put on *Master Olof* in its fourth ver-
> sion, which is a well-composed play, and if you were alert you would
> put on the mystery play, too! That would really have a role for you!
> The fourth version can be presented in Stockholm because the New
> Theater has bought only the rights to the play "in the form it has in my
> *Samlade ungdomsarbeten* [i.e., the 1872 prose version]." [4]

Of the various versions, only three and the short epilogue entitled
Efterspelet and called by Strindberg "Mysteriet" have, so far as I
have been able to determine, been performed to this day. They were
completed, according to available information, as follows: the prose
version in 1872; "Mellanspelet" (the middle version) in January,
1875; the so-called verse *Master Olof* in fall, 1876; *Efterspelet (The
Epilogue)* in 1877. Until the presentation of "Mellanspelet" in Göteborg in the season of 1958-59, only the prose version and the verse
Master Olof and the short epilogue were generally known. It is,
moreover, these three that are of primary importance to practically
all but Strindberg specialists.

The middle version is important, however, in that it not only
indicates a development in Strindberg's thinking about history and
historical dramas but reveals how far Strindberg was willing to go
in compromising his own standards to meet the demands of the
authorities in the Swedish theater. Strindberg reduced the number
of scenes, eliminated the superb subscenes, tried to eliminate un-
historical elements and anachronisms, transformed his play into a
drama of principle (with greater emphasis on the relativity of truth
and the necessity of giving up one's youthful ideals), and transformed the highly individualized characters of 1872 into typical
representatives of various brands of humanity. Master Olof becomes
in "Mellanspelet" a brutal, shortsighted pietist whose main desire
is to engage in the struggle; Gustav Vasa becomes a superhuman

realistic idealist; and Gert becomes a hidebound sectarian. Even these few details indicate that, in his frustration and human bewilderment and uncertainty over the fate of the prose *Master Olof* of 1872, Strindberg had gone far in trying to meet the requirements, demands, and advice of Frans Hedberg and the others who controlled the Swedish theater. It indicates, too, that Strindberg was wavering in his faith that the individual is exceedingly important and was suspecting that there is a possibility that humanity, not the individual, is the important fact.

Even with these concessions, the middle version was not accepted by the theater officials and, as we have seen, had to wait for over eighty years for its initial performance. Edvard Stjernström, director of the New Theater, wrote:

I have read the play *Olaus Petri* and take the liberty of telling you what I think of it. It begins with a highly interesting dialogue which arouses expectations—which are not fulfilled; the great universally known names are not sustained on the high level they deserve, it seems to me; one does not see the threads, does not get to know the causes of the actions presented. With full acknowledgment of the attractive tendency [idea, purpose] in the play, I cannot, because of the reasons I have given, present this play, for which reason I herewith have the honor of returning it [to you].[5]

No one could suggest better than Strindberg himself how he felt about his new defeat; on February 15, 1875, he wrote to Frans Hedberg:

If I were wealthy I should by all rights destroy the manuscript and rewrite the whole thing from the beginning. That is impossible. I cannot compose something different and yet I must, for dramatic art is certainly difficult and requires practice. I am twenty-six years old and have not been practicing [it on any other topic] for a long time. My play has become a fixed idea, for which I have given up everything and ruined myself economically. To repair this I am now a private teacher, work at the [Royal] Library, do translations, and manage the continued story in a daily newspaper. In my free moments exercise books have to be corrected and lessons prepared. Under such circumstances I cannot un-

dertake anything new and do not ask for that either. I surrender uncon-
ditionally and want to rewrite my play if I have any chance of getting
it performed.[6]

The indirect appeal had no appreciable effect on Frans Hedberg.
Strindberg wrote to Eugene Fahlstedt (April 18, 1875) when the
Royal Theater, too, had refused the play: *"Master Olof* has gone to
hell, too!" [7] The letters explain not only Strindberg's frustration and
torment and dedication to drama and theater but also the blindness
of Swedish theater directors to the most promising dramatic talent
that Sweden had yet produced.

By 1876, the final version—the so-called verse *Master Olof*—was
ready. The central figure was now, however, strikingly different
in conception and interpretation from the idealistic young reformer
in the prose play of 1872. Excerpts from two letters Strindberg wrote
in 1908 to Ivar Nilsson, who had then been called upon to play
the central role at the opening of the new Royal Dramatic Theater
building in 1908, will indicate what the differences were. In an undated letter, Strindberg says:

The historical Master Olof is, in a few words: "A hotheaded man" bent
on getting ahead, who relied neither on princes nor on the lower classes.
An anarchist in his youth, accused of knowing about the plan to murder
the king. Later on he wrote his chronicle, which displeased Gustav Vasa,
because Master Olof has depicted the Catholic bishops entirely too
sympathetically, from which the king concluded that Master Olof regretted the reformation and that his conscience had become Catholic
again . . . and Master Olof's moments of weakness are only moments of
temporary weariness, and are not part of his character. If you have been
given other instructions, toss them aside. I am the only person competent
to interpret the role.[8]

The letter of February 16, 1908, to Ivar Nilsson makes Strindberg's
points even clearer:

Master Olof is no elegiac Hamlet, but "a furious man." "The pale canon,"
sharp in logic, thinks a great deal, etc. . . . To fight with such a fellow
would take Satan himself. . . . A man of iron, with immeasurable self-

confidence, who is not congenial and does not bother about being so. Most of the actors who have interpreted the role have made the mistake of doing it with warmth instead of with fire, because they have not bothered about the author's characterization but have wanted to be winningly attractive or to play the coquette with the audience by showing themselves inwardly torn apart and touching. That way of misinterpreting a role subjectively has the inconvenience of being completely false. When the presentation of the character does not harmonize with the characterization suggested by the other actors, the interpretation of the role clashes with its depiction (sullen, insolent [to the?] king, etc.). Everything he says is arrogant, whether he is talking with a bishop, the king, or a servant. . . . Energy, almost brutality in his fire, but no so-called warmth; he is hard even at his mother's deathbed, but is overcome then by sleep and weariness, as he himself says. . . . The drama was written forty years ago; many have played your role, most of them as [if Master Olof were a] Hamlet. . . . Let us now have in the new White House [the new theater building] my Master Olof as our Luther! "For the first time?" [9]

If Strindberg meant that his advice to Ivar Nilsson concerned the verse *Master Olof* alone—the version in which the actor was to appear —what he says about the characterization of Master Olof is sound. If he meant that his advice applied to the prose version as well, his memory must have played him false. For the reformer in the play of 1872 is not characterized in the excerpts from the two letters, although the reformer in the verse play is.

A brief summary of the verse play will suggest not only the change in conception and interpretation of Master Olof but several other important matters as well:

> Act I (Strängnäs Cloister; one scene): Bishop Beldenacke, dined and wined on his visitation of the cloister, meets Master Olof, to whom he speaks briefly and promises his favor in spite of what he has heard and been told about him. Against a background of moral corruption, Olof rings the bell for forbidden vesper services, bluntly refuses Bishop Brask's offer of a chaplainship and challenges the bishop's order that he be confined for five weeks. Marshal Sparre appoints Olof secretary of Stockholm and sends

him to that city to preach in the Great Church. Olof, self-confident and arrogant, has definitely broken with the church.

Act II (the sacristy of the Great Church in Stockholm; one scene): Olof's mother persuades Brother Mårten to pray for her son. Having been assured by Mårten that Olof has not really become a Lutheran, his mother urges Olof to preach the truth about false prophets. He admits he is a Lutheran. She leaves, having cursed the forces he represents. Kristina, formerly his fiancée, comes in to warn him he will be stoned if he preaches. He does and is stoned. Olof tells his brother Lars he loves Kristina and will marry her.

Act III (Master Olof's study; one scene): Olof, busy with his chores as secretary of Stockholm and anxious about what the Riksdag will decide about the reformation he has been working for, is shown at home (after eight days of marriage) in a realistic marriage scene. His mother refuses to accept or approve his marriage. The Riksdag over, Bishop Brask sends his congratulations to Master Olof, warning him, however, that truth is relative. The old faith has not been abolished, but Master Olof has been appointed pastor of the Great Church. Olof determines to carry through the reformation; he joins Gert's group of conspirators without knowing its real purposes.

Act IV (a room in Master Olof's mother's house; one scene): Lars Petri and Kristina are keeping watch at the mother's deathbed. Friars Mårten and Göran are let in to pray for her soul. Olof comes; Mårten pleads with him to talk with his mother and to obtain her forgiveness. The friars leave. In his weariness, Olof uses the Catholic rites, but she dies before she can forgive him. Olof and Kristina come to an understanding of a kind. Gert confesses to Olof that he and his companions plan to assassinate the king. Gert is arrested for conspiring, Olof for having known about the conspiracy and not having revealed it.

Act V (in the Great Church of Stockholm; one scene): Göran and Mårten, the porter, Lars, and Kristina utter favorable judgments of Olof. In the presence of his confirmands, Master Olof is led in by the guards. Lars Petri, Marshal Sparre, and Bishop Brask try to persuade Olof he may not have understood what Providence called him to do. Sparre reads a letter by Martin Luther in which the latter says that worldly authorities must be obeyed. Master

Olof pleads for mercy, Vilhelm shouts "Renegade," and Olof soliloquizes about the inevitable fate of idealists.

Even this brief summary should suggest that the verse *Master Olof* represents not only a new play, rather than a revision of an earlier one, but also a new conception and a new interpretation of Master Olof himself. While the hero of the verse *Master Olof* is no more a glorified folk hero than the hero of the prose drama, he is not the very humanly weak and very moving young idealist of the earlier play. Friar Mårten, along with many others in his environment, sees Master Olof as "a schoolmaster prophet," who not only believes he knows the answers but also is "a pale canon . . . devilishly sharp in his logic, one who thinks much but eats little. Let Satan himself fight someone like that." But Friar Mårten, who is far less evil than in the prose play, testifies, "But he was a man of honor, a superb preacher and the best of enemies." Bishop Beldenacke judges him as "simple—insolent; very young, a type of schoolmaster; only needs discipline," but the Confessor, who knows Olof and would be more comfortable if he had nothing to do with him, says, "He's as proud as a king! . . . But he bites, is difficult and sullen." Both his mother and his brother Lars see in Olof a hard, hotheaded, gifted man. His mother says, for example: "My poor son! He has a violent temper—that has always been his misfortune—even as a child he always had enemies—he will always be violent—and he is good as gold—and manageable and gentle, if one only knows how to take him!" The beadle, who, like his wife, admires the handsome young reformer, says about Master Olof in the pulpit:

But then he caught his breath and raised his voice and then he said that the pope was Antichrist and called the Virgin Mary a mere idol. Then some of them began to yell and someone threw a stone at him. But you should have seen him then. He lifted his fist and struck it against the pulpit so the hour glass jumped, and then he went on, and you know— he sounded like thunder!

In general, as the few illustrations above suggest, the Master Olof of the "verse" play is an extremely able man who knows what he wants to do, who does not have to be stimulated to action by others, who is violently quick to act, who spares no words for the sake of tact—except on occasion in dealing with his mother, the young woman he loves, and his pupils—and who is going to do pretty much what he wants to do. It is significant, I believe, that King Gustav Vasa does not appear in this version. Two highly similar individuals brought into direct conflict with each other would have presented Strindberg with problems that could not easily have been resolved.

Master Olof's remarks about himself, in soliloquies and in speaking with others, and his actions clarify and support what the people about him think and feel about him. He is self-confident, has no sense of inferiority or inadequacy, believes he is the one who can carry through the Lutheran reformation, is blunt and brusque in dealing with his ecclesiastical superiors and equals, is not in the least reluctant about engaging in conflict, is kind to his mother usually only as far as his interests will permit, and yet is capable on occasion of feeling the need for companionship and love. It is an interesting Strindbergian characterization, but, by no stretch of the imagination, can the Master Olof of the verse play be called a weak and gentle Hamlet.

Master Olof, who is labeled "renegade" by his idealistic former pupil Vilhelm when he has asked for mercy and received it, has learned much about the practical facts of life. But he is not crushed by the idealistic "Renegade!" Martin Luther's letter in support of worldly authority and urging preaching first and reforming afterward fits in well with what Master Olof has suspected for some time: It is hard to be sure that one has the right answer to "What is truth?"

To present his changed concept of Master Olof—appreciably based on changes in his own ideas about God, man, and the universe and on the gradual loss of the strength of his youthful ideals—Strindberg went far toward meeting the demands and requirements of the Swedish theater of the time. In line with Strindberg's own definition of the typical Swedish historical tragedy (cited above in Chapter 2), he made the following compromises: five acts with one setting per act, the provision of "numbers," and use of soliloquies. With his use of verse for portions of his play and his avoidance of the reduction in stature of the historical Master Olof, the list is perhaps complete.

The results of these compromises are mixed. The firmer structure of the verse play with its greater attention to exposition and preparation does not compensate for the loss of the broadly humorous tavern scene and interlude and the lively variety of scenes in the prose play. The provision of "numbers," largely in the form of Master Olof's soliloquies, may have pleased audiences and particularly actors of the time, but the most that can be said for them is that in them is some of Strindberg's finest lyric poetry. The best result is the concentrated attention on Master Olof himself.

Strindberg did not manage to write the play entirely in iambic verse; it is instead a fairly strange mixture of colloquial prose and *knittelvers*.[10] An excerpt from Olof's soliloquy at his mother's deathbed can illustrate the kind of verse used:

> Sov, O sov; icke skall jag
> störa dina drömmar! Tag, o tag,
> heliga sömn, frid på dina vingar,
> du som allt lisar och plågan betvingar!

(He goes to the window, draws the curtain aside; one can see part of Stockholm and Lake Mälare in morning light. He opens the window.)

> Välsignade morgon, är redan du vaken,
> så kom då hit in och tag mitt Guds frid!
> Se rökarna stiga re'n över taken,
> likt offer, tända till dagens id
> av mödans barn på den svarta härden!

That which more than anything else makes the verse *Master Olof* an effective play for both the study and the stage is Strindberg's flair for making his characters come alive in spite of the need for meeting contemporary demands and requirements. With a cast of characters reduced from far more than twenty-eight (in the prose play) to some seventeen, the verse play brings alive some intensely interesting individuals, most of whom are quite different from their parallels of 1872. There are, for example, Bishop Brask, the intellectual and churchman who sees the significance of what is happening; Friar Mårten, a fairly well-intentioned poor sinner; pupils of Master Olof who are as boyishly inconsistent in behavior as one could ask; Lars Petri, who can quietly and calmly go about a task that will lead to the same goal as his brother's; a pleasant enough Bishop Beldenacke who likes his food and his comfort but who knows what he is about, nevertheless; Master Olof's mother (renamed Margareta), who still considers Master Olof as her boy who must be carefully managed; and the delightfully human couple, the beadle and his wife. A major improvement lies in the treatment of Master Olof's relationship with the woman he loves, both before and after marriage; it is a realistic treatment based on experience, not on reading or hearsay.

The verse play, carefully constructed within what Strindberg felt sure were the requirements of the contemporary Swedish theater but essentially Strindbergian in its basic realistic interpretation of man set within the framework of history, was submitted to Director Edvard Stjernström. In a letter to Karl Warburg (October 26, 1877), Strindberg says, among other things: "Stjernström declared that he can't afford to make new stage scenery. So the best five years are blotted out of my life." [11] Strindberg had to wait yet a few years.

But even the new defeat did not mark the end of Strindberg's interest in the reformer. Master Olof was to appear in later plays, particularly in *Gustav Vasa* (1899), but the most immediate treatment in dramatic form was *The Epilogue* (*Efterspelet,* 1877, first produced at Lorensbergs Theater in 1920), a curiously interesting fragment which Strindberg called a mystery play.

Fat and prosperous as the pastor of the Great Church, Master Olof sits with his two sons, Erik and Reginald, watching the open-air performance of a play called *The Creation of the World and Its True Significance* and consisting of conversations between God

(Evil) and Lucifer (Light, Good) in heaven; Eve, Adam, and Lucifer on Earth; Michael and God in Heaven; as well as a soliloquy by Lucifer in Hell; and human voices protesting against the way in which the world has been arranged.

The fragment has several matters of interest. There is, for example, good evidence of Strindberg's early preoccupation with the Middle Ages—the mystery play performed on three levels representing the visible heaven, the earth, and hell is just the sort of thing presented in the open air throughout Europe in the late medieval period. The content is decidedly Strindbergian but is at the same time close enough to that of the medieval mystery plays to be reminiscent of them.

For a writer who was to spend the most productive years of his life in producing one work after another in which the consideration of evil is a major factor, *The Epilogue* is highly significant. Readers who know Strindberg's *To Damascus,* III (1901) and recall the scene in which an attempt is made to trace evil to its ultimate source will find the ideas expressed there foreshadowed in the fragment of 1877. God is represented as the evil force who creates the earth and mankind for his own amusement, Lucifer as the force of good who does what he can by alleviating the lot of man, and Christ as the Son of Lucifer. Above both God and Lucifer, however, is *Den Evige* (the Eternal One), a term Strindberg was to use again and again in his post-Inferno plays.

The Epilogue apparently remained a fragment, but it illustrates Strindberg's loss of faith in the idealism of his younger days, a loss that can be traced not only to personal frustrations but to the closely related clearer thinking about the nature of man and the world in which he lives. One burgher's comment on Master Olof, the materially successful pastor no longer particularly disturbed by youthful idealism, can serve as an illustration: "There you see how fat and pious that man of God became after he got food in his craw; he used to roar with fear and trembling; but when his stomach got filled, his mouth became empty."

The verse *Master Olof* was published in 1878, but the prose version had to wait until 1880. It was shortly after that that Strindberg's basic conviction that the prose version of 1872 was a sound drama was confirmed. On January 28, 1881, Strindberg wrote humbly to Ludvig Josephson, director of the New Theater and the man who previously had rejected the verse *Master Olof:*

In the event that you still have any thoughts of producing my play *Master Olof,* I herewith send the first manuscript (printed) as it was written in 1872 and as it was refused then by the Royal Theater. . . . It is weak, I suppose and believe, but there are—in the prose Version— folk scenes that would do beautifully on the stage especially if you would take charge of them.[12]

On February 1, 1881, came Josephson's reply, a reply that must have warmed Strindberg's heart and that serves as an excellent commentary on other Swedish theater people of the time:

I hasten after finishing reading *Master Olof* in its original form, to declare that for many years I have not read a drama that has had such an overpowering effect on me. I assert bluntly that it must have been the most short-sighted, the most inartistic, the laziest, and most un-Swedish theater management which refused to accept this play for production.[13]

The *première* of the prose *Master Olof* came on December 30, 1881, at the New Theater. On February 18, 1882, Strindberg could write to Edvard Brandes: ". . . I have good reason to rejoice, for *Master Olof* at the New Theater has been a brilliant success!"[14]

The critical reception of this first production of *Master Olof* was mixed but, on the whole, favorable; the reaction of the audience was warm. Oddly enough, one of the most favorable reviews came from Carl David af Wirsén, the minor poet who in time was to become a member (1879-1912) and then secretary (1884-1912) of the Swedish Academy and a power in the awarding of the Nobel Prize in literature and, with little question, the nastiest and most persistent enemy of August Strindberg. In a long review, af Wirsén praised Strindberg's play for its technique of characterization, the sure touch for effective theater, and the life Strindberg had managed to instill into the whole play.[15] But af Wirsén objected to, among other things, the interpretation of Gustav Vasa, the allusions to Uppsala, and the pessimism of the conclusion, and he did it in the manner of a pedantic schoolteacher setting a very young but bright pupil straight. It is interesting that in examining the large collections of clippings in the Royal Library—notably, for reviews, the Nylin Collection— one comes across again and again the reviewers' fairly consistent recognition from 1882 on of Strindberg's intense interest in people, his ability to bring them alive, his skill in dramatic composition, and his sureness of touch in terms of the stage. It is equally clear that throughout his lifetime Strindberg was to be attacked again and again for alleged reduction of the stature of the great heroes, for his anachronisms, and for failing to abide by the accounts in the standard histories.

Since 1881-82, the prose *Master Olof* has gained an increasingly strong position in the Swedish repertory. Since 1890, its position has been supplemented and strengthened by the acceptance of the verse *Master Olof* as well. In that year that version was produced at the Royal Dramatic Theater in what became a rare personal-appearance triumph for Strindberg. The audience on March 16 was enthusiastic, Strindberg received an ovation, took, according to *Stockholms Dagblad,* seven or eight curtain calls, and received two laurel wreaths, then just as significant Swedish recognition as the warmest of applause.

Today *Master Olof,* particularly in the original prose version, is known by all Swedes beyond early childhood. They study it in the schools; they apparently accept—consciously or unconsciously— Strindberg's earliest interpretation of the Lutheran reformer, and they have frequent opportunities to see highly competent productions. Selecting among the hundreds of reviews, one can easily illustrate the changed attitude toward *Master Olof.* The great Swedish novelist, short-story writer, and dramatist Hjalmar Söderberg (1869-1941) wrote on February 3, 1920, in *Dagens Nyheter* of Stockholm, after having seen *Master Olof* at the Royal Theater in Copenhagen, that there were only a few plays he could see again and again without getting bored:

Hamlet, The Lady of the Camelias (forgive me!), *The Wild Duck* ... and even *Master Olof* is one of them. He [Strindberg] has caught the mood, the breath, and the life of the time he wanted to depict, because all that surged through *him* himself. And the varying scenes etch themselves into one's eyes and one's memory because they are filled to the brim by a dramatic life, which occasionally bursts its frame but is never allowed to exist for its own sake.[16]

In *Bokstugan 3* (1925), Oscar Olson made this pertinent comment:

It was the whole stupidity of the culture of conventionalism, represented above all by the Swedish Academy—naturally—and Theater-director Frans Hedberg, that Strindberg's youthful work tried to break through in vain. The literary criticism which set the tone in that time was hardly more intelligent than that of our days even if it took more polished forms.[17]

Too many Swedes humanly enough have apparently gone too far in accepting and labeling *Master Olof* as the masterpiece of Swedish historical plays. While *Master Olof* is a very good and even great play as Strindberg in his less bitter moments insisted, there are other Swedish historical plays that are even better. Strindberg himself was to write them.

5

The Secret of the Guild *and* Lord Bengt's Wife

Two Plays for Siri

THE blindness of Swedish theater men to the merits of the prose *Master Olof* in the 1870's undoubtedly enriched Swedish prose fiction, Swedish cultural history, and Swedish social criticism by turning Strindberg's major creative efforts away from drama. Such works as *Från Fjärdingen och Svartbäcken: Studier vid Akademien* (prose stories from life at the University of Uppsala, 1877) and *The Red Room* (the great novel of 1879) were major contributions to Swedish literature, and the latter, in particular, was highly influential in the development of the Swedish novel both in content and in form. Examinations and criticism of the environment in which he had found little more than disappointment and frustration, these two volumes belong with such concrete results of his study of Swedish social history and the contemporary community as *Gamla Stockholm* (*Old Stockholm*, written in collaboration with Claes Lundin, 1880-82), *Kulturhistoriska studier* (*Studies in the History of Culture*, 1881), *Svenska folket i helg och söcken, i krig och fred, hemma och ute, eller ett tusen år av svenska bildningens och sedernas historia* (*The Swedish People on Holiday and Everyday, at War and at Peace, at Home and Abroad, or a Thousand Years of the History of Swedish Culture and Customs,* 1880-82), and *Det nya riket* (*The New Kingdom,* 1882). Strindberg was fascinated by history in all its phases, and, when that interest expressed in dramatic form did not receive acceptance, the interest took other forms of literary expression.

Two factors kept him from absolute desertion of the historical drama, however. His conviction that he was by endowment a dramatist was undoubtedly one of these. The other was his marriage in January, 1877, to the beautiful Siri von Essen, by descent a member of one of the distinguished families of the Swedish aristocracy of Finland and, by her first marriage, Baroness Wrangel. Siri Strindberg has become a well-known figure in Swedish literary history largely because of her second husband's use of material from his own life and the lives of those about him in his creative work. Siri herself would have preferred to win recognition and fame through a career of her own as an actress in the theaters of Sweden and Swedish Finland. Among the results of her ambition and Strindberg's willingness and even desire to help her realize it are two historical plays— *Gillets hemlighet* (*The Secret of the Guild,* 1880) and *Herr Bengts hustru* (*Lord Bengt's Wife,* 1882). A clear statement of the fact that the plays were written for Siri is in his letter to Ludvig Josephson on March 22, 1882: "I do not have any new play ready, but am planning to bring in next fall a woman's play [*Lord Bengt's Wife*]— entirely for my wife's sake!" [1] In Volume IV of *The Son of a Servant* he says just as bluntly: "To provide pleasure for the mother [Siri], who was now beginning to be uneasy partly about her career, partly about their child's [Karin's] future, he [Strindberg] wrote a play so she would get a role." [2] His approach to the problems involved in the dramatic composition of the two plays was practical, with due regard for the prejudices of Swedish theater men.

The immediate choice of the subject for *The Secret of the Guild* lay in a contemporary controversy about the restoration of the cathedral at Uppsala, seat of the Archbishop of Sweden, in the 1870's and 1880's. Two leading architects, Helge Zetterwall and Claes Grundström, had presented plans for the restoration. The former's was based on the conviction that the original model for the cathedral was French Gothic, the latter's on the opinion that the model was North German. Engaged in extensive reading in both primary and secondary sources involving the late middle ages—the construction of Uppsala Cathedral had been begun in the late thirteenth century—for his cultural histories, Strindberg became actively interested in the whole matter at issue, read widely, considered active participation at least in the newspaper phase of the debate, did some research, and corresponded with several people, including Grundström, about the question.

That Strindberg himself wrote the chapters on the guilds in *Old Stockholm* and all of *The Swedish People* also helps explain why he chose a phase of the building of the cathedral in his university city as the general subject for the first of the plays written for Siri. It is not the complete explanation, however. In *The Son of a Servant* (Vol. IV, chap. ii), Strindberg suggests what he attempted to do in the play and what his approach was:

In *The Secret of the Guild,* he glorifies faith, as the driving force in life, and he symbolizes it in the old symbol of the cross, the cross form of the Gothic church. With the birth of his child he had, you see, regained a sense of life's relative worth for an individual when things go well for him, and the child's future gave him a desire to work for the future, so that his child would have a better time of it with contemporaries than he had had with his.[3]

Strindberg's marriage was relatively happy when he wrote the play.

The Secret of the Guild, which Strindberg himself classified as a comedy, may be summarized:

Act I (the cathedral dean's study at Uppsala, 1402; one scene): For 150 years the building of the cathedral has proceeded. Time and again sections have collapsed, been rebuilt, and collapsed again. For twenty years nothing has really been accomplished. In the presence of Cecelia, lovely young ward of the Builders' Guild of St. Lawrence, is revealed the intrigue by which the unworthy Jacques has made the guild elect him, instead of the highly competent Sten, master builder as a successor to Jacques's eighty-year-old father, Hans. Distressed by the election of Jacques, who swears falsely that he knows the secret of the guild, Sten prepares to leave Uppsala for France, but is dissuaded from doing so by Cecelia and the dean. Cecelia and Sten declare their love for each other. The dean sends a monk with a message to Archbishop Henry, who is in Rome.

Act II (Jacques's living room; one scene): Although he is fortunate in his marriage to Margaretha, Jacques is unhappy. His conscience is uneasy because of his selfish actions, among them his resentment and treatment of his father and his injustice to Sten, who should be the master builder. When Margaretha goes out to visit friends, Jacques—in the presence of Gerhard, who has managed Jacques's election—opens the guild's chest, which he hopes contains the secret of the guild. The box is empty except for a strip of parchment, the writing on which Jacques cannot read. When Sten then comes, Jacques tells him he will do what no one has ever done before—complete the north tower by laying the brick in winter. Sten accuses Jacques of having had the north tower constructed so that it leans and of having sworn falsely that he knows the secret. Sten leaves when Jacques becomes furious. Cecelia brings in the old master, Hans. The dean's jester presents imaginatively what Archbishop Henry's report to the pope on the building of the cathedral could have been, and thereby exposes the whole situation. The dean comes to present the chapter's charges that Jacques and his father before him have deserted the original plan and have wasted the efforts of fifty years. Jacques shows the dean the strip of parchment and swears that by the end of April (Walpurgis) the tower will be complete with spire, cross, and bells. The dean leaves, Cecelia takes Hans away, and Margaretha returns.

Act III (outside the Guild House; one scene): Only the last stone remains to be added to the tower. Jacques lets Gerhard read the strip of parchment, but Gerhard refuses to tell him what it says. Supported only by his wife, Jacques continues to be tortured

inwardly. Jacques buys a supply of mercury when he leaves.
Margaretha is told that Sten has been given the honor of ringing
the bell in the new tower only because Jacques does not dare to
climb the tower. Cecelia and Sten come to a misunderstanding:
Cecelia believes Sten has been unjust to Jacques. At dusk in
stormy weather on Walpurgis Day and in the presence of the
people, Jacques takes the banner of the guild to climb the tower.
The bell rings. The last stone—commemorating Jacques's achievement—falls. The tower collapses.

Act IV (the interior of the Guild House; one scene): Margaretha
rebukes the people, who have turned against Jacques because of the
collapse of the tower. Jacques attempts to poison Gerhard and
tries to have his father killed. Old Hans reveals that he has pre-
tended to be blind and deaf and pleads that Jacques humble himself in work and in penitence. Jacques is tried by the guild for
having departed from the plan of the cathedral and for having
destroyed the preceding generation's work on it. The cathedral
dean reads a message from Pope Boniface IX dissolving the Guild
of St. Lawrence. Sten reveals the secret and is made the master
builder; Jacques is exiled from the city. The jester reveals that he
has substituted calcimine for mercury. Purged of evil selfishness,
Jacques looks forward to a humble but useful future with his
ever-forgiving Margaretha.

Strindberg's reading of the primary and secondary sources on the
building of the cathedral gave him a fairly detailed knowledge of
its history, striking aspects of which were the numerous difficulties
and disasters that accompanied it. Probably started in the late 1250's,
the building proceeded slowly but not always surely over some two
hundred years. French master builders and French stone masons,
brought to Sweden to plan and execute the construction of the
Gothic cathedral, apparently did their best to complete the structure
fairly quickly, but their efforts and those of their Swedish fellows
were on one occasion after another hindered by errors in judgment,
faulty materials, and the Black Death. To cite two examples of the
kind that interested Strindberg: In 1331 when the cathedral was considered almost complete, not only did the Black Death break out
and so delay the completion but an appreciable portion of the build-

ing collapsed; in 1402 one of the towers collapsed. Strindberg re-
acted to such details as he usually did: He fixed his attention on
what might well have been the human situations that undoubtedly
arose in both the good and the unfortunate periods in the building
of the cathedral and on the human personalities that must have been
involved.

The widespread contemporary discussion of the restoration, centering as it did on the nature of the basic plan of the cathedral and involving not only architects but many others as well, made Strindberg
keenly conscious of the possibilities of quick exploitation in a drama
that not only would provide Siri with a role but could quite possibly
interest the theaters because of the timeliness of the topic. At no point
in the composition of *The Secret of the Guild* was he primarily concerned, however, with the historical aspects of the construction of
the cathedral. Similarly general was his use of his wide knowledge
of the medieval guilds. His preparations for writing both *The
Swedish People* and parts of *Old Stockholm* had made him very
well informed about guilds, associations of either craftsmen or mer-
chants organized for the protection of the particular group involved.
Among the Swedish guilds, the relatively slight records of which
Strindberg examined, were those of the builders' guild of St. Lars
[Lawrence] at Uppsala.

Strindberg used his knowledge of both the guilds and the construction of the cathedral in *The Secret of the Guild* to provide a
historical setting and a historical atmosphere. He did not, however,
concentrate his attention as he had done in *Master Olof* on a
specific figure from Swedish history. Instead he used the historical
materials as a means of illustrating a problem of great concern to
himself personally and perennially of consequence to people in any
period. As we have seen, Strindberg in his early plays glorified
idealists who fight for their particular faiths. The prose *Master Olof*
of 1872 belongs essentially with these apprenticeship plays as far as
the treatment of idealism goes. But in the years that followed Strindberg learned exceedingly well the lesson that the way of the un-

compromising idealist in a world such as this is nearly unbearably difficult if not impossible.

Strindberg's conviction that it is the grasping and unscrupulous opportunist and not the sensitive and richly endowed idealist who reaps both opportunities and other rewards in this world is a key to *The Secret of the Guild*. Strindberg was sure, for example, that he was by endowment and achievement the Swede who could compose great dramas for his countrymen; yet, his *Master Olof*—in 1880 without question the greatest play written in Swedish up to that time—neither had been accepted for production nor had received anything but qualified praise at best from anyone who had read it. Other Swedish playwrights, far less competent and much more opportunistic, could get their plays read, presented, and praised. There is no need, however, to stress the personal implications in the major idea of *The Secret of the Guild,* although Strindberg did not conceal this particular conviction during the late 1870's and 1880's, the years when he was directing concentrated attention to the flaws in the society of his time. The plot of the play illustrates within the loose framework of a medieval setting what could happen in any period and in any place. Sten was obviously the man who had the skill and faith to become the master builder, but it was Jacques, the unscrupulous opportunist, who was elected.

That Strindberg labels the play "a comedy" represents his concession to audiences' preference for a happy ending and to Siri's desire for a role that would suit her. Nor was this the only concession Strindberg made in *The Secret of the Guild*. The prose *Master Olof* of 1872 had startled the theater men of the 1870's for many reasons, not least because of its highly unconventional structure. There was nothing in the composition of *The Secret of the Guild* that could startle any director or critic of the early 1880's. Aside from the fact that it has only four acts, the play fits very well the qualifications necessary for the successful submission of a new play in the 1870's: one setting per act; a beginning, a middle, and an end per act; places for applause; "numbers," emotional outbursts, speeches of condemnation, exposures; the narration of an event; and rewarding roles. All these are there. It is as if Strindberg deliberately composed the play so that the theater managers and directors and potential critics would get exactly what they were used to and wanted.

In making such concessions, Strindberg displayed little or no sign of progress in dramatic composition nor in his skill in making history come alive on the printed page or the stage. The play is instead little better structurally than his apprenticeship plays of the late 1860's and very early 1870's. It has little of the strength and the richness and naturalness of the prose *Master Olof,* and a great deal of the artificial structure of the drama of intrigue that contemporary critics and audiences apparently sincerely preferred. Even the dialogue and the manner are frequently oratorical and declamatory.

The play is not without merits, however. Even in a play composed without much enthusiasm Strindberg did not fail to become actively engaged with the characters themselves. Always keenly interested in people, Strindberg managed to make both of the rivals—Jacques and Sten—complex and dynamic. Apart from the artificial manner and declamatory dialogue, neither Jacques nor Sten is presented as a type merely representative of an idea. They are flesh and blood, as human and credible as Strindberg himself.

Jacques is no mere grasping, unscrupulous opportunist. While he is quite capable of securing through intrigue his own election as master of the guild in succession to his father, he is inwardly disturbed by what he has done to his father and by what he has done to others, including Sten, the rival who has the qualifications for the task. He boasts and brags, but his boasting and bragging amount to little more than whistling in the dark, concealing his own sense of inadequacy. A man without ideas of his own, he grasps desperately at any means of getting what he wants and feels he should have. Note, for example, one speech by Jacques (in reply to Cecelia's plea that he spare his father's feelings) :

Spare? Has he spared anyone? Has he spared me? Has he spared you? Hasn't he trampled on everything that has got in his way? No, no one is going to be spared! He has trampled on me for thirty-eight years— now *I* am the one who'll trample! You've thought I was meek and gentle because I haven't blocked anything or complained, but you have been wrong! Here I am—this is what people have made me and how they will have to take me. You won't reap figs from the thistles you've raised yourselves! Don't grimace, Gerhard; I don't need your apron strings any longer; now I can walk by myself. Open the door for Jacques the Master Builder.[4]

A product of his heredity and his environment, Jacques lies, forces his father out of his position, purchases poison and plans a murder, and mistreats Sten. But the dean senses that Jacques has good qualities, too, and his wife Margaretha and he love each other. As Strindberg was to write a few years later in the preface to *Lady Julie* (1888): "I do not believe . . . in simple stage characters; and the summary judgments of authors—this man is stupid, that one brutal, this jealous, that stingy, and so forth—should be challenged by the Naturalists who know the richness of the soul-complex and realize that vice has a reverse side very much like virtue." [5]

In developing the character of Sten, the man who should have been the master builder and who—in keeping with the happy ending— becomes that ultimately, Strindberg did not present a paragon with all his attendant virtues. Sten has the knowledge, the faith, and the training to direct the completion of the cathedral; he has the insight into what is needed: "I have practiced humility so long, *Domine,* that I find it sinful—shameful! I know—these are proud words— that no one else has as great an insight into the secrets and funda- mentals of the cathedral as I do; they have forgotten the great truths in their drinking bouts—that's why the cathedral will never be com- pleted." His humility is somewhat superficial; he is resentful and envious and not a little smug, to mention only those matters Strind- berg emphasizes.

What Strindberg has done with the two major characters is in keeping with what he had already done in *Master Olof* and was to do superbly in the realistic *The Father* in 1887. It is basically the technique of characterization he was to explain and justify in the preface to *Lady Julie:* he made his characters characterless, that is, dynamic and complex. But the characterizations in *The Secret of the Guild* are, when compared to those in *The Father, Creditors* (1888), *The Dance of Death* (1899), and the post-Inferno historical plays, obscured because of the lack of care with which the play was composed.

Close examination of the other characters reveals a potentially interesting lot: Hans, the old master builder, who in spite of his selfish retention of his position understands to a considerable extent his son and what is at fault in the completion of the cathedral; the two conniving rascals, Jurgen and Gerhard, who manipulate the actions of others because of disappointments and frustrations, deserved and undeserved; the basically dedicated dean of the cathedral; Claus, the archbishop's jester—one of several important jesters in Strindberg plays and the man who understands the other characters well and furnishes a commentary on their actions; the choirboy Olof, just coming into embarrassing adolescence; Helvig, the dean's gossipy housekeeper; and the two principal women characters—the lovely and very human Cecelia, and Margaretha, the faithful and loving wife of Jacques.

As interesting as anything in the play is Strindberg's broad and symbolic conception of the whole drama, which can be interpreted as concerning the achievement of any ideal goal. Consider, for example:

DEAN: Sten, you dreamer, who believe it is the spirit that gives life to the stone and that love is more than wisdom, come forward! You are the one we need, we, who have hardened our minds; step forward and tell them why the cathedral collapsed and why it has stood as a cripple with broken arms stretched toward heaven without receiving an answer. Tell them the secret so that it may be revealed, for now it is to take place and now it shall be said!

STEN: Gracious lord, the beautiful words you have spoken make me ashamed, but I will obey you and will interpret the secret of the guild as I understand it. Jacques, you say the secret has been lost, and you, Jurgen, think that the basic plan of the cathedral has been forgotten. Take your parchment, Jacques; examine it—you see a cross on it. That is the secret. If you had been present when the foundation was laid, you would have seen how the founders placed their stone cross in the earth—that is the basic plan of the Christian church. The cross has come to life in the hallowed ground and has grown, we have seen that— and it has shot forth branches and unfolded leaves—but farthest up, nearest heaven, on every tower's highest point and gable roof, it has blossomed and put forth a flower in the shape of a cross. Do you understand? Or shall I read the lines the unknown master builder wrote on your parchment: "You who build this church do not depend on your own strength. Build on the cross: That is Faith!"

DEAN: That is simple enough; too simple for you, Jacques, for what is great is simple and so you will not understand.

There is another important matter in *The Secret of the Guild* which recurs in the great post-Inferno historical plays, not least in *The Saga of the Folkungs* (1899). Consider:

HANS: No signs, but the naked truth. I have heard and seen everything, and now I am punished—perhaps not enough yet, for my sin was great; I sought power and honor, I wanted to make my name great and famous, and my family powerful, and I swore—as you did—falsely. The cathedral was built in sin and that is why it lies in ruins as my life and yours do. Your guilt is less than mine, for you became the sacrifice and that was the hardest punishment I could get!

And:

HANS: You were born to be a tyrant, that is, to trample the weak; the real ruler protects the weak from the strong. You have not done that. Bend! Bow down! Your life has not been thrown away as mine; but you still have half of yours left. Use it! And let me now begin my pilgrimage toward the unknown, where even the sinner can hope—for punishment and for atonement.

In these speeches and elsewhere in *The Secret of the Guild* are implicit Strindberg's ideas about the relationship between man and the jealous and avenging deity, guilt and atonement, and the deity's punishment of pride and arrogance on the part of a mere mortal, all ideas which he was to develop further in post-Inferno plays.

One of the fascinating problems in comparative literature that remains to be studied with care but that has been little more than touched upon is the influence of Strindberg and Ibsen on each other. That Strindberg owes something in *The Secret of the Guild* to Ibsen's *The Pretenders* (1863) may well be true. Sten's interpretation of the secret has much in common with the "king's thought" in the Ibsen play, but the essential idea was an old one, happily rephrased by Ibsen to be sure, and the statement of borrowing needs to be investigated before the point is labored. But Strindberg's own conviction that Ibsen borrowed more than a little from *The Secret of the Guild* (1880) in composing his great play *The Master Builder* (1892) has enough validity to warrant further investigation. The parallels are obviously there.

As a historical play, *The Secret of the Guild* represents no development or progress. The effective use of history as a means of creating atmosphere and mood is no better than it had been in *Master Olof,* and it is significant that, while the earlier play has definitely influenced understanding among Swedes of the reformation and its great leader, *The Secret of the Guild* has had no discernible influence on Swedish understanding of the early fifteenth century.

The play's record on the stage has not been impressive, and there is no evidence that Strindberg himself considered it particularly good. Accepted quickly enough at the Royal Dramatic Theater in 1880, its *première* came in May, 1880—with Siri von Essen Strindberg in the role of Margaretha—and the play was given that season only six times. The critical reception then was fairly friendly but, understandably enough, far from enthusiastic. Since then it has been revived occasionally for short runs; the most important of these were the Stockholm productions of 1906, 1909-10, and 1916. It has had short runs as well in Oslo, Copenhagen, Berlin, and Helsingfors.

The other historical play Strindberg wrote for his wife, within two years of the completion of *The Secret of the Guild,* is a decided improvement over that play. Even a brief summary of *Lord Bengt's Wife* will indicate that Strindberg was intensely interested in what he had to say and concerned about how he was to say it:

Act I (the discipline room of the cloister; one scene) : Although she has taken the vows, aristocratic Margit is unhappy and rebellious. She receives letters from Bengt, the knight with whom she had fallen in love before she entered the cloister. Commonborn Sister Metta tries to persuade Margit to conform to the rules; the Abbess tries to have the evil whipped out of her; the Father Confessor tries to deal with her, only to be infected with her thoughts and passions. Bengt arrives to reveal that the Lutherans have won and the novices and nuns have been released from their vows. Margit and Bengt declare their love for each other.

Act II (a room just outside the master bedroom of the castle; one scene) : On the morning after the wedding, Margit's thoughts are all on pleasure; Bengt, however, is soon reminded of his everyday duties. The king's bailiff brings him the news that Bengt owes the king for five years' neglect of his duty as a nobleman to keep both man and horse ready for military service. Loss of nobility and of freedom from taxes can be prevented only by the payment of six hundred *marks*. Bengt mortgages the estate to secure the sum from the witness who accompanies the bailiff. After conferring with the Father Confessor, Bengt decides to spare Margit from the worry of knowing that they may lose everything.

Act III (the common room; one scene) : Their daughter Margit has been born. Lady Margit, up for the first time, finds that her flowers have not been watered and that Bengt has cut down her favorite linden. The fact that no rain has fallen for three weeks and that the crops must be harvested and brought into shelter does not strike her as important. She orders the servants to haul water from a distance for her flowers. Almost beside himself with worry over rescuing the crops and thereby having a possibility of paying the debt, Bengt rebukes her and is on the verge of striking her. The rains come. They quarrel. She decides to seek a divorce through an appeal to the king.

Act IV (the same room; one scene): The judge's wife tries in vain to persuade Lady Margit to think twice before she divorces Bengt. Margit rises to the occasion in Bengt's absence and manages the business of the estate well. Margit finds consolation through what she thinks is good advice from a childhood friend, the king's bailiff. She is suspected of being the bailiff's mistress. Bengt appeals in vain for reconciliation.

Act V (two scenes).

Scene 1 (the room outside the bedroom): The king grants the divorce. The bailiff tries to seduce her; she had thought his intentions honorable. The Confessor saves her. She takes poison, then regrets doing so, having learned that life is both good and evil, that there are duties and other serious matters as well as pleasure. The Confessor goes to seek an antidote.

Scene 2 (the nursery): Lord Bengt and Lady Margit reach an understanding as the Confessor brings the antidote: "Let us teach our child heaven is up above, but that this is the earth!"

What Strindberg intended in *Lord Bengt's Wife* he has stated clearly in the preface to *Giftas* (*Married,* 1884):

INTERVIEWER: You've written a play about Woman that I don't understand!

AUTHOR: That may be my fault, but it may be yours. You mean *Lord Bengt's Wife!* Well, first of all, it's an attack on the romantic bringing-up of women. The cloister—the *pension!* He is the knight; all men are knights to young girls. Then they face the realities of life, and she learns he is a farmer. He thinks she is a fool, but reality develops her into a woman, which the *pension* could not do. In the second place, it's a defense of love as the natural force which survives all nonsensical notions and conquers free will. In the third place, it's a defense of woman's love as higher in quality (with the addition of maternal love) than man's. In the fourth place, it's a defense of a woman's right to be her own. Fifth, it's a play for the theater, and that's too bad.[6]

Even this brief summary and Strindberg's statements show that his primary interest while writing this play was not the historical elements; they amount to very little indeed. There are, to be sure, details about life in Swedish cloisters in the early sixteenth century, impressionistic hints about King Gustav Vasa's closing of the convents and monasteries, and a few illuminating touches concerning life in a sixteenth-century Swedish castle; but what little "history" there is is nothing more than a very thin cloak for a plot illustrating a theme with universal and timeless interest. That the theme of marriage with emphasis on the conflicting interests of husband and wife had been the subject of discussion in Swedish literature from the publication of Carl Jonas Love Almqvist's controversial novel, *Det går an* in 1839 (translated by Adolph B. Benson as *Sara Videbeck*), and the discussion had been intensified because of Ibsen's social problem plays of the 1870's and early 1880's, are facts significant in the development of Strindberg as a historical dramatist.

Lord Bengt's Wife, with its conventional five acts, its use of conventional intrigues, and its conventional dramatic devices such as soliloquies and frequent romantic expressions of love and hate, not only belongs to the traditional Swedish concept of dramatic composition against which Strindberg had rebelled in writing the prose *Master Olof* (1872) but is in several ways—both in form and content —a precursor of the great naturalistic-realistic plays of the late 1880's. Such matters as the Strindbergian treatment of universal, timeless human problems; his dominant concern with people and his technique of characterization; his use of intense but usually conversational dialogue; and the peculiarly Strindbergian techniques of dramatic composition are all on the way to full development in *Lord Bengt's Wife.* That they were to be polished and perfected in such plays as *The Father, Lady Julie,* and *Creditors* is important in the consideration of the post-Inferno historical plays. All these matters stood him in remarkably good stead when he composed the plays from *The Saga of the Folkungs* (1899) to *Earl Birger of Bjälbo* (1909).

Strindberg's theme—the relationship of husband and wife and, for that matter, the whole institution of marriage—was to occupy his mind and receive unforgettable treatment not only in a whole series of realistic-naturalistic plays from *The Father* to *The Bond* (1892), in all of his expressionistic plays, and in the transitional plays, *The Dance of Death,* I and II (1899), but to a remarkable degree in the historical plays as well. The searching and intense study of marriage, of the natures of man and woman, and of the family—shocking in an age very much committed to the conspiracy of silence—is foreshadowed in *Lord Bengt's Wife*. It is, after all, the dramatization of a marriage entered into because of romantic love by both principals, disrupted by the desire of the idealistic husband to shield the woman he loves from some of the facts of realistic life and by the wife's Nora-like rebellion against what she considers encroachment against her as a person, complicated by misunderstanding, ignorance, and lack of common sense on the part of both, and, finally, resolved through the acceptance of the facts of the human condition. Strindberg was to deal in many variations with the same theme in his subsequent plays, historical as well as nonhistorical.

Nor can there be any doubt about Strindberg's genuine interest in his major characters. Lady Margit, for example, has been studied and considered with care, and the result is a complex character who can bear comparison with Laura, Lady Julie, and Tekla in *The Father, Lady Julie,* and *Creditors,* as a credible human being. Interpreting her in terms of heredity and environment, Strindberg presents her as a human being handicapped by her training and her nature but potentially capable of making the adjustments necessary for living in an adult world. There is relatively little or nothing of either the half-woman or the vampire in Lady Margit, however. Created as a role for his wife, Lady Margit was undoubtedly—as most Swedish scholars have insisted to the point of excess—modeled on his wife as he saw her in 1881. Only in an extremely superficial sense is there anything that stamps her as a woman of the reformation period. Much the same can justly be said about Lord Bengt and the other characters.

What is important for our present purposes is that in this so-called historical play there are the elements of Strindberg's realistic technique of characterization, the intense interest in human beings and their problems, the approach to the natural Strindbergian conversational dialogue in many of its nuances, and—in spite of a relatively small number of artificial devices such as declamatory soliloquies and the contrived saving of Lady Margit's life—the components of the peculiarly Strindbergian method of dramatic composition.

Although it is definitely superior in form to *The Secret of the Guild, Lord Bengt's Wife* has fared little better on the stage. Siri Strindberg found in Margit a role apparently particularly suited to her. She was given good reviews for her acting during the seven performances (November 22, 1882, on) at the New Theater in Stockholm, and most of the critics were fairly friendly to the play as well. The reception by the audience was good, according to all accounts; one of the reasons for this was undoubtedly the fact that Ibsen's *A Doll's House* (1879) was then becoming the sensation of the theater and Strindberg's play was rightly considered a contribution to the controversy about the woman question. Since 1882, *Lord Bengt's Wife* has been rarely revived; in 1908-9 it played forty-eight times at the Intimate Theater; in 1920 the great actors Gösta Ekman and Tora Teje appeared in it at the Swedish Theater in twenty-two performances. The play has been performed by a touring company in the provinces and has had short runs in Finland, Denmark, and Germany. At no time has it become a thoroughgoing success at any theater.

6

The Saga of the Folkungs
The Lamb, the Shepherds, and the Wolves

BETWEEN *Lord Bengt's Wife* (1882) and *The Saga of the Folkungs* (1899), Strindberg wrote no historical plays. But that fact does not mean that the seventeen years were without significance for the development of Strindberg as a historical dramatist. On the contrary, it is doubtful if he would ever have become the one modern rival of Shakespeare in the genre if he had not lived through the experiences of those years and if he had not in his great nonhistorical plays of the late 1880's refined his realistic-naturalistic dramatic techniques to Strindbergian finish and if he had not in his Inferno years gained his own intense insights into man, God, and the universe. Without these developments the superb blend of realism and expressionism in Strindberg's post-Inferno historical dramas could obviously not have been achieved.

Three such plays as *The Father* (1887), *Lady Julie* (1888), and *Creditors* (1888), nonhistorical, extremely realistic, naturalistic (if the definition of the term is loosely used to cover all three although Strindberg labeled only the middle one so), and among the relatively small number of plays that cannot be disregarded by anyone interested in modern drama, have in them matters of intense importance to the later historical plays. They include, for example, such Strindbergian elements as realistic dialogue, the psychologically timeless and universal concept of the characterless character, the sureness of plot construction, the penetration beneath the merely superficial, and the at once remarkable similarities and profoundly rich variety that bear the peculiar stamp of Strindberg. The best exposition of most of these matters is, of course, Strindberg's own —the indispensable preface to *Lady Julie*. In terms of dialogue, characterization, plot construction, and penetration below surfaces the preface is as applicable to the post-Inferno historical plays as to the great plays of the 1880's.

Strindberg's Inferno experiences of the 1890's—mental, emotional, and physical suffering extending at least from 1894 to 1897 and recorded in rich detail in autobiographical volumes—are just as important to the development of the later historical plays.[1] Strindberg's renewed faith in a deity and supernatural powers, never frozen in the form of dogmas; his feeling that the search for truth is perhaps more successful if the emphasis is laid less on the evidence that five distressingly limited senses can provide and more on such inner sources of knowledge as the imagination, the memory, and all those forms of the dream experience that can function only when conscious control no longer functions; his heightened appreciation of color, atmosphere, and movement; and his renewed concept of human nature in a form very much like that of unsentimental Christianity—these attitudes are among the results of the Inferno years of suffering that are indispensable to the understanding of his later historical plays.

By 1899, spurred on by the urging of friends,[2] the belated success of *Master Olof* on the Swedish stage, the renewal of intense interest in Sweden and its history, and, perhaps above all else, his own fascination with people of the past and the present, Strindberg returned to the composition of historical dramas. He was quite well aware of the fact that no matter what he wrote there would be critics and pedants among his countrymen who would be delighted to belittle and to pick flaws, but he was also convinced that his insights into the history of his people, his understanding of the nature of man and of human society, and his skill as a dramatist could give Sweden an outstanding historical dramatic literature.

It is significant that Strindberg now selected the story of the Folkungs, the great royal dynasty of the middle ages, as the subject of his first post-Inferno historical play, and that he chose the last of the Folkungs on the Swedish throne as the tragic hero. Strindberg had in the course of his Inferno years examined the middle ages and, among other things, had accepted the medieval willingness to distinguish between good and evil, the medieval tendency to see life as a possible pilgrimage toward an ideal goal of self-conquest, the medieval acceptance of the idea of freedom of choice, and the medieval understanding of the universe as a moral universe in which supernatural forces representing good and evil struggle for the control of the world and the possession of man's soul. Anyone who knows Swedish history knows that Strindberg could not have selected a happier historical subject for a study of both good and evil than the saga of the Folkungs, who, by all historical accounts, were with one exception men not only of great gifts, genuinely capable of great achievements, but also of distressingly strange combinations of good and evil.

It is the one exception that Strindberg made the tragic hero of the five-act historical tragedy, *The Saga of the Folkungs,* without question one of the greatest glories of the Swedish drama and theater. Preserved in cartons in the manuscript division of the Royal Library in Stockholm are a great number of Strindberg's notes jotted down while he was thinking through, planning, and finally composing the play. Too numerous to be considered in detail here, these notes throw a great deal of light on Strindberg's method of creative writing, the development of his understanding and his final interpretation of the whole Folkung period, his examination of his tragic hero King Magnus and the other characters from St. Birgitta to the court barber, and his final perception of, and insight into, the whole subject.

In what are apparently early notes, the play is called *The Sacrifice of the Folkungs (Folkunga-Blot)* and, in still others, simply *Magnus*. Two notes containing provisional plans for plot construction reveal how carefully and painstakingly the author worked out the final structure (Carton 1, Number 4): [3]

Plan A

Act I: *The courtyard of Stock-holm Palace.* The bailiff. The window to Prince Magnus' prison can be seen. Soldiers spread a red carpet. A block; a broadaxe. The place is haunted. Tournament.

Act II: The mother is exposed.

Act III: *The courtyard.* The bailiff. The son's rebellion. His father Duke Erik is exposed. Birger was right, but was the sacrificial goat. Separation from Blanche.

Act IV: The plague. Erik's death. The human sacrifice demanded for the plague's being brought to an end.

Act V: *The courtyard.* The bailiff. Vadstena Cloister.

Plan B

Act I: *A room in Stockholm Palace.* The portraits. Birgitta prophesies. The square. Entry (procession).

Act II: Funeral commemoration at the palace. Plots (intrigues).

Act III: Erik's rebellion.

Act IV: The plague announced by grasshoppers, earthquakes. Flagellants. Famine. Human sacrifice.

Act V: Magnus excommunicated. Vadstena Cloister.

Compare these early outlines with this brief outline of the finished play:

Act I (two scenes).

Scene 1 (the court barber's shop): exposition, foreshadowing, intrigues. The rivalry between Knut Porse and Bengt Algotson. The introduction of co-King Erik.

Scene 2: The procession celebrating King Magnus' great achievements. The Madwoman; her exposure of the corruption at court; her prophecy about Magnus' fate.

Act II (one scene): Lady Birgitta's selfish activities. Magnus and Birgitta's discussion of the problems facing him and the kingdom. His insight into Birgitta. Her and Bishop Styrbjörn's decision to excommunicate King Magnus.

Act III (a hall in the palace; one scene): The king's mother and her lover. The queen and her friend. Magnus' seeing the corruption. Erik used by the king's enemies. The Madwoman revealed as Algotson's wife.

Act IV (two scenes).

Scene 1 (the square): Intrigues, plots. Magnus as an excommunicated penitent exposed to humiliations. The open-air festival disturbed by the religious fanatics. Erik's unwitting giving of the signal for the replacement of King Magnus. The king taken prisoner. The appearance of the Plague Girl. The Madwoman and Algotson killed. The plague. Porse and Ingeborg's plan to take the throne.

Scene 2 (the square with the dead, the dying, a monk, and a choirboy): The bishop's union of Princess Ingeborg and Porse in marriage. The lords' exile of the two and going over to the Mecklenburg nephew, successor to Magnus.

Act V (the same hall as in Act III; one scene): Full-length portraits of the Folkungs. King Magnus and Queen Blanche. Discussion of the significance of the whole saga of the family. The death of Erik and Beatrice. The Mecklenburger and the lords at the city wall, King Magnus—humbled and resigned—waiting for the last token of the fulfillment of the destiny meted out to him by the Eternal One and the Powers.

Even an examination of the sketchy preliminary outlines suggests that while Strindberg was primarily concerned with his tragic hero he was interested as well in the tragedy of that hero's family— not at all surprising when one thinks of Strindberg's concentration on the family in the great realistic plays of the 1880's or, for that matter, Strindberg's never-flagging attention to the family throughout his lifetime. In considering the long period when the Folkungs dominated the Swedish scene (from 1248, when the first Folkung Earl Birger of Bjälbo came into power, until Magnus lost the throne in 1364), Strindberg came to an interpretation of history that was to provide the pattern for the interpretations in all the later historical plays.

Strindberg's assertion that he began the final composition of a play with the writing of the last act [4] provides help in understanding what Strindberg was saying about the historical significance of the Folkung family. Consider, for example, what King Magnus says to Queen Blanche in the great hall of the palace (where full-length portraits of the Folkungs, from Earl Birger of Bjälbo on, are displayed) :

MAGNUS: Who can understand the ways of Providence? . . . Blanche, since you came from another country, you probably don't know the saga of our family.

BLANCHE: I've heard bits of it, but not the whole story.

MAGNUS: If you turn your chair, you'll see the whole line on the wall . . . It's not an attractive family you married into, Blanche. It certainly has provided strong instruments for the hand of Providence—it has brought order out of chaos in our country, it has unified our laws, and made a Christian kingdom out of a badly split and unhappy country. But the Lord sometimes uses dirty instruments . . . Why? That we're never told.

These statements are supplemented by concise and colorful accounts of each of the great Folkungs in Act V and by richly colorful reminders of King Magnus' own admirable achievements earlier in the play, and *The Saga of the Folkungs* presents a fascinating interpretation of one epoch of greatness in Swedish history that can and does, within the frame of reference of western history in general, provide Swedes with an insight into their past. That recent Swedish historians' interpretations of the Folkung period are, aside from details, in general broad agreement with Strindberg's is a tribute to his capacity to understand the essential significance of his country's past and to make it come alive both on the printed page and on the stage.

It was not a highly civilized period, as Strindberg understood it, and much of what promised progress toward civilization was directly attributable to the Folkungs, "the dirty instruments" of Providence. The Folkungs' civilizing influence, manifested by their interest in unifying and strengthening the country, their protection of the commons from the oppression of the lords, and their support of two institutions—the church and chivalry—as tools in their struggle against chaos and disorder, is one of the two major historical factors for Strindberg in this play; equally important to him is their failure to achieve within themselves individually and among themselves what they were more or less consciously fighting to achieve for their countrymen. All but one Folkung ruler failed to apply more than superficially the tenets of the two civilizing forces they had supported, protected, and used. Strindberg's tragic hero alone has taken the doctrines of the church and the ideals of chivalry seriously, and they in turn have taken root in him, so that he is essentially as close to a practicing Christian and a knight beyond reproach as a human being can be—in other words, an appreciably civilized human being. That, in brief, is what Strindberg believed he discerned in the historical Magnus when he read the popular and scholarly sources and applied to the subject his renewed faith and his insight into man and society.

The notes in manuscript form suggest as much. One apparently early one reads, "The sacrificial offering, who was to be pure. Blood on the crown. Everything he does is twisted—besmirched"; another, in part, "King Magnus wants to avoid the danger of dukes, and makes [his sons] kings instead."⁵ But the most significant note follows:

MAGNUS: Good, considerate, right-thinking; Christian. Thinks what is good, out of principle speaks well about everyone: Therefore becomes stepped on and despised by all parties, [much] later has been generally liked for the first time. He has to pay the penalty for other people's cruelty, stupidity, and arrogance. Is so used to being blamed that it never occurs to him to find out if he is to blame or not. . . . Crushes the lords: is overthrown by the people. Punishes no one; a fine man without any pettiness; is called slack. Everything he does is criticized. All his virtues are interpreted as vices: If he is condescending, he is considered shabby; if he is generous, he is called a spendthrift; if he is thrifty—miserly; if he is gentle—weak; if he is stern—cruel.⁶

It is an instrument of Providence, a practicing Christian, and a king in whom the ideals of knightliness have come into flower who is Strindberg's tragic hero. Strindberg made that point even clearer in his *Open Letters to the Intimate Theater:*

To represent the bloody saga of the Folkungs which very much resembles the War of the Roses in England and the struggles of the Sköldungs in Denmark in the thirteenth century was my object in *The Saga of the Folkungs.* Magnus Eriksson, the last reigning Folkung, who in my schooldays still had an ugly nickname, has been washed clean by more recent historical research. In his textbook Odhner has eliminated the nickname *Smek* and recalled that the Norwegians called him Magnus the Good. He supposedly got the nickname because he let Scania *(Skåne)* slip out of his hands, even though the king—without money and troops—was in no position to defend a country without means of defense against superior enemies. According to all that I can learn from history Magnus was really a good man who had learned to bear his fate with humility, and for that reason was despised by evil people in an evil age. It was easy for the author to consider him a sacrifice for the guilt of others, which was to place the question on a classical and Christian foundation. And thereby the basic idea of the tragedy was obvious.[7]

As he was to do again in *The Last of the Knights,* Strindberg selected for his tragic hero a man who is both good and great and a man who not only believes in the Christian and chivalric codes but also practices them. But in *The Saga of the Folkungs* he was dealing with a family as well as with an individual and placing the emphasis directly on a Biblical basis. When Strindberg said that he considered Magnus a sacrifice for the guilt of others, he meant exactly that. From the second speech in Act I, when the Barber calls the king Pharaoh, to the final speech, Magnus' resigned "It is fulfilled," the play is permeated with the spirit of the Bible and liberally interspersed with Biblical allusions.

The statement in Exodus (20:5), "For I the Lord thy God am a jealous God, visiting the iniquity of the fathers upon the children unto the third and fourth generation," was undoubtedly Strindberg's point of departure, for that Old Testament idea fits Strindberg's King Magnus perfectly. He is the one member of the fourth generation of the great Folkungs. Add to this the Biblical ritual sacrifice of the innocent and the atonement by the innocent. The Madwoman says:

There is blood on your crown, King Magnus! But you are innocent—you weren't among those who had the lawful heir to the throne . . . beheaded. You *had* to take your throne over his dead body; you have Folkung blood on your royal purple; your soul is white as ermine—so you can't see the black tails on your enemies.

> You're gentle as the lamb
> in peace and on holy days;
> you're skilled as the lion
> in combat and war:

Poor lamb, you live among wolves and dragons, but the flame of your innocence blinds you so you see only the glow of your innocence. You see only love and friendship, faithfulness and goodness, where you sit up to your neck in falseness and evil, and where all the vices, even sodomy, flourish. . . .

Strindberg adds, moreover, Job-like trials and tribulations to suggest that there is profoundly tragic experience for the innocent lamb, the practicing Christian, who, chosen by the Eternal One to perform great deeds for his people, to serve a historical purpose, carries through his assignment brilliantly, only to be plunged from the heights of greatness into the very depths of the human condition. In few other works of literature are the miserable state of man as well as the undying hope of the Christian as effectively presented.

Strindberg does not make Magnus another Christ, but he does present him as one of the few who not only try to lead the Christlike life but succeed appreciably in doing so. A faithful son of the church, King Magnus relies both on the authorities (the shepherds) of the church—Bishop Styrbjörn and the priests—and, above all, Birgitta (who was to be canonized) for his pattern of Christian behavior. It is ironic that the bishop, who is nominally a servant of the Lord, is actually a selfish egotist obsessed with the conviction that he must root out the Folkungs, that Birgitta is too blinded by pride and ambition to think through clearly the implications of the moral and political situations at court, and that the ordinary priests have only the formal and legal ecclesiastical answers to give Magnus, not the warm comfort he richly deserves and that the professional servants of the Lord are supposed to provide.

As the fourth-generation representative of a great family, King Magnus can look back to ancestors who, in an age unsurpassed in brutality since Viking times, were in spite of their selfish barbaric behavior in dealing with one another and with enemies, apparently instruments of Providence in making Sweden a united country. This they did by supporting the two civilizing forces of the church and chivalry. Through their own individual efforts they freed the slaves and, by supporting the commons against the lords, spared Swedish men and women from serfdom and kept them free participants in the state. King Magnus has not only continued the *good* program of his family but has expanded it and made its spiritual and moral implications part of his way of life.

The king, who as a Christian knight has learned the idealistic teachings of the two institutions, has until shortly before the first act—Strindberg restricts the action of the play to its catastrophe—served effectively and brilliantly as a military leader, opposed injustice and reduced it within his realm, and defended and strengthened law and order. He has had the active approval of "the shepherds" in these major pursuits of kingship. A practicing Christian suddenly exposed to disaster upon disaster, humiliation upon humiliation, and now assured by the shepherds that he is to be the Providence-selected sacrificial atoner for the sins of his fathers, he is so conditioned to obey spiritual authorities and his well-trained conscience that he commits one Christian act after another in direct opposition to his own human and royal interests. In Act I he disclaims all honors and credit for his great achievements, releases the prisoners, blesses the Lord even when He takes away, counts himself blessed because of the people "nearest" him, and refuses to levy the excessive taxes and issue the brutal orders that might have saved his crown; he later accepts excommunication and performs the prescribed penance, refuses to believe ill of others even when he hears and sees evidence, and accepts his role as sacrifice and atoner.

Yet Strindberg knew that no human being can be so good a Christian that he does not doubt and question, think and wonder. Like anyone who accepts the Christian doctrines, Magnus admits that there is much that he cannot understand. But there is no question about his capacity to understand what the Christian and chivalric codes permit him to consider (his great achievements provide numerous illustrations), what his human imperfection makes him consider (his analysis of Birgitta and her ambition is superb), and what he is forced to see (he orders his mother and her lover to marry when his eyes observe them in a compromising situation).

Strindberg places his tragic hero at what is for him the center of his earthly life outside of which move in successive and ever-widening circles the people nearest to him—his queen, his son and his daughter-in-law, his mother, his closest friend, and his counselor, Lady Birgitta; representatives of the court and its servants ranging all the way from the Butler, the Baker, the Barber, and the Hangman to Duke Porse; the bishop and the priests and choirboys; a motley crowd of representatives of the Swedish people; and the rest of the western world, never quite unnoticed. Beyond all these are Providence and the Powers, invisible but ever present. The characters, with the notable exception of the child co-Queen Beatrice, to a degree the very young co-King Erik, and Lady Birgitta in her better moments, are, as the Madwoman says, evil and sinful. In other words, Strindberg's Magnus exists in a world that pays lip service to God and to what is moral and good but practices evil in many forms; it is a barbaric and bloody and brutal world in which the good man must go on his lonely pilgrimage, serve as the atoner for the sins of his fathers, and through his atonement—meted out by Providence and the Powers—purge his people of their guilt.

The very nature of his interpretation of King Magnus undoubtedly prompted Strindberg to make ritualistic elements dominate the play. In addition to the central thematic ritual of sacrifice and atonement, there is a whole series of rituals and rites, all in keeping with the theme and with the richly colorful medieval setting: the celebration of the king's victory and great achievements with processionals, songs of praise, prayers, and invocations; the rite of confession; the rite of excommunication and the ritual of penance; the monumental medieval scene with the two rival forces of good and evil in symbolic conflict as the worldly festival clashes with the litany and the flagellants who whip themselves and dance in open repentance; the ritual of the mass for the dead; the formal ritual of marriage (Christian in form, barbaric in spirit); and the final bowing in humility and resignation.

As all these ritualistic elements are permeated by biblical symbolism, the whole play is permeated by symbolism as well. Consider the appearance of the Madwoman (or the "possessed woman"), her revelations, realistic and expressionistic in turn, of conditions at court and of King Magnus' role as the sacrifice and the atoner, and, in the scene where she comes to warn her husband of his impending death, her characterization of the nature of this world as something very much like that of the dream state. "Everything we live through is only a dream," she says. Note, by way of example, this highly suggestive symbolic passage:

Comfort, comfort his spirit, for evil days, the days of wolves, are dawning! The hunting of the gods, the plague boy with his rake and the plague girl with her broom, the cup of poison and the fever of hunger, the refusal to pay taxes, and the bed of adultery . . .

> Oh Lamb of God, that taketh away
>   the sins of the world!
> The sacrifice is ready.
> The fire burns as reeds.
> The knife is drawn,
> The lamb shall die!

Though written, aside from a quoted ballad and short bits of verse, in Strindbergian conversational Swedish, the play is the author's poetically conceived interpretation of Magnus and his age penetrating far below the surface chronicle and using symbol and imagery to convey his decidedly poetic conception.

What has been said throws valuable light on Strindberg's concept of tragedy. Basic to an understanding of it is Strindberg's concern with the nature of God and the nature of the relationship between God and man. Emphasizing as he does on many occasions the idea that finite human beings cannot in all honesty pretend to understand and grasp these matters fully or satisfactorily, Strindberg nevertheless was convinced that there are creative and guiding supernatural, external forces that are interested in the soul of man, in his moral perfection, and in using selected men as instruments for the achievement of their purposes, sometimes more or less vaguely discernible to the most perceptive of men. Strindberg's Providence *(den Evige, the Eternal One)* and the Powers *(Makterna)* are symbols of these creative or guiding forces.

How they communicate with man is illustrated in detail in *The Saga of the Folkungs:* through revelations, human representatives, and the individual's conscience. The revelations may take many forms extending from the Bible and nature to the visions that come to such instruments of the Deity as the Madwoman, who in her state of spiritual possession sees into past, present, and future, and Birgitta, who not only believes that the Deity reveals the truth to her in mystic ecstasy but is accepted by her environment as a seeress and prophetess. Since the supernatural revelations are frequently obscure, and natural disasters (the visitation of the plague, for example) can be hard to understand, there is a need for interpreters of revelations, natural and supernatural. Bishop Styrbjörn, Lady Birgitta, and the priests serve as officially recognized interpreters, but at best they are finite human beings, imprisoned within the limitations of their five senses, their human intellects, and their moral and spiritual imperfection. Even the Madwoman, who sees life as a dream state and human beings like herself and King Magnus as sleepwalkers, ironically enough can do little to make the significance of her vision clear to either the lamb, the shepherds, or the wolves. The promptings of King Magnus' sensitive conscience, conditioned as it is to Christian and chivalric ideals of behavior, seem inadequate and contrary; while they seem to be in keeping with the ideals, they are destructive in their effects. As the Barber says, "The king's behaving like a fool in his goodness! Letting wild beasts loose on the streets! He hurts everybody else with his goodness."

There is, moreover, King Magnus' heroic vision of his calling as king. It is a vision that is at once Christian, chivalric, and kingly. The king's very good mind and common sense make it possible for him to know what is demanded of the strong and effective worldly ruler; in the days and the years that the representatives of Providence and the Powers assured him that he, the believing son of the church and the practicing knight, was the divinely chosen instrument for governing and had the favor of divinity in his pursuits, he had amply demonstrated that he could plan wisely and execute his plans brilliantly. But as the obedient follower of Christ he is also subject to the apparently authentic demands exerted through His human representatives. As Strindberg presents King Magnus' tragedy, that tragedy is brought about by his being unable to obey the contradictory imperatives of what he should do as a temporal ruler and what he should do as a submissive Christian.

It is the appearance of the Madwoman and the stunning revelation through her vision of King Magnus' new role as the lamb to be sacrificed that precipitates his tragic experience. Lady Birgitta not only confirms the validity of the Madwoman's vision but amplifies, extends, and interprets it with crushing effect on Magnus' power to act. Furthermore the bishop, the priests, and the general populace are only too willing either to accept the vision as an authentic revelation or to use it for their own purposes or both.

What Strindberg considered King Magnus' tragic experience on both a classical and Christian foundation is precisely what he gives us in the play. After an expository and preparatory scene in which he makes both the past and immediate situation fairly clear and suggests what is to come, Strindberg shows us King Magnus at the height of his career as king. The grandeur of his achievements and the touching recognition he receives from the representatives of the people he has ruled and served well is illustrated in the magnificent procession and victory celebration, the significance of which is stated by his young son and co-king:

Lord, priests, burghers, and farmers! My royal father's great achievements have been completed. Scania, the most precious jewel in the Swedish crown, has been reunited with the motherland, without the shedding of blood, through voluntary agreement. The laws of the realm, formerly and since time immemorial as many as there are provinces and, for that reason, sundering and sundered, are now collected and united into one single code for the realm, so that from now on the law is one as the kingdom is one.

Miners in Dalarna, who in their legal occupation have been burdened with oppressive taxes, can look forward again to the future with security. The farmers of the realm—without protection and at the mercy of the traveling lords—knights of the highways and castle scoundrels plundering —the farmers, I say, can again plow and haul, and themselves reap what they have sown!

The slaves, since the day of our great ancestor Earl Birger of Bjälbo free in name, but not in practice, are now legally and actually freemen, so that the kingdom of Sweden for the first time is a free nation with a free people.

Nobles, priests, and commons from city and country, no other Swedish king has ever done so much for the welfare and benefit of the realm as King Magnus Eriksson, my fellow ruler and father . . .

A new era of unity and peace, of good times and progress, is dawning; someday the historians will hail our royal father as fortunate in peace, fortunate in friends, fortunate in years, and fortunate in victory. Fortunate even in victory, for he has defeated the barbarian Russians to the east, and Finland is again ours as it had been since the days of St. Erik and Torkel Knutsson. We have gathered today to celebrate that victory in songs of praise, in prayer, and in invocation.

From the heights of greatness, King Magnus is immediately brought low as the whole structure of his deeds seems to collapse about him. He incurs guilt, slight though it must seem to most: he counts himself fortunate in his children, his wife, and his friends; he releases the prisoners; he questions, on occasion, the implications of the events caused by the strangely inscrutable and jealous Powers, who apparently resent even the slightest expression of arrogance and pride.

Providence and the Powers strike him with one test and humiliation after another, and the play becomes a moving illustration of King Magnus' suffering and passion in richly conceived scenes until in the final act, tested and humbled like Job but not to be recompensed like him, King Magnus has expiated for every shred of arrogance, has lost his son, his daughter-in-law, and his friends, and sits beside the queen whom he has never really understood, waiting —humbled and resigned—for his successor to take him prisoner. With the suspension of disbelief in what has been called a naïve faith,[8] reader or spectator will undoubtedly feel both fear and pity for Strindberg's tragic hero.

In dramatic technique, *The Saga of the Folkungs* represents a return to the prose *Master Olof* of 1872 and an advance beyond it. In *Open Letters to the Intimate Theater* Strindberg emphasizes the similarities to his first great play:

When I returned after twenty-five years to the historical drama, I did not have to bother with the scruples of 1872 when I wanted to depict historical men and women so I went back to my dramaturgy from the first *Master Olof.* My purpose was as it was my teacher Shakespeare's to depict human beings both in their greatness and their triviality, not to avoid the right word; to let history be the background and to compress historical periods to fit the demands of the theater of our time by avoiding the undramatic form of the chronicle or the narrative.[9]

He has avoided the loose form of the chronicle play and, as in the first *Master Olof,* managed to inject life and atmosphere into *The Saga of the Folkungs* by the use of folk scenes that are far more effective than anything of the kind he had done before. Consider, for example, the opening scene in the court barber shop and the plague scenes. They not only provide atmosphere, exposition, and preparation for what is to come but are at the same time integral and indispensable parts of the story he has to tell.

The use of the parallel subordinate actions goes back partly to *Master Olof* and partly to other plays, notably to *The Secret of the Guild;* but in *The Saga of the Folkungs,* these are developed as strikingly integrated parts of the whole action. The idealistic love story of the very young King Erik and Queen Beatrice is treated with a sensitivity and tenderness surpassing anything in the earlier plays. The story of the love between Queen Blanche and the king's friend Bengt Algotson is developed with quietness and restraint and with touches of the ideals of romantic and chivalric courtly love, a decidedly illuminating technique suitable in a play about the particular period. The love-hate relationship between the Dowager Duchess Ingeborg and Knut Porse, decidedly reminiscent of the nonhistorical plays of the late 1880's, serves, with the other two parallel actions, as devices for clarifying the whole substance of a drama devoted to a sacrificial lamb, guided by selfish or inadequate shepherds, in a society populated by wolves and dominated by them.

A first reading may give the impression that *The Saga of the Folkungs* is a loosely constructed play, but such an impression is deceptive. Careful examination will reveal that the play is exceedingly carefully composed. It is not a mere linking of loosely related and loosely connected episodes, but rather a broadly conceived and imaginatively executed structure which suits well Strindberg's broad panoramic depiction of history and which permits him to bring an age and an impressively large number of its representatives alive for both reader and spectator. By means of such a structure, centered as it constantly is on the central theme of the sacrifice and the atoner, Strindberg not only succeeds in bringing the age alive in all its horror and promise, but succeeds as well in making his characters live.

Strindberg has depicted human beings in both their greatness and their triviality and, in so doing, has surpassed what he had done well in *Master Olof*. The technique applied in that play and refined in his so-called naturalistic plays of the 1880's was, for some of the characters, supplemented by aspects of what has been generally labeled expressionism. But the theory of characterization so clearly and emphatically stated in the preface to *Lady Julie* (1888) is the one that dominates; the characters in *The Saga of the Folkungs* are, with the exceptions of the Madwoman, the Plague Girl, and, to a slight degree, King Magnus, characterless characters, i.e., dynamic and complex human beings.

In addition to the challenging characterization of King Magnus, Swedish actors have rich and rewarding roles in a cast of intensely human characters who not only come alive as individuals in their own right but also illuminate and clarify the characterization of the tragic hero: the beautiful and worldly Queen Blanche, who is not without sympathy for her husband; the barbaric vikinglike royal mother, who wants every worldly advantage for herself and who considers her son as little more than a child; the intelligent but grasping egotist Knut Porse, who understands the difficulty of King Magnus' role as a force for good in a predominantly evil world; Bengt Algotson, the friend who does not understand what friendship implies but who is capable of rising above himself; young King Erik, out of whose childish mouth comes the truth about his father's great achievements as well as—without his understanding them—the words which bring his father the greatest humiliation; the potential saint, Birgitta, who is a thoroughly convincing blend of good and evil and who both uses King Magnus for her own purposes and comforts him on occasion; the subtly individualized court employees, all of whom usually judge King Magnus according to the waning of his popularity and fortune but, occasionally, see into the truth about a good man in an evil world. All these, the Hangman, and the two maids are sufficiently characterized as individuals to provide challenging roles. Nor must the minor characters—monks, choirboys, the spokesmen and their companions, the archers, the flagellants, the foreign prisoners, and the populace in the folk scenes be neglected; they add much to the color and the movement of the whole epic panorama.

Three of the characters are decidedly expressionistic—the Madwoman, the Plague Girl, and the Plague Boy. The latter two are types, personifications, as it were, of elements in medieval legends, but the Madwoman is much more subtly conceived, reminiscent to be sure of what Strindberg had already done in *The Journey of Lucky Per* (1882) but much more closely akin to characters in the expressionistic plays from *To Damascus, I* (1901) on.[10] On the basis of a minimum of realistic detail—she is the estranged wife of Bengt Algotson, she is an expressionistic sleepwalker and seeress who in her state of possession, a sort of dream state, is able to strip the truth about King Magnus and his environment bare of all confusing realistic details. The Madwoman has indeed been poetically conceived, and the critics as well as the audiences who have witnessed her re-creation on the stage agree about Strindberg's successful conception of this fascinating being.

The dialogue is realistic with touches of Strindbergian expressionistic dialogue here and there. At no time does he avoid the right word. Varied and adapted to fit each situation and each character, the dialogue has all the nuances from the harsh and brutal exchange of blunt thought between Queen Blanche and her mother-in-law:

INGEBORG: You are lucky, you slut!
BLANCHE: And you, you bitch of a mother!
INGEBORG *(slaps the queen)*: Can you blush, or shall I help you?

through the common human patter designed to conceal thought—

MAGNUS: What's your opinion, Bengt Algotson?
ALGOTSON *(cautiously)*: Porse's the man, I think.
MAGNUS: What's wrong with you? You aren't saying much and you're depressed.
ALGOTSON: Aren't the misfortunes of the realm and of Your Majesty mine, too? Don't I have the blood of the Folkungs in my heart?

through the deliberately phrased speech designed to attain an end in speaking with the very young and gullible—

> INGEBORG: Save the kingdom and by so doing spare your father from the humiliation of having the lords of the realm formally dethrone him.
>
> ERIK: You talk too fast, grandmother! Let me grasp . . . what you've said. "My father, the king, has in reality lost the throne, because the people have rejected him." So it's not a question of dethronement?
>
> INGEBORG: No, since he has already lost it.
>
> ERIK (*childishly*): What shall I do?
>
> INGEBORG: Use your royal prerogative and save the country!
>
> ERIK: Who will help me?
>
> INGEBORG: The Duke of Halland, Bishop Styrbjörn . . . and I!
>
> ERIK: So that's what those men meant tonight! Yes, then I will!

through the tender poetic prose assigned to the dying young king—

> ERIK (*awakens*): Where am I? (*Looks about*) Why did you awaken me? I was so far away, I was far, far up with the cranes on their way to the south where the sun was shining on silver mountains and blue lakes, and I saw the golden apples I had never seen before . . . I don't remember anything else. . . . Why did you awaken me?
>
> MAGNUS: Erik, my son, look at me . . . it's your father . . .
>
> ERIK (*raises his arms, embraces Magnus, and kisses him*): Yes, it's you, but how young and handsome you are . . . as when you played with me once under the lindens and people thought you were my brother . . . How did you change? Wait, I remember something else . . . Whose hand was I holding when I crept under the vines in the violet bed? (*Sees Beatrice*) Ah, my little bride who's so pale and still. Has she left me? (*Takes Beatrice's hand and lies back*) Sh-h! I'd like to sleep again so I can catch up with her in my dreams . . . It's so delightful to walk through clover in bloom with the one whom one loves and to hear the larks singing up there . . . sh-h!

to the dreamlike utterances of the Madwoman—

> THE MADWOMAN: I don't understand . . . in the spheres where I live we don't use words like that, for we don't have thoughts like that. Do you mean he was to blame? No one can be blamed for what *is*

to happen. Besides, everything we live and suffer through is only a dream . . . there, she's beating me again *(makes a gesture as if she were warding off a blow from an invisible being)* . . . but that's only because I'm telling you this . . . and one mustn't tell the children that it's only to frighten them . . . It isn't so bad on the other side . . . in the grave . . . for God is good and forgives everything, but one mustn't tell that. *(To the invisible being)* Don't pinch me!

The *première* of the epically and poetically conceived *Saga of the Folkungs* took place on January 25, 1901, at the Swedish Theater in Stockholm with the great Anders de Wahl playing King Magnus before a packed house and an enthusiastic audience. The critical reception was for the most part favorable, ranging all the way from faultfinding about anachronisms to the enthusiastic review by Tor Hedberg in *Svenska Dagbladet:*

The effect of the drama increased from act to act to gain its culmination in the violent and exciting scenes in Act IV and in the contrasting restrained and gentle scenes of Act V, which are among the most beautiful Strindberg has ever created. . . . Personally, I consider this the best of all Strindberg's historical plays. There is a kinship, an inner affinity, between the material and the imagination, which has transformed it, that I sometimes miss in the other plays. With what a long-husbanded power, what sureness of grasp, what joy in again recognizing one's own strength does not that imagination seize its subject and hold it fast afterwards in a wild and stormy struggle! . . . What I admire above all else is Strindberg's way of presenting the masses, his ability to inject life into these "people," whose purpose on the stage usually limits itself to filling it and in unison, without character, shouting "yes" or "no" to the heroes of the drama.[11]

Written by a critic who was an able dramatist in his own right, the quotation represents a most valid judgment.

7

Gustav Vasa

The Wonder Man of God

WHEN Strindberg turned from his historical tragedy about the gentle medieval Magnus the Good to the writing of a serious drama about Gustav Vasa, he was dealing with a heroic figure decidedly different from Magnus. Instead of being a king the close of whose reign was to mark the end of his dynasty on the throne, Gustav Vasa was to found a great dynasty and in the process create in Sweden the makings of a great power. While Magnus came at the end of a great epoch and was to go down in humiliating defeat, Gustav had to deal with results of that defeat and to lay, to a great extent by the sheer force of his own strength, the firm foundations for a still greater epoch and to go far toward building the sound structure of a nation whose power was to be felt throughout Europe for generations to come. Both had been men with substantial achievements to their credit; both had been men of their times. Both were rulers who saw clearly what Sweden needed, who believed that they did what was best for the Swedish people, and who believed that they were called upon to serve as instruments of Providence in bringing order out of chaos.

But the similarity ends there. The powerful Gustav Vasa, who freed his nation from a highly unpopular union with its neighbors and then proceeded to build his kingdom from foundation to rafters, was neither a highly sensitive and obedient son of the church nor a chivalrous knight beyond reproach. He was instead a remarkably self-reliant man, who believed not only that he knew what should be done but that he was the man to do it, and who acted upon his belief. A builder of a nation, self-confident, brilliant, not too sensitive to means, ever aware of an essentially idealistic purpose—the welfare of the nation—Gustav Vasa presented Strindberg with both problems and a challenge. The problems lay primarily in the wealth of historical records and popular legends, the essentials of which all Swedes beyond early childhood knew. The challenge lay in presenting an interpretation that would at once be in keeping with both the Gustav of history and legend and Strindberg's post-Inferno insights into men and history.

Strindberg had, to be sure, already presented Gustav Vasa as a character in the prose *Master Olof* of 1872. In that play Strindberg had presented the king as a realist about the achievement of his idealistic goal to make Sweden strong and unified, driving toward the attainment of that goal without illusions about himself, his fellows, or his environment. Above all, the Gustav Vasa of *Master Olof* is a practical hardheaded realist who values enthusiastic starry-eyed idealists only in so far as they can serve his purposes. By 1899 Strindberg felt sure that he understood Gustav Vasa very well indeed, and, while his understanding had not changed radically, it had deepened.

The influence of his recently completed *Saga of the Folkungs* is discernible in two of the undated manuscript plans for the play (Carton 1, Number 8):[1]

The Vasa Saga.
Act I: The palace terrace. King Gustav I's birthday is celebrated with tableaux representing the most important events in his life.
Act II:

Act III:
Act IV:
Act V:

The next sheet is headed *Gustav I:*

Act I: The palace terrace. The tableaux go wrong so that by mistake
          a horror tableau comes like a warning. His birthday = rejoices
          over his good fortune. Pause: Nemesis hears. He speaks well
          of someone: immediately struck down. The misfortunes fol-
          low. *The Hanseatic Office:* Israel = is plotting. The False
          Sture. Dacke. Merchant ethics.
Act II: The king's study = John. Erik. Mutual accusations. Eskil's
          chambers = Israel = the bells: church silver.
Act III: State room. Magnus and Cecilia = Playing with the crown. In
          John's quarters = astrology. A Catholic.
Act IV: A room in the palace = stroke = meeting with Måns Nilsson
          and Anders Persson. The False Sture is supported by Lübeck =
          Israel. In Erik's quarters.
Act V: Bedroom. The stepmother's power is at an end.

These fragmentary plans indicate, along with several others for
which there is no space here, that Strindberg weighed and considered
many means of presenting Gustav Vasa. There are, in the first fragment, definite suggestions that he considered a modified use of the
chronicle form and, in the second, that he speculated on presenting
Gustav as struck by misfortunes much as Magnus had been because
he rejoiced over his good fortune. The number of plans indicate,
moreover, that Strindberg considered many other technical possibilities before he finally decided on the final plan.

   Strindberg himself has most happily stated both the dilemma and
its solution:

The destiny of Gustav Vasa begins like a legend or a miracle story,
develops into an epic, and is impossible to survey completely. To get this
gigantic saga into one drama is impossible, of course. Therefore the only
answer was to find an episode. That was the one centering in the rebellion
led by Dacke. The king was then in his second marriage with children
by two wives, and at the height of his power. But Providence wanted to

test him and temper its man, to whom the building of the kingdom was entrusted, and for that reason it [Providence] struck him with all the misfortunes of Job. That time of despair gives one the best opportunity to depict the great human being Gustav Vasa with all his human weaknesses.[2]

The major keys to an understanding of *Gustav Vasa* are all implicit in this quotation.

Again the approach is Biblical. Just as the idea of guilt inherited unto the third and fourth generations had served Strindberg superbly in *The Saga of the Folkungs,* the Old Testament story of Job served Strindberg equally well in the new play. Not only were almost all of his fellow Swedes members of the Church of Sweden, but, as such, they were trained in Biblical history and the Bible; the misfortunes of Job were therefore an illuminating parallel. They were, moreover, eminently suitable in the depiction of the middle-aged king at the height of his power and on the verge of achieving his ultimate goal. The Book of Job after all presents a man of integrity who, though he is tried and tested, overburdened with suffering, disaster, doubts, and humiliations, and driven to temporary despair, endures the tests and trials. The Gustav Vasa in the episode Strindberg selected seemed to him to bear a striking resemblance to Job not only in these ways but in such matters as the roles his family, his friends, and his enemies had to play in his destiny. It seemed to the post-Inferno Strindberg that Gustav Vasa must have suffered both anguish of spirit and bitterness of soul as well. The Book of Job does unfold Job's inner life, and the Strindberg of 1899 was far more intensely interested in his hero's inner life than he had been when he wrote *Master Olof* in 1872.

Although Strindberg does not neglect either the historical background or its significance in *Gustav Vasa,* he meant exactly what he said: "That time of despair gives one the best opportunity to depict the great human being Gustav Vasa with all his human weaknesses." That is, his major interest was the man as the instrument of Providence "to whom the building of the kingdom was entrusted." It is important to note that Strindberg considered Gustav Vasa both *great* and *human,* therefore neither simple nor static but complex and dynamic. As Strindberg understood him, Gustav Vasa was quite different from the Master Olofs in the plays of the 1870's as well as from Magnus the Good. Needed for his interpretation in a drama was an approach technically different from that used for the central characters in the earlier plays.

With the misfortunes of Job in mind, Strindberg fashioned a play strikingly different from the earlier ones in both form and substance: This brief synopsis, compared with the two early plans already quoted in this chapter and to the synopses of earlier plays, may suggest Strindberg's extreme care in adapting the structure of the whole play to his interpretation of Gustav Vasa:

Act I (the living room of Måns Nilsson in Dalarna; one scene): The king's arrival in Dalarna to settle his difficulties with the Dalesmen, who were among those who helped him gain Sweden's independence a generation earlier but who on occasion have rebelled against his program for unifying the country and for making it economically sound. Through Master Olof, whom he has forced to come to terms, he brings three leaders of the Dalesmen to trial and liquidates them; through Master Olof and Herman Israel, representative of Lübeck, which had helped him in the war for independence, he investigates conditions in Dalarna. Måns Nilsson and Anders Persson are invited to confer with him in Stockholm.

Act II (two scenes).

Scene 1 (Herman Israel's headquarters): The Lübeckers are weighing the confiscated church vessels. The crown prince meets Herman Israel's son Jacob there; Prince Erik is revealed as one of King Gustav's major problems, Jacob as a hero-worshiper of the king. When the prince leaves, Herman Israel enters. Lübeck's attempt to control Sweden and its intrigues with the king's enemies are discussed.

Scene 2 (the Blue Dove Tavern): Prince Erik and Göran Persson discuss themselves, life, and the king. The prince insults Agda, the girl Jacob Israel loves. Prince John comes to appeal to Erik to come home; shortly after John goes, the royal guard appears—

arresting Göran, taking Erik to the tower, and closing the tavern.

Act III (the king's study; one scene): The king appears for the first time. He rejects the queen's pleas for Göran Persson and the Dalesmen. Erik talks with the queen and is reprimanded by the king because of his behavior. Herman Israel tries to exert pressure on the king to enter an alliance with Lübeck but, as a result of the king's frank and moving analysis of his own problems, reveals that the two Dalesmen are plotting with the rebellious *smålänningar*. Jacob Israel comes to warn the king that Herman Israel is plotting against him. Israel condemns his son to death. The queen's mother, now a nun, complains that she has been mistreated. The king deals with her. Master Olof urges the king to execute the two Dalesmen. The king condemns his former friends to death.

Act IV (two scenes).

Scene 1 (outside the Hanseatic headquarters): Agda and her friend Karin Månsdotter appear; the former is looking for Jacob. Prince Erik falls in love with Karin and breaks with Göran. Göran befriends Agda. The king and Prince John find that the Lübeckers have left; the king is confronted by the widow and the daughter of the executed Måns Nilsson. Agda is told that Jacob is dead.

Scene 2 (Master Olof's study): The reformer's home life as a marital hell. His son Reginald's rebellion against what Master Olof had fought for earlier. The king's coming to Master Olof: the latter's frank appraisal of the king's problems.

Act V (the terrace of the royal palace; one scene): The king prepared for flight. Småland rebels approaching Stockholm from the south, Dalesmen encamped to the north. Master Olof's belief that the outcome is not yet clear. Family problems. The arrival of Engelbrekt, representative of the Dalesmen, with assurance of help.

If such a brief summary indicates nothing else, it does show that Strindberg wanted to reveal his interpretation of the hero king in terms of himself, his family, his friends, his enemies, and his people in general, in terms of both his great achievements and his equally great tribulations, and in terms of his time and his place in the history of his nation.

What it does not indicate is Strindberg's skillful device of having everyone in the play constantly aware, directly or indirectly, of the king. In none of his other historical plays does Strindberg make his central character so completely dominate every scene. The proud Dalesmen assembled in Måns Nilsson's living room do not forget King Gustav for a moment; their feelings for and about him are a complex blend of suspicion, distrust, resentment, fear, admiration, liking, and appreciation. Måns knows that Gustav Vasa is a wonder man of God, that his life is precious to his country, and that nothing should be said against him behind his back. The Dalesmen think of him as a gadfly and feel that he purrs like a cat before he strikes. They have not learned their lesson as well as Master Olof has learned his in his earlier bout with the king: "I don't permit myself to judge my king's acts, both because I'm not equal to the task and because I know that above him he has a Judge, who guides his destiny."

Jacob Israel believes King Gustav is infinitely great and is reminded of the prophet Isaiah when he sees the king. Prince Erik, who says he hates his father, nevertheless thinks of him as a giant and a god, whom he can not forget or disregard: "I think he resembles the god Odin, I said. The Odin who returns and lays waste the temples of the Christians as once they plundered his. . . . And, you know, he's lucky in everything; if he's sailing, the wind's good; if he's hunting, the game appears; if he's fishing, he gets fish; if he gambles, he wins." Göran Person agrees: "He's an extremely unusual man." Jacob Israel summarizes the general awareness: "Always this giant hand, which one never sees, only feels." The device is sustained throughout the whole play. Even though Gustav Vasa—like Molière's Tartuffe—does not appear in either of the first two acts, he is constantly felt. On stage or off in the last three acts he is the center of attention.

The unfolding of the dominant character's inner life is Job-like. In 1899, Strindberg saw Gustav Vasa as an instrument of Providence to whom the building of his nation was entrusted and as such a man of basic integrity. Note:

QUEEN: The country first!
KING: First and last . . . the country!

and, insisting on his central purpose—

MASTER OLOF: If it were a private matter, yes; but since it concerns the whole country. . . .
KING: I take care of that! I take care of the whole country.

and, when he believes he will lose everything he has worked for—

I don't believe anything any more but this: God is angry with me, and I'm only expecting the axe. Fine! I have served and have been given notice. So I'll leave before I'm driven away. . . . A generation ago I made my entrance into my capital: that was the greatest moment of my life! I thought the work of liberation was done, and I thanked God. But it wasn't done, and I hadn't arrived at my goal. The Dalesmen rebelled; I defeated them, and I thought I had arrived, but I hadn't. The Dalesmen rebelled twice more; I thanked God and thought I had arrived, but I hadn't. The lords of Västergötland rebelled; I defeated them, and I was happy, because I thought I must have arrived; but I hadn't! And now, Olof: we'll never arrive before we've come to the end. And I'm there now.

As Strindberg interprets the king, not only is he an instrument of Providence but he believes that he is, that he can do what he has had assigned to him, and that he has done just that.

It is only on rare occasions that Strindberg's Gustav Vasa ever speaks about his inner self, and then it is only to someone with whom he has been or is emotionally involved. To his unstable heir, who is anything but the sort of person he would have liked as successor, he admits, "To this day I have to go about picking up old bits of carelessness of my own." To Queen Margareta, whom he loves, he says: "Margareta, if you have confidence in me, stop trying to judge in this matter of state. I have investigated it for two years, and I haven't quite made up my mind yet. How then can you understand it?" To Prince John, whom he would like to have succeed him: "Humiliation beyond compare! There you see, son, that no one is ever in so high a position that he doesn't have to step down occasionally. But I never dreamt it would come to this." In checking up on Master Olof, the Lutheran reformer whom he had brought to terms but who still reminds him of one of the greatest but never fully settled problems, King Gustav learns that Master Olof is loyal: "Really, Herman. I'm glad to hear that. Really, Herman. Well, you know about the old trouble between him and me and how it was settled. Yes, yes. It was settled. Yes, it was." On all of these occasions Strindberg emphasizes that Gustav Vasa is not an insensitive man of action and suggests that, though he may give that impression, he is far more complex than that.

It is to Herman Israel, the official representative of Lübeck and the individual who has befriended the king on crucial occasions, that Gustav Vasa reveals his anguish of spirit and his bitterness of soul. For example:

I have so much that lies heavy upon me anyway. So very much! . . . Herman, old friend, believe me: I never make a decision or pronounce a sentence without having asked the Eternal One, the Almighty, for counsel. When I've fasted, prayed, and considered, and I've received the answer from above, I strike cheerfully even if it should cut me to the heart. But . . . you remember Jon of Svärdsjö, Jon, the friend of my youth, who helped me in my first bout with Christian. He changed his mind and he raised the Dalesmen in rebellion against me. He had to go, so he was executed! *(Gets up)* . . . I don't regret what I did, I mustn't, because I was right; by God, I was right! But just the same—I don't have any peace of mind any more.

Master Olof, who dares tell the king exactly in what he has failed and who has come to have the greatest faith in him as king, classifies himself as "A humble instrument of God made to serve what is great: the great miracle man of the Lord, to whom it was given to unite Swedish men and Swedish lands into one." It is an instrument of the Lord that Strindberg presents but a very human one. The king, with his simple faith in deity and his belief in the direct approach to God through prayer, fasting, and careful consideration, is no King Magnus in subtlety or depth of religious experience, but he is a genuinely religious man for whom dogma and outward form mean very little. Gustav is rather one who deals directly with God.

Strindberg presents his wonder man of God at the time when he was struck most heavily by misfortunes reminiscent of Job's. The presentation of his trials and tests is contrapuntal. In Act I the major emphasis is placed on the group of misfortunes stemming from his relationships with the Dalesmen, who had helped him free Sweden and keep it free but who were not ready to accept subordinate roles by sacrificing their historical semi-independence. Friendship and gratitude were in conflict with Gustav's basic goal, the unification and strengthening of Sweden. The men who come to Dalarna to investigate and to help Gustav settle the problem of the insubordinate Dalesmen are, moreover, representatives of two other problems. One of them—the Lutheran reformation and the king's settlement of the religious problems (including his confiscation of the church bells, silver, and other property)—has been uneasily settled so far as the once enthusiastic Lutheran leader Master Olof goes but is still a cause of rankling dissatisfaction to the Swedish people, not least the Dalesmen. The other, merely introduced in Act I, is the pressing problem of Gustav Vasa's and Sweden's future relations with Lübeck; it is a problem which also brings friendship and gratitude into direct conflict with Gustav Vasa's major aim.

In Act II the Hanseatic problem is directly presented through Herman Israel's clerks, weighing and appraising the church vessels which Gustav had confiscated, Jacob Israel discussing with Crown Prince Erik the king and the relations between Lübeck and Sweden, and Lübeck's plotting and intriguing to retain and if possible to extend every advantage gained through helping Gustav in his war for independence. Equally important in Act II is the presentation of another of Gustav's misfortunes and trials—the complex problem of his family, particularly those aspects involving the unfortunate crown prince, unstable, antagonistic to his father, his stepmother, and his half brother John, and, in general, undependable as the prospective successor to the throne. Introduced but not developed is the latest and most immediately pressing problem, the revolt of the *smålänningar* and its steady progress under the leadership of Dacke and with the support of Gustav's enemies elsewhere, including such friends-enemies as Herman Israel and the two Dalesmen, Måns Nilsson and Anders Persson. Over all these interwoven matters in Acts I and II is constantly what Jacob Israel calls "this giant hand, which one never sees, only feels."

In Act III, King Gustav appears, gentle and human in his dealings with the queen he loves, very much concerned as a family man with the problems caused by his queen's desire to decrease the harshness of the king's acts, Crown Prince Erik's unhappy behavior, his preference for Prince John, and his mother-in-law's unwillingness to obey King Gustav's church laws. The following is only one of many illustrations of the king's driving compulsion to bring order out of chaos through his own concept of what must be done:

> KING: However, if you don't want to obey me as my son, you'll obey me as a subordinate.
> ERIK: The crown prince isn't a subject.
> KING: That's why I said subordinate; everyone's subordinate to the king.
> ERIK: Am I to obey blindly?
> KING: Yes, as long as you're blind, you'll obey blindly; when your eyes have been opened, you'll obey with your eyes open; but you are going to obey! Just wait until the time comes for you to give orders, and you'll see how much harder that is, and how great the responsibility.

Next seen in direct dealings with Herman Israel, who proposes to use Sweden for Lübeck's welfare, Gustav Vasa skillfully analyzes their relations past, present, and future and, by sincere and open appeal to Herman Israel's friendship for him as a man (not as king), secures the information he needs about the two Dalesmen, reveals his innermost difficulties, and comes to the decision to execute them as traitors. But in deciding to do so—with Master Olof's approval—he prays: "Oh, eternal God, who directs the destinies of peoples and princes, enlighten my understanding, and strengthen my will so that I may not pass judgment unjustly!" Once convinced he is right, he acts, but, having acted and alone, "sinks down and buries his face in his hands."

In Act IV, the problems involved in the areas of the crown prince, the Lübeckers, the widow and the daughter of the executed Måns Nilsson, and his need for Lübeck's help in resisting the Småland rebels are blended naturally in keeping with Strindberg's conviction that everything repeats itself and in keeping, too, with the historical evidence that Gustav Vasa unified his country and strengthened it without ever succeeding fully in settling any major problems completely and finally. Scene 2 presents not only the parallel unhappy husband-wife-child relationship in the Petri household but the clarifying exchange between Master Olof, "the humble instrument of God made to serve," and Gustav Vasa, "the great miracle man of the Lord, to whom it was given to unite Swedish men and Swedish lands into one." It is a humbled miracle man of God who decides to try to negotiate with Dacke, leader of the Småland rebels, now approaching Stockholm.

In the brief final act, Strindberg presents Gustav Vasa prepared to abdicate and flee, with thousands of Dalesmen encamped north of Stockholm and perhaps ready to join the southern rebels. His family continues to cause him difficulty; reminders of many matters that weigh heavily on his conscience drive him to despair; only Master Olof has the confidence that the wonder man of God still has much to do to fulfill his assignment from Providence. Engelbrekt, representative of the Dalesmen, arrives to offer the Dalesmen's help and utters the summarizing judgment: "That's a hell of a fist, but it's clean!"

Although the characterization of Gustav Vasa is highly different from Strindberg's characterizations of the major characters in his other Swedish historical plays, some of the technical devices and some of the human qualities of the king of necessity have their parallels in other plays. Strindberg's post-Inferno faith in the Eternal One, in His plans for man, and in His role in the lives of individual men plays a basic part in *Gustav Vasa* just as it does in the other post-Inferno plays written after 1897.

Obvious parallels between this play and others are the use of self-revelation; revelation in terms of relatives, friends, associates, and enemies; revelation through action; clarification and illustration through parallel actions (father-son: Gustav-Erik-John, Herman Israel-Jacob, Master Olof-Reginald; husband-wife: Gustav-Margareta, Master Olof-Kristina; love between man and woman: Gustav-Margareta, Jacob Israel-Agda, Erik-Karin, Master Olof-Kristina); careful exposition and preparation; subtly varied realistic dialogue adapted to each character and each occasion; and the concept of the characterless (i.e., complex and dynamic) character.

The devices by means of which the central character is placed in his own time have their parallels not only in *Master Olof* and *The Saga of the Folkungs* but in the plays written after *Gustav Vasa* as well. The devices are, to be sure, scrupulously adapted to the character and the time. The brilliantly conceived and executed first act, with its Dalarna setting, its suggestions of a typical Dalesman home, the muffled drums, the tolling of the bells, the ballad, and the give-and-take of proud Dalesmen's talk in their hour of misfortune, has parallels in earlier plays. Other techniques used elsewhere by Strindberg are the use of intimate scenes from the lives of the characters at home and the deliberate omission of actual dates, which serves as an effective means for compression of time.

The difference lies in Strindberg's deliberate and sustained directing of primary interest to Gustav Vasa no matter who is on the stage. As Strindberg understood Gustav Vasa, he was the one historical Swede who more than anyone else in the long line of powerful rulers had dominated his environment. The brilliant, astute, hot-tempered king has one major purpose—the building of Sweden by himself; everything by way of politics, economics, family and other social ties, religious and ecclesiastical affairs, and laws is dealt with in terms of that goal and subordinated to it. It is because of this singleness of purpose and his well-nigh constant pursuit of it that the self-reliant Gustav Vasa can make Erik say, "When he's furious in the attic, people say they feel it all the way to the cellar just as when it thunders."

While Gustav Vasa by his very self-reliance, his lack of illusions about people and the world in which they live, and his pursuit of his goal does not arouse the love of very many of his fellow human beings, he does arouse their alert attention and retains it. That their reactions to him run the whole gamut from fear and hate to admiration and even love is an indication of Strindberg's remarkable insight into human nature. Strindberg is not content with demonstrating and illustrating only Gustav's striking qualities but reveals his inner doubts and conflicts and his weaknesses. It is a remarkably brilliant characterization superbly revealed through a plot and a dramatic technique suited exactly to the revelation of a man who, in spite of all difficulties, dominates his environment and as far as humanly possible controls it. The choice of the single episode "centering in the rebellion led by Dacke" was indeed a wise one.

It should be noted that Strindberg in his characterization of Gustav has illustrated the king's occasional departures from the guidance of Providence, whose servant he is, when he for personal reasons deviates temporarily from the pursuit of the fulfillment of his mission. His failure to close the cloister at Vreta because his mother-in-law wanted it to remain open, his egotistically inspired pursuit of Erik's courtship of Elizabeth of England, and his many moments of carelessness are illustrations of Strindberg's application of the concept of a divinity testing and setting straight its human instrument.

Nor should it be forgotten that Strindberg thought of *Gustav Vasa* as a companion play to his *Master Olof* of 1872 and that he planned to write another play which would serve as the final member of a Vasa trilogy. The third play was to be *Erik XIV*. These facts help account for the relatively great attention that both Olaus Petri and Crown Prince Erik receive in the middle play, although that attention does not in any way detract from either the unity or the independence of *Gustav Vasa* as a drama. Instead, the one permits

Strindberg to clarify Gustav Vasa's Joblike trial through a principal member of his difficult family, the other to clarify the never quite settled problem involved in Gustav Vasa's highly individual approval and use of the Lutheran reformation, and both permit Strindberg to characterize the king more fully through two of his principal protagonists.

Master Olof is no longer an idealist who believes that making Sweden Lutheran is the means of creating a religious Utopia, or that a marriage of love will necessarily succeed, or that awakening the spirits of men can lead to happy solutions quickly and surely. He is instead a middle-aged believer who no longer has any particular enthusiasm about dogmas and formulas, who is involved in a dance-of-death marriage, who has no final answers to give to his rebellious son, and who has few if any illusions about either man or society. But he does believe in the need of a strong king with good intentions and the ability to achieve them and has resigned himself to the subordinate role of serving the great miracle man of the Lord to the full extent of a remarkable endowment. Strindberg's characterization of Master Olof, accomplished through his presentation as a brilliant emissary and adviser of the king, as the disillusioned husband of an unhappy frustrated woman who married for romantic reasons, and as an understanding father, is superb.

Equally striking is the interpretation of the unfortunate crown prince, a primary source of annoyance and trouble for the great king. In every scene in which Erik appears, Strindberg makes it abundantly clear why, as Jacob Israel says, the prince was doomed to misfortune. The hereditary and environmental factors are as carefully suggested as in any of the great nonhistorical plays of the late 1880's. The great intellectual endowment, the lack of emotional balance, his resentment of everyone in his family, his suspicions of almost everyone, his need for affection and understanding, and his predictable behavior pattern are all illustrated again and again both as they cause his great father Job-like difficulty and as they help explain what was to become the future Erik XIV's personal tragedy. It is an exceptionally full and well-rounded case report, fitted so naturally and carefully into *Gustav Vasa* that instead of serving as a distraction from the theme of that play it helps in rounding it out.

Just as Master Olof and Crown Prince Erik come individually alive in their own right but serve at the same time to characterize Gustav Vasa, the Israels, the Månssons, the other Vasas, Lady Ebba Lejonhufvud, Kristina Petri and her son Reginald, Agda, and Karin Månsdotter come alive as people, yet serve directly or indirectly or both in advancing Strindberg's central purpose. It is an intensely varied group of human beings: a beautiful and gentle queen who loves her husband but who would, out of the kindness of her heart, reduce if she could the harshness of her husband's acts; the stubborn and self-centered mother-in-law, not only proud of her ancestry and her status as a nun but inclined to look upon her son-in-law as somewhat of an uncouth upstart; Prince John, with his preference for formalism even in speech and not really a paragon of filial loyalty; Kristina Petri, middle-aged and frustrated in her dreams of marriage, motherhood, and the Utopia that she thought the Reformation would bring; Reginald Petri, the very young man who sees no hope in a bewildering intellectual and religious environment; Jacob Israel, the brilliant young idealist who sees a great deal of hope in love and in the miracle man of God but who at the same time has the inner strength to abide by the traditions of his people; Agda, the naïve waitress whose future is decided indirectly by her lover's hero; Karin Månsdotter, the teenage commoner whose beauty and charm were to help her to take a place on the throne; the Dalesmen, each of them an individual representative of qualities that at once mark them as Swedes and yet a very special kind of Swedes; the richly endowed Göran Persson, unfortunate in his social antecedents but even when young involved with the Vasas; and Engelbrekt, the somewhat tipsy Dalesman, who on two occasions brings the miracle man the good news he needs in his hour of distress.

Assigned to all these characters and to the Hanseatic clerks and the beggars is dialogue subtly adapted to each character and each situation. The dialogue, moreover, ranges from what Strindberg calls the "hard accents" in *A Dream Play:*

> KRISTINA: Even if I did have any doubts, I wouldn't want to bother you with them.
> MASTER OLOF: As charming as ever! Would you ask Reginald to come in?
> KRISTINA: I always obey your orders.
> MASTER OLOF: As I never give orders but ask . . .
> KRISTINA: If you'd give orders to that son of yours, for once, he'd probably be a little politer and more obedient to his mother!

to gentle "accents"—

> KING: Say something bad about the king!
> BARBRO: No! Father said we mustn't, even if we heard others say it.
> KING: Did father say that?
> BARBRO: Yes.
> KING: Go in peace. I'll talk with the king, and you'll get justice, for he wants what is just and does what is just.

Much of the dialogue is, of course, like that in his realistic and other historical plays; since they deal primarily with human beings in conflict with each other, a dominant characteristic of the dialogue is the bluntness of bickering, quarreling, and argument, but the dialogue is by no means restricted to that sort of exchange.

The superbly composed serious drama about Gustav Vasa is not only a monumental realistic study of the king but also a remarkably fine presentation of his period in terms of Sweden and of Europe in general. Following his general practice, stemming from his conviction that no nation can be completely isolated historically or culturally from others, Strindberg carefully places Sweden in relationship with such neighbors as Lübeck and Denmark, with England (through Erik's courtship of Elizabeth), and with events on the continent and their effects on Sweden (Luther and Wittenberg, for example). Nor does he present Gustav Vasa's period as isolated from the Swedish past. For example, the king's reminding the queen of her royal ancestry serves as a simple and very natural means not only for clarifying Gustav Vasa's story but for placing it in proper historical perspective.

Even more prominent than the allusions and references to foreign countries are the Strindbergian details that help bring sixteenth-century Sweden alive on the stage. The superb first act with its setting in Dalarna is, among other things, a vivid and colorful re-creation of a special setting and time, unsurpassed in Scandinavian literature. The other acts, in turn, present a poetically conceived interpretation of aspects of sixteenth-century Stockholm. Strindberg's great knowledge of the Swedish past, certainly not least of the city that he loved, is revealed. There are historical and dramatic implications, for both spectator and reader, in every detail in, for example, the following stage directions:

The king's study. Large windows consisting of painted panes at the back; some of the windows are open. No door at the back. Outside can be seen trees green with the foliage of spring; above the trees, the masts of ships with flags flying and the spires of towers. Benches attached to the walls and covered with many-colored pillows under the windows. To the right a large open fireplace richly decorated and with the national coat of arms above it; on the same side a door leading to the waiting room. To the left a throne chair with a canopy; in front of the chair a long oak table; on it a green cloth, a folio Bible, writing utensils, candlesticks, a steel hammer, etc. On the same side farther away a door opening into other rooms.

On the floor, fur rugs and carpets.

On the walls paintings of scenes from the Old Testament; the most striking depicts "God visiting Abraham in the grove of Mamre." The Abraham closely resembles the king.

An Arabian pottery decanter with a silver beaker on a cupboard table. By the door to the right hangs a large, long, blue cape and a very large black slouch hat; next to them stands a short wild-boar spear.

The king is standing in deep thought by an open window in the middle of the sunlight; he is dressed in a black Spanish costume lined in yellow, which shows in the slits and seams; his cape has a sable border. His hair is blond and his giant beard, which extends down over his chest, is somewhat lighter.

Queen Margareta enters from the left; she is dressed in yellow trimmed with black.

The publication of *Gustav Vasa* in 1899 led as usual to a mixed reception from the critics. In general those who objected to the play concentrated their attention on anachronisms (there are some), the presence of coarse expressions, Strindberg's subjective interpretations of the characters, his subjective dialogue and his ideas. Carl David af Wirsén, by then Strindberg's inveterate enemy and undoubtedly the member of the Swedish Academy who more than any one else kept Strindberg from receiving the Nobel Prize, had to strain to belittle *Gustav Vasa* in his review in *Vårt Land* (November 21, 1899).[3] In *Nordisk Revy* (Vol. V, No. 10, 1899), Erik Thyselius presented a thoroughly sound but not complete analysis of the reviews of *Gustav Vasa* not only as literature but as theater; he comments on the great continuing success of the first production of the play at the Swedish Theater that should have been the occasion of nationwide joy and on "an unquenchable underhanded hatred of Strindberg à la C. D. W. or the petty views and reservations of coteries."[4] Commenting on the altogether too common practices of searching for flaws, although finding them only through the application of set theories and habits of thinking, barely mentioning the great merits of the play, and forgetting completely the total impression of the play, he raised two highly appropriate questions: What is the proper and balanced critical method for presenting the merits and flaws of a significant literary work? Should a play written for the theater be judged as such or as a work to be read? He agreed with Hjalmar Branting, who in *Social Demokraten* had written: "When the miserably poor judgments of our time's coteries of esthetes have long since been forgotten, *Gustav Vasa,* with its fellow dramas, will have its unchallenged place among the classics of Swedish drama."[5] Branting was right.

Since the first highly successful production in 1899-1900, *Gustav Vasa* has been produced in the leading cities and the provinces, and it has proved its exceptionally high quality as theater. Swedish audiences have been enthusiastic from the beginning; numerous Stockholm and other Swedish productions have given many actors and actresses challenging and rewarding roles and audiences a delightful and credible stage interpretation of the king and of the period that marks the beginnings of modern Sweden.

It is an interesting fact that with the years both academic and nonacademic critics have become increasingly less addicted to "unquenchable underhanded hatred of Strindberg." Three brief quotations will perhaps suffice to illustrate the point. In *Arbetet* of Malmö on April 4, 1911, a reviewer wrote:

Academic esthetes will in the future study Aug. Strindberg's Vasa Trilogy, with happy amazement that the docents in literature of [Strindberg's] time limited themselves to scolding with human anger about what they were not able to understand. Not because the future geniuses in that field would have gained greater understanding naturally, but they will be forced to acknowledge the master after his death. That is, even academic docents have to acknowledge dead geniuses.[6]

In *Social-Demokraten* of Stockholm on December 30, 1922, a critic wrote: "Life pulsates as strong as ever in the Strindberg drama. No theater dust in the world will ever dim the monumentality of the central figure. That comes from . . . the dramatist's happy grasp on the human qualities of the builder of the kingdom." [7] And in *Helsingsborgs Dagblad* on February 25, 1927, when *Gustav Vasa* was being presented at the City Theater, appeared this testimony: "It is, quite simply, our classical national drama." [8] Since then that has become more and more the general judgment.

8

Erik XIV
Doomed to Misfortune

THE success of *Master Olof* on the stage in the 1890's confirmed Strindberg's conviction that his method of composing that historical play was right. It did more than that, however; it gave him the idea of composing what he calls the Vasa trilogy, the first part of which was to be the prose *Master Olof* of 1872, the second, *Gustav Vasa,* and the third a play about King Gustav's successor, Erik XIV. As we have seen in the chapter on *Gustav Vasa,* Strindberg deliberately linked that play with *Master Olof,* presenting many of its characters a generation later, shifting the major emphasis from the reformer to the king, but, in general, dealing with the same basic personal and social problems in keeping with the shift in emphasis and with the changes in time. The two plays can be said to be studies in the contrast, on the one hand between youthful enthusiasm (Master Olof) and youthful drive toward a definite goal (King Gustav) in the play of 1872, and on the other between middle-aged resignation to the well-nigh inevitable (Master Olof) and middle-aged determination not to lose the achievement of his goal (King Gustav).

In composing *Gustav Vasa,* Strindberg was aware of the final play in the trilogy. One of the most important secondary characters in *Gustav Vasa* is, as we have seen, Crown Prince Erik. Used in that play as the principal embodiment of one of King Gustav's major misfortunes—family troubles—Erik is characterized in such a remarkably full fashion that there can be little doubt about Strindberg's intention to complete the trilogy by writing a play about Prince Erik which, among other things, would make it a thoroughgoing companion play and which might in the uncertain future induce an imaginative and daring Swedish producer to put on all three plays as a trilogy.

In writing a play about Erik XIV—again removed roughly a generation from the time of action of its predecessor—Strindberg faced a set of problems that he had not faced in composing any of his earlier historical plays. The very nature of Erik, for example, tended to obscure the central issues involved in the plays about Master Olof, King Magnus, and King Gustav; even the historians, scholarly and popular, tended to pay more attention to the bizarre behavior of King Erik than to the continuing struggle for power and to the king's plans for Sweden's future and for the development of its present.

Even more disconcerting was the evidence in all the sources that if one were to consider King Erik one must consider his favorite and adviser, Göran Persson, as well. The one was as important as the other; the interests and the actions of the one were curiously intertwined with the interests and the actions of the other. As Prince John says, "No Göran without Erik. . . ." Of all the great figures of the Swedish past whom Strindberg considered for treatment in historical plays, Erik XIV alone could not be presented as the unquestionably central character; he had to share that role with Göran Persson.

Strindberg found an illuminating and helpful parallel in Shakespeare rather than in the Bible for his interpretation of Erik XIV, but, because of the close relationship between the king and his favorite, it was at best only a partial parallel. As he says in his essay on *Hamlet:*

Erik XIV is a Hamlet. Stepmother (= stepfather); murders Sture (= murders Polonius); Ophelia = Karin Månsdotter; Erik XIV dies poisoned as Hamlet does; insane or simulating insanity as Hamlet; vacillating; judges and rejects his judgment; his friend Göran Persson— faithful unto death; Fortinbras = Dukes John and Charles; Hamlet was loved by the uncivilized masses. Erik, too, a hater of the lords and the people's king.[1]

So Hamlet himself is only made up of apparent contradictions, evil and good, hating and loving, cynical and enthusiastic, cruel and lenient, strong and weak; in a word: a human being, different at every moment, as human beings are, of course.[2]

Elsewhere Strindberg wrote, "My *Erik XIV* is a characterization of a characterless human being." [3]

The unprinted notes preserved in the manuscript division of the Royal Library suggest that Strindberg considered many possibilities for dramatizing the story of Erik XIV before he decided on the final plan. Of the many preliminary plans and sketches that will be considered elsewhere two may be used to throw some light on the difficulty of Strindberg's problems of composition. (His plans ranged from making the play a Swedenborgian drama with the emphasis placed on the occult to giving the story an extremely realistic interpretation and treatment.) One apparently fairly late plan is this (Carton 1, Number 9):

Erik XIV: half-German, stepchild, Nero.
Act I: Nils Sture's return with Renata's "no." (Renata the grand-
       daughter of Christian II, [has] right of inheritance to Norway
       and Denmark.) Sture is insulted. Karin and the people defend
       him. John is ordered to marry Catherine Jagellonica [of
       Poland]. Göran P. plays up to Karin. Is reconciled with Erik.

Nils Gyllenstjerna from England. Ten thousand *dalers* for Leicester's life.

Act II: Karin's friend discovered and drowned. Maximilian an ensign. Erik burns and harries in Blekinge. Nils Sture refuses to cut down Danes in Västergötland. John is imprisoned. Erik hates and envies John who has made a better marriage than he.

Act III: Alchemy, black magic. The murder of the Stures. John is released. Göran is imprisoned. Erik thinks he has been dethroned and imprisoned.

Act IV: The marriage with Karin. No guests come; only the father-in-law and his relatives. Erik poses as a democrat, waits on the guests. Afterwards becomes drunk and kicks them out. Erik and Göran's *nachspiel*. Karin has to go to bed: after Erik has discovered that Karin has warned the dukes.

Act V: Erik is taken prisoner. Göran is tortured. The dukes come. Göran P.: Has anyone a good word to say for him: Agda answers.[4]

The other and much briefer plan (also in Carton 1, Number 9):

Act I: Erik's courtships are rejected.
Act II: John is imprisoned.
Act III: The murders of the Stures.
Act IV: The marriage.
Act V: Erik's being taken prisoner.[5]

Present in one way or another in all the extant plans and sketches are the implications of King Erik's bewilderingly complex character; his close relationship with Göran Persson; the problems centered in the king's courtships and marriage; and, obscured largely by the attention-provoking actions of the king, the basic struggle for power.

Having weighed and considered many possibilities, Strindberg settled on one that permitted him to write a play that is both a companion play for *Gustav Vasa* and an independent play that interprets the king's complex character, his unusual relationship with Göran Persson, his courtships and his marriage, the most striking events of his reign, and, with deliberately obscure effects, Erik's struggle with the lords and his own half brothers for power. A brief outline of the four-act tragedy will help clarify that:

Act I (the terrace of the royal palace—the same setting as in Act V of *Gustav Vasa;* one scene): Max and Karin. Göran Persson's news that Erik's ambassador Nils Sture's mission for Queen Elizabeth's hand has failed. Erik and Karin and the crown he has had made for Elizabeth. Erik's approval of John's plan to marry Catherine of Poland. Erik's fury with the Stures. Erik's urging Gyllenstjerna to murder Leicester. Göran Persson in love. His advice that Erik marry Catherine of Poland. Pursuit of John. Göran appointed procurator.

Act II (Göran Persson's home; one scene): Göran at work as procurator. Agda and Maria (Jacob Israel's daughter) befriended by Göran. Svante Sture's insult of Göran. Max sent to his death. Göran's plan for overcoming the Stures, the other lords, and Duke John. King Erik confronted by his mistress' father.

Act III (two scenes).

Scene 1 (a bridgehead): Göran and Gyllenstjerna's arrest of lords in act of paying homage to Duke John now sentenced to death for treason and rebellion.

Scene 2 (a room in Uppsala Castle): Göran's plan for prosecuting the case against the lords. Karin and the children. King Erik misplaces his speech. Furious upon failure to present the case Göran has carefully prepared. Dowager Queen's persuasion of Karin to take children and flee with her to the stronghold of the Stures. Göran's engagement broken. The assassination of the imprisoned Stures and other lords.

Act IV (three scenes).

Scene 1 (Måns Knekt's kitchen): Karin and her father. Erik, after temporary derangement, asks for Karin's hand.

Scene 2 (a tower room): Dukes John and Carl agree to dethrone Erik and to share the throne.

Scene 3 (a room in the castle): celebration of King Erik and Queen Karin's marriage. Lords and dukes not present at wedding or banquet. Common people called in to take part in banquet. The arrival of the dukes. The taking prisoner of King Erik and Göran Persson. John hailed as King John III.

Even this brief outline should suggest that Strindberg had hit upon a structure and a form that was essentially different from any that he had previously used and that was at the same time peculiarly suitable for his interpretation of a king whose story was thoroughly interwoven with that of his favorite and adviser.

Without for a moment neglecting exposition, preparation, the development of the plot, and gradual but sure characterization, Strindberg presents King Erik in the presence of a group of people, all of whom have decided opinions about the king and about whom Erik has decided opinions: his young mistress, whom he loves and who likes but pities him; Nigels the goldsmith, who is merely a servant and who does not contradict him and has his favor; his half brother John, who deliberately conceals his dislike and contempt for the king and who in everything, including his manner, furnishes a source of irritation, distrust, suspicion, and hate; his second stepmother, who finds him more pitiable than bad but who infuriates him; the Stures, who are somewhat condescending in their manner toward him and whose every act annoys him; Lord Gyllenstjerna, who is loyal to the Vasas and likes Erik, but has self-respect enough not to be the blindly obedient executor of Erik's impulsive offers; and Göran Persson, the one person in his environment who comes close to understanding Erik and who can work with and even to some degree manage him.

Act I is King Erik's, designed deliberately to show King Erik in action, with the major emphasis placed on his personality, temperament, and behavior. It is clear from the first exchange of speeches between Max and Karin that King Erik is no Gustav Vasa who dominates his environment through singleness of purpose, strength of character, and dedication to a goal greater than himself. Erik, it is clear, is no instrument of the Lord chosen for the performance of a great task. Instead he is one of those doomed to misfortune, as Jacob Israel says in *Gustav Vasa,* and doomed, too, not only to going "about picking up old bits of carelessness" but to ever creating new ones. While some of the others like him, none of them respects him, unless it be Nigels the goldsmith, and his role of servant does not permit him to express an opinion. Karin believes he is dangerous and pitiable; she says he believes in every evil power but not in any good;

she knows that when he is in a bad mood, he is unhappy and will hit out at anyone. Max wonders if the king is not crazy, and Svante, head of the Stures, frankly calls him a madman. Göran Persson knows that the king can easily be upset, that he needs to be entertained and cheered up, and that when he becomes irritated or bored he becomes dangerous. But the first act reveals Erik's inner disturbance (he easily becomes lost in his thoughts), his dependence on others (Karin, Göran), his suspicions of others (the stepmother, John, and the Stures), his conviction that he is hated by his enemies, and his capacity for hatred.

Two patterns become fairly clear in Act I, one centers in suspicion, distrust, and hatred, the other in Erik's typical pattern of behavior—beautifully illustrated in his approval of John's marriage plans—whimsical decision, irritation when he finds that the act was unfortunate, fury, and—prevented in this case by Göran—unfortunate action based on impulse. Act I serves as a splendid introduction to King Erik; one does not need to refer to Strindberg's careful examination of him in the companion play, *Gustav Vasa*. Erik is revealed as an unfortunate human being who does not approach his Strindbergian predecessors either in health or wholeness: he is no starry-eyed enthusiast like young Master Olof, no dedicated and knightly Christian like Magnus the Good, no miracle man of God like Gustav Vasa.

Just as Act I is Erik's, Act II is Göran Persson's, constructed as a parallel to Act I to permit the audience and the reader to take a close look at the second member of the strange duo. Göran is presented in self-examination, at work, in action, and in dealings with a group of people important to him for a variety of reasons: his practical mother with her common sense; Agda and her fatherless daughter, both of whom he has taken under his protection; Svante Sture, whom he quickly controls; Karin's suitor Max, whom he deals with realistically after having tried persuasion; the king, whom he handles with care so that he himself will not be thrown; Karin's father, Måns Knekt, whom he treats with common sense; and his one-eyed nephew Peder Welamsson, whom he treats openly and honestly. In every situation he acts with insight and intelligence; he deals with each person in terms of that person's particular nature. As a result he controls each situation sensibly and calmly when he has a chance to do so.

It is a strangely contrasting pair that emerges from Acts I and II: a brilliant, richly endowed king without any substantial sustained control of either himself or his environment, and a brilliant, richly endowed adviser with as great a control over himself and his actions as a human being could have and in substantial control of his environment.

It is in this way that Strindberg makes clear the nature of the relationship and affinity between these two sharply different men, both of whose backgrounds have been unfortunate. Erik says to Karin, "Where's Göran? I long for him every time you're contrary. Göran alone knows all the secret ways in my soul; he can say what I think so I hardly need to speak in his presence . . ." Göran tells his mother, "We're bound to each other by invisible bonds; it's as if we had been born in the same litter and under *one* constellation. His hate is my hate, his likes are mine, and things like that bind people to each other." But it is Göran who comes close to understanding both himself and the king. Erik, on the contrary, has brief moments when he can forget his own concern with his own ego and sense what Göran is and is trying to do.

Strindberg obviously considered Göran Persson the one person about Erik who has a program akin to the one Erik, instinctively as it were, favors and who can carry it through. Göran states, "I don't rely on anyone but myself! I wasn't born to wear a crown, but to rule; since I can rule only through my king, he's my sun." He tells the king, "Your great father, the master who built this nation, always observed the judicial rule of not taking any special regard for relatives, friends, or other associates. First the country, then that crowd!" Göran's program is much like that of Gustav Vasa but modified to fit a new age: "The lord of the realm must be one, and

one only, and no lords shall stand between the king and the people!"
And, in rebuking Svante Sture, the highest ranking of the lords and
unfortunately static in his political and social thinking: "You despise
the man with the pen, but the pen has created this new age that has
passed you by and that you don't understand. Human rights and
human dignity, respect for the unfortunate and forgiveness of sin—
these are new ideas that are not yet recorded on your escutcheons."
King Erik, too, favors this program, but all too often he is so
emotionally disturbed that he cannot give his full attention to it.
Note, by way of clarification, what Strindberg says about Erik in Act
IV:

> GYLLENSTJERNA: God protect and preserve the good king, the friend
> of the people, the people's king!
> ERIK: Do they call me that? Do they say anything good about me?
> GYLLENSTJERNA: Yes, and, when Erik comes with grain, the farmer sees
> St. Erik's broadaxe on the king's staff and says, "God save King
> Erik!"

Acts I and II establish the basic struggle between King Erik and
his enemies as a struggle for power and establish, too, the three
major problems that face King Erik and his procurator: the problem of Duke John, intent on gaining power; the lords, intent on
becoming the dominant element in the country; and the king's marriage, a possible means of strengthening and even expanding the
royal power. In these two acts, moreover, the contrast between King
Erik and Göran Persson when they consider these problems and their
solutions is suggested, illustrated, and amplified.

Scene 1 of Act III presents Göran Persson carefully, logically, and
legally solving the problems involving both the duke and the leading
lords; when Göran is in charge, everything goes well. Scene 2—the
trial of the lords—undoes everything Göran has accomplished, for
the king must then nominally take over. Then nothing goes well.
It is this contrast that Strindberg illustrates in one colorful episode
after another throughout the whole play, culminating in the tragic
end of the reign of the king in a wedding banquet that is an ironic

and humiliating confirmation of the king's conviction that everything he touches becomes stupid and twisted.

Numerous Swedish writers have presented their interpretations of King Erik XIV in poems, prose fiction, and dramas, but no other has approached Strindberg in making the unfortunate king take on the dimensions of a living, breathing human being, doomed, as Strindberg understood him, to misfortune because of both his heredity and, more particularly, his early environment. Strindberg did not see in Erik a believing and practicing Christian, like King Magnus, or a miracle man of God like Gustav Vasa, with a simple direct faith in Providence. Instead he saw in Erik a man who was at least partially the victim of the religious discord and intolerance that had for all practical purposes deprived him of a much-needed point of reference outside and above himself. Erik lacks religion, as Duke Carl says; what Strindberg implies, however, again and again, is that Erik lacks a faith that might have helped him bring some order into the chaos of his inner life and a good measure of sense into his external acts.

Scattered throughout the whole play are the details which taken together make up Strindberg's highly realistic case report on the king, whose behavior must have struck all those with an opportunity to observe it as not a little like that frequently encountered in nightmares. There are, to be sure, reminiscences of Hamlet-like behavior as Strindberg himself said in the passage quoted toward the beginning of this chapter. If one takes into account the material about Erik in *Gustav Vasa,* the similarities become even more striking. Note, for example, Erik's suspicion that his mother was murdered, his vacillation, his simulation of madness or madness itself, the role of enemies in his tragedy, his treatment of the woman he loves. But the most important statement pertaining to this matter is this: "So Hamlet himself is only made up of apparent contradictions, evil and good, hating and loving, cynical and enthusiastic, cruel and lenient, strong and weak; in a word: a human being, different at every moment, as human beings are, of course."

Strindberg's explanation of his characterless character is very much like that of the major characters in *The Father, Lady Julie,* and *Creditors:* the unhappy formative environment, the lack of adjustment to life, the emotional insecurity, the deep-rooted and abnormal suspicions of others, anxiety, brooding, fears, irritability, feelings of inferiority and the need for compensating for them through rationalization and striking out at the human being closest at hand, and, above all, the tragic obsession with his own ego. But Strindberg's Erik is no neatly dissected and classified monster emerging from a case report on a thoroughly abnormal human being. He is kind as well as cruel, he can love as well as hate, he can be sensitive and tender as well as insensitive and brutal, he can admire what is admirable as well as despise what he considers despicable, and he has a moral sense by means of which he sits in judgment on himself. The pattern of behavior that Strindberg illustrates again and again—fury, hasty and impulsive action, remorse, and an attempt at setting things right—is only in degree not typical of general behavior. But that difference of degree and Strindberg's dramatization of it has provided Swedish and other actors with a fascinating and rewarding challenge.

Nor is the characterization of Göran Persson much less challenging. Interpreted in terms of both his heredity and (primarily) his environment, Göran Persson is without question among the most subtle and most satisfying characters in Strindberg's dramaturgy. Not merely a foil for Erik XIV, Strindberg's Göran Persson exists as a vital characterization in his own right. Because of his humble origins —he was the son of an ex-priest and even in a Lutheran period therefore considered the offspring of an impure union—Göran Persson has from the beginning been inured to humiliation and suffering, but nature has endowed him with a mind superior to that of others and the related capacities to think clearly, to play carefully, and to act realistically and logically. He has, moreover, a set of basic values, a capacity for thoughtful kindness and love, an understanding of himself and others unsurpassed by anyone in his environment, and the ability not to let himself become embittered because of mistreatment by his fellow human beings.

Strindberg's Göran Persson is a complex and dynamic individual, not a type roughly sketched by means of a few characteristic traits. Note his understanding of Karin, her role in King Erik's life, and her role for the Swedish people; of the unfortunate Agda and her Maria; of Max, the young idealist who would rescue Karin from a life of shame but who will not compromise his ideals; of his kindly sensible mother, who knows that food must be paid for; of his one-eyed nephew, modestly ambitious but willing to execute an order; of Duke John, whose secret ambitions and jesuitical behavior make him the king's leading enemy; of the loyal Lord Gyllenstjerna; of Svante Sture, condescending and insulting in his treatment of one he considers the lowest of the low; and of King Erik, whose impulsive acts undo everything Göran has accomplished.

Note, too, how he deals with each of these characters in a manner adapted both to the individual and the occasion. To the beautiful teenager who was to become Queen Karin, he speaks gently and simply, appealing to her genuine desire to do what is right and good for King Erik and others; to Agda, he speaks with kindness, brushing aside her expressions of gratitude; to little Maria, he speaks playfully but sympathetically; to his mother, he speaks in a kindly and frank manner befitting a son who appreciates a fine mother; to Max, he ranges all the way from an appeal to his feelings for Karin to threat, and the brusque execution of his threat when neither appeal nor threat alone accomplishes his purpose. The greatest range comes, however, in his dealing with Svante Sture and with the king. A courteous reception of Sture becomes a blunt warning and a frank putting Sture in his place when courtesy and sincerity of appeal do not suffice. Göran's dealing with King Erik varies with the king's mood from the deliberate effort to play up to the king in order to get him out of his state of boredom (in the opening scene) to unqualified frankness:

GÖRAN: My God, then we're lost! Yes, Erik, whatever you put your
hand to, goes wrong.
ERIK: Can't you straighten this out, Göran?
GÖRAN: No, I can't straighten out your messes any more. Everything I
build up, you tear down, you unfortunate soul!

Strindberg has very carefully motivated Göran's every action. As
important a matter as any in Strindberg's interpretation of Göran is
Göran's need for a human point of reference and for a supernatural
one as well. The love of an unidentified woman supplies the former
and is on its way to helping supply the latter when the woman
rejects Göran for another man. The loss ultimately strips Göran of
the power to act and even to doubt that there is any point in acting:
"No, I know absolutely nothing, understand nothing, and so I'm done
for. There was a time when I dreamt I was a statesman, and thought
I had a mission in life: to defend your crown, inherited from your
great father, given by the people—not by the lords—and worn by
the grace of God. But I must have been mistaken." It is a rich and
sympathetic interpretation.

Of all the sufficiently individualized secondary and minor characters that have essential roles to play in the story of Erik and his
favorite before their fall from power, the royal mistress and later
queen needs to be singled out as a striking illustration of Strindberg's
insight into human nature and his ability to make historical figures
come alive. Strindberg's Karin is not a romanticized idealization in
keeping with the dominant Swedish literary tradition; she is instead
a very real and credible young woman placed in an extremely difficult position, whose beauty, natural charm, and goodness of heart
do not suffice to make her the king's "good genius"—as tradition
has it—but whose frailty and gentleness provide her neither the
sharpness of mind nor the experience to affect the king's erratic
pattern of behavior except to a very much limited and indecisive
degree. Lovely and well intentioned though she may be, she, unfortunately enough, does not appreciably understand either the king
or his environment. But she is a decidedly attractive and sympathet-

ically conceived character, and as such one of many women characters so understood and interpreted by Strindberg in the historical
plays.

The insight Strindberg demonstrates in his interpretations of his
two principals and of Queen Karin is demonstrated as well in the
other characters, from little Maria and the two royal children—all
three the offspring of irregular unions—through Måns Knekt with
his understandable insistence on having irregularity replaced by reg-
ularity, to Lord Gyllenstjerna, who knows that irregularities are,
unfortunately, parts of a highly imperfect world, a world at best
not too far removed from madness.

For the composition of his drama about the king and his adviser,
"bound by invisible bonds," Strindberg had employed a structure that
is strikingly different in some basic ways from any that he had used
in his earlier plays. A close examination of the structure of *Gustav
Vasa* reveals that that play is built carefully and scrupulously about
one central character and the Job-like misfortunes by means of which
that miracle man of God is tried, tested, and not found wanting.
There is a concentration in *Gustav Vasa* that makes the play admirably suited, even from the point of view of dramatic structure, to the
interpretation of a king who was the unifying center of attention in
his environment. It is significant that neither scholar nor critic nor
theater audience has ever seriously objected to the dramatic structure
of *Gustav Vasa*.

Many have, however, objected to the composition of *Erik XIV*. It
is episodic and to all appearances loose structurally; a first reading
gives one an impression of the fragmentary, the inconsistent, and
the illogical. Yet, an unbiased reader or spectator, who judges without cut-and-dried, static notions of how a realistic historical play
should be written, will have to come to the conclusion that *Erik XIV*
is another example of Strindberg's genius for varying his dramatic
structure to fit the particular subject. Strindberg deliberately, I suspect, devised the loose and irregular structure of *Erik XIV* to fit the
chaotic and extremely irregular nature and behavior of his Erik and

the great chaos and disorder such a character would make of his immediate environment. The royal wedding banquet can serve as an illustration. Could a happier device have been conceived for demonstrating how everything in the life of the king doomed to misfortune became soiled and twisted? Note the very effective contrast between Strindberg's banquet and its Biblical source of inspiration. No one has objected to the impact of the scene when presented on the stage, and no one can deny its culminating share in giving strangely compelling consistency to the structure of the rest of the play and to Strindberg's concept of Erik.

In this play the primary concentration is on character and only to a limited extent on history and historical background and atmosphere as such. There are, to be sure, allusions to Erik's courtship of foreign princesses, above all Elizabeth of England; to Finland, Poland, and the whole Baltic area; and to the contemporary religious chaos; but the significance of all these matters is far more obscure than parallel matters were in the earlier plays. Nor is there any specific religious concept or idea that helps give meaning to conflict and to life beyond the immediate to either Erik or Göran Persson.

The latter fact will have to be considered by scholars who attempt to establish the main features of Strindberg's highly complex concept of tragedy. For Strindberg considered Erik XIV as tragic a figure as Hamlet, and his Göran Persson merits detailed consideration as a tragic character. It is Göran who challenges traditional values and morals; it is Göran who has the power to be free in his thinking, voluntarily selecting his goals, examining the mystery of his universe, and, up to an obvious point, acting. Erik XIV, however, is a fairly close parallel to Lady Julie as a naturalistic Strindbergian tragic character. Note the implications of the following exchanges:

> ERIK: Have you ever noticed, Göran, that there are matters we don't understand, and may not understand?
> GÖRAN: Yes. But haven't you often and finally felt yourself a bit better than the others?

ERIK: Yes. And you?

GÖRAN: I have always thought my acts were right . . .

ERIK: I, too; and most likely the others do, too. Who has been wrong, then?

GÖRAN: Who knows? Imagine how little we know!

and:

ERIK: Göran, is life more to be laughed at than to be wept over?

GÖRAN: As much the one as the other, I suspect. For me, the whole thing is nonsense, but that doesn't mean there mayn't be a hidden meaning to it.

But the Göran who says that has not cynically rejected all values, as the context proves. Both he and the king are keenly aware of the tragic implications in man and in the world in which he has his being.

Whatever objection may be made to *Erik XIV*, it is certain that it is highly successful theater. The superb characterizations, the thoroughly realistic dialogue, the fascinating plot, and its very structure have appealed to audiences since it had its *première* at the Swedish Theater in Stockholm on November 30, 1899. On the following day a reviewer for *Stockholms Dagblad* wrote, among many other things about the triumph for both Strindberg and the actors:

The performance, which was attended by Prince Eugene, was over just before eleven o'clock and was followed by an almost uncountable number of curtain calls. Mr. de Wahl [Erik XIV] and Mr. Svennberg [Göran Persson] appeared again and again and were greeted with enthusiastic applause. As the calls for the author continued for a long time, Producer Ranft announced that Mr. Strindberg was not on stage. Finally Mr. Molander [the director] was called forward and became the object of the audience's appreciation.[6]

The critic did express regret that Strindberg had not paid attention to King Erik as a lover of art and literature and as a learned and literary man; he regretted, too, the use of "nasty words." The testimony of the press is, in general, that the audience liked the play.

It is interesting to note that among the contemporary critics and reviewers who did not bless *Erik XIV* as literature or drama, Carl David af Wirsén had as early as November 21, 1899, in *Vårt Land,* damned the play both as literature and theater. He acknowledged no real merit and ended his lengthy attack thus:

Perhaps the flaws in the play would have been emphasized less fully if the fanatical storm of jubilation with which witless admirers praise anything of Mr. Strindberg's to the skies did not make it a duty to do a little sifting. Those who with genuine thoughtfulness read Strindberg's *Erik XIV* cannot avoid acknowledging the accuracy of the criticism which has been expressed here. It may be the lot of someone else on this paper's staff to express himself about the play when it is produced. No manner of acting, even if it were superior, could change the judgment which—after reading the play again and again—has been pronounced on the work itself.[7]

Fortunately for both Strindberg and the Swedish stage, af Wirsén's judgment has not been accepted. An examination of the many reviews in the Nylin Collection at the Royal Library leads to one conclusion: that audiences have appreciated *Erik XIV* and critics have gradually learned to appreciate the play both as theater and as literature the farther they have been removed in time from the violently personal anti-Strindberg feelings of the early years of the century.

The record of *Erik XIV* on the Swedish stage and abroad confirms its value as drama and theater. At home the play has been revived again and again; touring companies have carried it to the provinces. Abroad *Erik XIV* has enjoyed more successful productions than any other of Strindberg's historical plays. The Danes, the Norwegians, the Germans, the Finns and the Swedes of Finland, the Russians, and even the French have found *Erik XIV* intensely interesting and stimulating theater.

9

Gustav Adolf

Deliverer from Bondage

HAVING completed his Vasa trilogy, Strindberg turned to the history of a Swedish king who had never aroused his enthusiasm in the pre-Inferno years but who had since his conversion come to his attention in subtly disturbing ways. The tercentennial of Gustav Adolf's birth had been celebrated in 1894, in public ceremonies and memorial services and in numerous printed articles and books. In keeping with the general Swedish attitude of the 1890's toward Sweden's history and its great historical figures, most of these accounts reinforced and supported the accepted apotheosis of the seventeenth-century king as a genius, a saint, and a martyr for the cause of Protestantism. Suspicious as he always was of the exaltation or deification of any human being, past or present, Strindberg in 1899 had good reason for examining deliberately and fairly painstakingly the king who was being glorified as the savior of the whole concept of religious freedom.

By 1899, as we have already seen in the discussion of earlier plays, Strindberg believed in a deity who took immediate interest in his human creatures and interfered in their affairs, largely through chosen men who were sent on missions to guide historical development. From that point of view there could be no question but that some developments exceedingly important to mankind had taken place in the seventeenth century and that Gustav Adolf had played a highly significant role in them, in more ways than one. The possibility that his earlier lack of interest in the king, because of his generally accepted exaltation as a Lutheran saint and the protector of the faith, might not be soundly based on logical conclusions led Strindberg to read widely, not only in the popular sources he generally used for his historical material but in less widely known source material about the king. In his reading he found a confirmation of his earlier suspicions that Gustav Adolf must have been anything but a saint, and at the same time he developed a profound appreciation of Gustav Adolf as an effective champion of ideas Strindberg himself favored in 1899. He believed that he found historical proof of the accuracy of his conviction that there have been and are human beings chosen by the Lord to perform great tasks.

It must never be forgotten that Strindberg was keenly aware at practically all times of what was happening in the world about him. The twentieth-century efforts to unify the various Christian denominations, led for many years by Strindberg's personal friend Nathan Söderblom (1866-1931), archbishop of Sweden from 1914 to 1931, had predecessors throughout Strindberg's lifetime and even before that back to the days of the post-Reformation at least. Gustav Adolf's father, Charles IX, and uncle, John III, for example, had had inclinations in that direction. Such contemporary moves as were made within Protestant ranks in his own time and promises of even wider efforts attracted Strindberg, whose particular brand of religious faith can be classified as syncretism. The fact that his study of the sources indicated that Gustav Adolf had progressed far toward religious tolerance and toward a syncretist point of view confirmed Strindberg's own conviction that human enlightenment would ultimately lead to religious unity and monotheism.

Equally important is Strindberg's preference for peace and dislike

of war. In 1898 and 1899 Strindberg's hope and the hopes of count-
less others for the elimination of war were concentrated on The
Hague International Peace Conference, which promised to become a
landmark in the history of mankind. Strindberg, who insisted that
disarmament was the social reform he would have liked to see
realized before any other in his time, believed he found in his search
of the sources no evidence that Gustav Adolf loved war for its own
sake but rather that he was a military genius who used war in pursuit of a real peace. That developments at The Hague promised to
carry further what Gustav Adolf had achieved toward the ideal of
coexistence in peace and the ideal of religious freedom and tolerance
helped Strindberg appreciate the seventeenth-century king, who, he
was convinced, was not the saint presented in the official Swedish
textbooks but a very human chosen instrument of the Lord.

In *Open Letters to the Intimate Theater,* Strindberg has stated the
practical result of his extensive reading in the literature about Gustav
Adolf:

Gustav Adolf. A Lutheran saint, who has almost become a school text,
had no attraction for me. But then came the Jubilee of 1894 and the
memorials in [his] honor. In an unpretentious little [booklet] I happened
to read that Gustav Adolf, who had begun his career by torturing Catholics (see Cornelius' *Church History*) had finally come so far that he
hanged his own men who had disturbed a Catholic service in Augsburg
(or Regensburg?). Then I saw at once his whole character and the whole
drama, and I called it my *Nathan the Wise.*
The blond man with the gentle spirit, who always had a joke ready even
in dark moments, very much a statesman and a little of the musketeer,
the dreamer about a universal monarchy, our Henri Quatre who loves
beautiful women as much as a good battle, half Swedish and half German, with a mother from Holstein and a wife from Brandenburg, related
to Pfalz, Prussia, Hesse, Poland, Hungary, Bohemia, and Austria itself,
sinful enough to be human, gets into such disharmonies and inner conflicts as make a drama rich and interesting. Supplied by Cardinal Riche-
lieu with 400,000 a year on the condition that he leave the Catholic
League alone, he participates for a couple of years in the Thirty Years'
War against the House of Hapsburg and involves himself, as a dramatic

character namely, in insolvable difficulties when it comes to telling friend from enemy, and only death on the battlefield can restore harmony and cut the tangled threads.[1]

Strindberg's reading, in other words, destroyed his old idea of Gustav Adolf as an exalted saint and replaced it with a concept of a great man who was highly human and moreover exceptionally interesting.

It is highly significant that Strindberg says, "I saw at once his whole character and the whole drama, and I called it my *Nathan the Wise.*" Lessing's *Nathan the Wise* (1779) is a very long, loosely constructed five-act dramatic sermon on religious tolerance and brotherly love; it includes representatives of Christianity, Mohammedanism, and Judaism against the somewhat vague historical background of the third crusade in Palestine in the 1190's. There can be little doubt that Lessing's example may have, as we shall see a little later and as I have tried to show elsewhere,[2] led Strindberg to present his modern realistic study of tolerance in dramatic form on a broad and even monumental scale.

From the beginning Strindberg conceived a play about Gustav Adolf that was not limited to the conventional two to three hours for performance. Though he did decide to concentrate his attention primarily on the crucial last two years of the king's life, the years in which Gustav Adolf played his role as a decisive factor in world history, Strindberg linked those years (1630-32) with the past by means of exposition and preparation and did not confine himself to a relatively small number of episodes for dramatic treatment. For, unlike *Gustav Vasa,* for example, *Gustav Adolf* was to be as much a drama of ideas as a drama of character.

The new play was to present the Thirty Years' War as one of the periods in which world-shaking events occurred in keeping with a plan not always clear to mere men, to demonstrate and explore intolerance in its various manifestations and the nature of tolerance and its achievement, and, in the process of doing all this, to present Gustav Adolf as the one chosen by the Lord to become the man of tolerance who curbed intolerance at one of the most crucial points in the history of western civilization. The most ambitious of all his historical plays, *Gustav Adolf* is a five-act play with fifteen settings that, if performed in its entirety would require approximately seven hours for performance. It has more than fifty characters with lines to speak and many, many others without lines. The list of settings suggests the scope:

Act I: The shore on Usedom.
Act II: A wealthy burgher's home in Stettin; a room in a farmhouse; in the camp outside Frankfurt an der Oder; the palace park in Berlin; in the fortress at Spandau.
Act III: A churchyard on a hill; in Auerbachshof in Leipzig.
Act IV: A pass in Thuringia; the terrace of a palace outside Mainz; the market square in a village near Ingolstadt on the Danube; in Munich.
Act V: The camp outside Nuremberg; a shed at Lützen; the castle church at Wittenberg.

A reading of the play confirms what this list can only suggest: This play was planned on a far greater scale than any other of the historical plays, and, strangely enough for a playwright as keenly conscious of the stage and its limitations as Strindberg, it was written with little or no regard for the realistic facts about available stages in 1900.

An analysis of the play, act by act, will reveal in some detail, however, what Strindberg attempted to do and will suggest what he succeeded or failed in doing. In justice to Strindberg, one must at all times remember that, while concentrating primarily on Gustav Adolf himself, Strindberg was developing three closely related and interwoven themes—war in all its horror as exemplified in the Thirty Years' War, the problem of religious intolerance, and the achievement of tolerance in areas that go all the way from religious tolerance to the brotherhood of man.

It must be remembered, too, that Strindberg's dramatic technique is the extremely realistic one he discusses at length in the preface to

Lady Julie. The scenes, the dialogue, the exposition, the foreshadowing, and the characterization are essentially applications of what he says in that preface. To illustrate the development of his central character, Strindberg has selected (1) crucial episodes in the development of the king from an intolerant Lutheran leader to the point where he has become a genuine man of tolerance and (2) episodes from both civilian and military life, which supply the broad background.

In the first act, Strindberg introduces his themes, the religious, racial, political, and personal conflicts, and many of his characters. To provide the extensive background needed for his massive subject, he paints boldly, creating sweeping effects and almost unlimited panoramas without neglecting telling detail.[3] The physical setting for the coming action in an environment of starvation, want, plundering, and brutality, all stemming from Gustav Adolf's enemies, and the hope of the Germans that the Swedish king is about to deliver them from chaos and restore order, are quickly conveyed. The Swedish herald's reading of Gustav Adolf's initial proclamation, promising the Germans protection of personal freedom and property rights and guaranteeing the persecuted German Protestants religious freedom, contrasts in its implications of order and quiet delivery with the chaotic and disorderly atmosphere of the opening. That contrast is emphasized by the entrance of representative common Swedish soldiers and noncommissioned officers in orderly fashion, in keeping with the high standards of conduct set up by a respected leader. The dramatic effect is further heightened by the orderly entrance of the men closest to Gustav Adolf—his commanders and his confidant, Erik Rålamb. Throughout this opening of the first act Strindberg manages to convey the very important fact that, devoted to the king as these soldiers and officers are, not one among them fully understands the king and what he has set out to accomplish.

Against a background of a devastated Germany with its despairing people and a background of his very human followers and assistants and their own great poverty, Gustav Adolf makes his first appearance. He comes on stage as a confident idealist, a firm believer in the Lutheran God, a leader sure of having been chosen by God to perform a great mission. He comes on stage embodying the people's hope, able to instill in them the conviction that he can perform the mission in good faith, order, and discipline. Cheerful even in adversity, Gustav Adolf nevertheless reveals that he has much to learn: He thinks of his mission as a Lutheran crusade, but, having learned that even a Catholic woman can welcome him to Germany and that her handshake does not remind him of having taken hold of a snake, he admits, "I'll be wiser with every day that goes."

It is a superb first act, brilliantly conceived and brilliantly executed. It is, however, an act that would need a stage far beyond any available in the Sweden of 1900 for its fully effective presentation; it is the sort of act that would provide an imaginative and highly competent film director material to conjure with.

Act II is something else, lacking dramatic intensity and concentration in its five long leisurely scenes. It makes excellent reading, however. It makes vivid the progress of the war; clarifies the complexities of the religious situation and its resulting intolerance; suggests the Strindbergian solution—syncretism; demonstrates that Gustav Adolf's crusade cannot be a clear-cut Lutheran crusade for the protection and security of German Protestants; shows both Swedes and German allies in action; and shows that not even the disciplined and generally orderly Swedes can be anything but human.

The Gustav Adolf of Act II has grown and developed. Far from remaining the naïve idealist of Act I, he has become increasingly aware of the fact that religious, political, and economic matters are not simple. He has been forced to sacrifice his anti-Catholic ideals by allying himself with Catholic France, since soldiers must be fed, clothed, and sheltered, and waging war involves other expenditures as well. He has learned that he himself is not certain any more of the real nature of his mission; he has learned that he, too, can be tempted—the imperial thought of uniting all Germans suggests that he may aspire to more crowns than that of Sweden. He is reminded, moreover, that he has sins to repent—his illegitimate son appears.

When read, the second act is highly satisfactory; it develops the themes presented in Act I, and it advances the characterization of Gustav Adolf himself. In the hands of a gifted director, the act could be an intensely interesting part of a movie; on the contemporary stage, it would present serious problems.

Act III, with its two long scenes, the first set in the churchyard overlooking the battlefield at Breitenfeld and the second a victory celebration that becomes anything but a celebration, serves the reader well in the development of the themes of religious tolerance and the futility and brutality of war. The two gravediggers' argument about religious faith and the confession of faith by representatives of the Mohammedan, Romany, Jewish, and Christian (Calvinistic, Catholic, and Lutheran) religions demonstrate effectively the essential basic unity of beliefs on the part of all these faiths (and denominations) and suggest that tolerance and syncretism are solutions to the problem of religious intolerance.

The complexity and the brutality of war are, for the reader, beautifully clarified by exposition in the form of discussion by observers and commentators. There is, however, very little dramatic action.

Most important for the development of Gustav Adolf's character is Johan Banér's explanation of the significance of the victory at Breitenfeld: the Swedish king could then have had peace and have gained his initial goal—securing religious freedom for the Protestants. We learn, however, through the discussions of the great commanders, that Gustav Adolf has changed; from a dedicated crusader with a noble if limited mission he has become a leader more and more tempted to unite all the Germans and to secure the imperial crown for himself. The king, who appears only briefly at the end of this long act is, moreover, isolating himself from most of the brilliant Swedish leaders who had served him and his cause well.

Act IV gives more direct attention to the central character than the two preceding acts, but even so we learn most of what Strindberg has to say about him through the expository talk of others. In scene 1, Tott and Rålamb's conversation not only clarifies a great deal of the Swedish background but suggests that Gustav Adolf is becoming a Lutheran renegade, that is, he is becoming tolerant of other faiths. In scene 2, the commanders discuss the outwardly successful progress of the war and the changes in the king's thinking about himself and his future. Strindberg presents the king himself in revealing conversations with Banér, Oxenstjerna, Queen Maria Eleanora, and Marcus the Jew as well. In scene 3, the increasing corruption in the Swedish camp is related to Gustav Adolf's growing tendency to think about gaining greater power for himself rather than about his country and his role as a deliverer. But the scene closes with the highly dramatic entrance of the king after he has been wounded at Ingolstadt. Note what the king has learned at last: "*My* plans, *my* objectives, which haven't been mine and which I'm just beginning to understand . . . as I understood that I have been only a blind subordinate of the Lord, whose plans we are never permitted to understand." In scene 4, Gustav Adolf has become a man of tolerance, knowing that his role is that of deliverer from oppression, but, even though he suffers inner distress and outward isolation, he does not fully succeed in bowing before the Eternal One in humility and resignation.

Act IV is, like Acts II and III, excellent reading, but its lengthy discussions would undoubtedly make it difficult for staging except under inspired direction, inspired acting, and discreet cutting.

The final act is the shortest of all. Scene 1, set in the camp outside Nuremberg, illustrates Gustav Adolf's extreme difficulties when he has invaded purely Catholic territory outside the limits of his original goal. Demonstrated are the king's increasing inner tensions and conflicts in terms of his initial mission, his temptation to extend his mission for selfish reasons, and his tormenting doubts about what he is doing. Scene 2, one of the most touching scenes in dramatic literature, presents the death of the orphan trumpeter, symbolically representative of the horrors of war. Scene 3, with its setting at Lützen just before the final victory in which the king loses his life, presents

the king, pale and hollow-eyed, chastened and resigned as he goes
into battle for the last time: "Is it Golgotha? Into Thy hands I com-
mend my spirit, Lord Jesus!" And in anguish: "The battle begins!
The horses, the horses! *(Falls to his knees at the back with hands
folded)* Oh Jesus, our Saviour, who has conquered death and the
kingdom of death, have mercy upon us, have mercy upon us all!"

In scene 4, Strindberg presents what Swedes in general had been
used to—an apotheosis of Gustav Adolf! The funeral is set in the castle church; the scene, effective in its own right as colorful theater, concentrates largely on presenting the summarizing verdicts on the great
king and his achievement. The tributes, carefully worded in keeping with each giver, range from "To the good blond man from a
Catholic woman" to "To the restorer of freedom of conscience. The
colors are seven but the light one."

The play would make an excellent film, and, if the day comes
when there are stages adequate to permit full justice to such a monumental play, it would probably give spectators a theatrical experience
never to be forgotten. Considered from the point of view of literature
alone and not from that of the stage, *Gustav Adolf* must be judged
a masterpiece. There is no other literary work in Swedish literature
that can begin to compare with it, in the first place, as a brilliant
interpretation and depiction of the Thirty Years' War, one of the
most significant segments of Swedish history. Strindberg has naturally and economically treated the particular war itself and the
theme of war in general. Fitted naturally and painlessly into the long
expository discussions and into other parts as well are the elements
of historical information that clarify the causes of the war, reaching
back to before 1618 when the war began, the issues involved, the
physical setting, the progress of the war (particularly, of course, from
the Swedish point of view), the major participants, and the sweeping effects of that war until the death of Gustav Adolf in 1632.

The presentation carries with it a highly persuasive consideration
of war as an activity largely compounded of inevitable brutality,
horror, senselessness, and futility. Illustrations of this are, in Act I,

the miller's description of a Germany devastated by the imperial
mercenary armies as they apply the scorched-earth policy, and the
gradual deterioration of the conduct of Gustav Adolf's Swedish and
Finnish troops as they are exposed to the ugly facts of war. From an
unusually high level of discipline, order, and idealistic purpose (even
if its implications are only vaguely grasped by most of the Swedes
and the Finns), many of the men descend to beastlike behavior. Take
the king's analysis of war by way of illustration:

My friends, you know I feel how someone has taken me by the hair to
drag me where I don't want to go. Those cries out there . . . they're not
the cries of want and suffering; they're the evil passions that war has let
loose . . . I know where it will lead; I know I don't want to go there;
but I'm being dragged there. *(Gets up, moved)* For twenty years I've
been at war, but I can never get used to the horrible smoke of powder;
it smells of the devil, sulphur and saltpeter, and it makes people evil as
if it rose from hell to mock the thunder of heaven; but it brings only
showers of blood and tears instead of blessed rain for the crops of the field.

Suffering and want are included, too; so are deterioration and disintegration. Note in Act V:

QUARTERMASTER: I'm ashamed, but not because of that; but because
we've become a disgrace to Sweden, because from having been the soldiers of the Lord in discipline and honor we've become as bad as our
enemies. All vices, all crimes flourish in our camps, and we have just
as many pagans as Christians, but we have still more corpses than we
have living men. The whole country about us stinks, and our friends
curse us! *(At the back of the stage goes a procession of green stretchers
for the living and black stretchers—covered with white—for the dead,
carried by white-clad attendants.)* The angel of death's procession of
triumph! *(Fabricius can be seen in the procession.)* And the chief priest
. . . who has to bury both Christians and pagans. All become alike in
the great pit! *(The queen can be seen in the procession; she is dressed
in white and is carrying a little child in her arms; a crowd of white-clad
children follows the queen.)*
SERGEANT MAJOR *(moved)*: The queen!
QUARTERMASTER: The good angel of mercy and suffering! The mother
of the abandoned children! Yes, the deserted and the orphans! Not an

accurate birth certificate any more . . . only "parents unknown." The
king strikes, and the queen heals; he punishes, and she comforts. Bless
her! *(The queen goes by; children tug at her skirt; the procession is
continued by wounded with bandages and crutches.)*

SERGEANT MAJOR: The dark sides of war. You know, I can't remember
the bright ones any more . . . Everything smells, everything tastes of the
dead! even the wine in the goblet! *(A procession of ragged people)*

QUARTERMASTER: There come the hungry. No bread and no money.

SERGEANT MAJOR: It's as if there were a curse on the French money; it
never lasts.

Illustrating and explaining such matters again and again, *Gustav
Adolf* is indeed an effective indictment of war as part of man's in-
humanity to man.

The presentation of the Swedish historical background is brilliant, too. The historical, dynastic, political, economic, military, and
religious factors in Sweden, as they relate to the war and to Gustav
Adolf himself, are clarified when needed. That fact is important, not
least because of Gustav Adolf's strong conviction of blood guilt and
the necessity for his personal atonement for his father's crimes and
sins. The gnawing fear that his claims to the Swedish crown may be
anything but legal helps, for example, to explain his inner conflicts
and the reasons for the intimate, familylike relationship between
him and many of the men on his staff. Note, for example, in scene
4 of Act IV, that in talking with the queen the king identifies the
blood guilt he has had to carry and classifies himself as a usurper.
All such historical details are presented, of course, in keeping with
Strindberg's particular concept of the king and his time, but a comparison of Strindberg's account—in spite of its compression and rearrangement and a few inaccuracies—with the account of the king
and the period of the Thirty Years' War in any standard history of
Sweden (for example, Ingvar Andersson's *History of Sweden*) will
prove Strindberg's account amazingly accurate and thoroughly vivid.

In *Gustav Adolf,* as in most of his historical and many of his nonhistorical plays, Strindberg demonstrates that he knows his Bible
exceedingly well, and in this play, as in *The Saga of the Folkungs,*

that knowledge is used as an effective part of the historical background. The Calvinists and Lutherans know their Bible, the Catholics know their church doctrines and history, and the non-Christians know their respective faiths—each one according to his capacity and to his particular point of view. In a play that deals especially with the problem of religious intolerance, it is appropriate that Biblical and other religious references and information permeate the play. From the conversations of the characters, women as well as men, comes what amounts to a comparative examination of several denominations of Christianity and several other religions. All this is highly in keeping with Gustav Adolf's time, a period when controversy about religious faiths raged just as violently as controversy about political faiths does today.

It is on this basis that Strindberg develops his theme of tolerance. From this point of view, the play is an examination, in human terms and on various social and intellectual levels, of the nature and forms of intolerance. The examination ranges all the way from the attitude of Gustav Adolf, who lands in Germany naïvely convinced that he is tolerant and the Catholics intolerant:

I can't tolerate intolerance . . . and so I hate the Catholics . . . You know I can smell a Catholic within gunshot, and when I've had to take one by the hand I've felt as if I were taking hold of a snake! That's why, you see, my position is so clear, my task is so simple. That's why I didn't need any declaration of war, that's why I needed no alliances, because the sheep know their shepherd, and the shepherd knows the wolves. And the one who is not with me is against me.

through the attitude exemplified in the mixed marriage of the Protestant miller and his Catholic wife to the narrowness of the ordinary soldiers and gravediggers:

QUARTERMASTER: Do you know, children, why there's such a deplorable division within the church?
GRAVEDIGGER 1: No.
QUARTERMASTER: Well, because you don't accept the same interpretation.
GRAVEDIGGGER 1: Whose interpretation?

QUARTERMASTER: Mine! Ours!

GRAVEDIGGER I: That's what Luther said, too!

QUARTERMASTER: And Luther was right! And do you know how this deplorable division within the church can end? Well, only through this, that you all accept my interpretation, our interpretation. It would be so easy, so natural, so . . . what shall I say . . . ?

GRAVEDIGGER II: Simple!

QUARTERMASTER: Shut up! I can't stand criticism! What are they up to in that church?

GRAVEDIGGER I: Celebrating morning mass.

QUARTERMASTER: Papal inventions, human tricks, vanity, superstition, foolishness.

Intolerance as Strindberg presents it stems largely from ignorance, lack of understanding, stupidity, selfishness, indoctrination, or a combination of several of these factors. He illustrates all these and demonstrates the results of intolerance that stem from them.

The Strindbergian answers to the problem are crystal-clear. In Act III, scene I, for example, he demonstrates through the religious services of the Mohammedans and the Jews that the basic doctrines of the denominations and the major religions are essentially the same. Consider such matters as Fabricius' translation of the Afghans' prayer:

FABRICIUS: There is no god but God; the only true, great, and highest God has His being in Himself, is eternal, is not born and does not bear, is perfect in Himself, fills the universe with His everlastingness, omnipotence, omniscience, goodness, mercy, and immutability.

GRUBBE: Why, that's the same God as ours!

Johan Banér's words express Strindberg's point of view: "Yes, the devil take Luther and the pope and Calvin and all the other wranglers; I'm a Christian and would preferably be a syncretist if I should be anything. A syncretist is one of those who think it's all one, if you can only say the Lord's prayer with a fairly clear conscience." That monotheism and syncretism need not be universally accepted but that tolerance—religious, nationalistic, and racial—should be, Strindberg feels. Note, by way of merely one illustration, Gustav

Adolf's speech when he has developed from a fairly bigoted defender of one branch of the Christian faith to a genuine champion of tolerance:

> I have finally heard the defendant, something I ought to have started with; and I have learned something! Out of these unsolvable contradictions in which I had been caught at the beginning of this war, I have finally worked my way; I have found myself and my task, which I didn't understand until now. . . . From now on it will be the deliverer against the oppressor!

In this tragedy there is, as in all Strindberg's major historical dramas, a gallery of memorable individualized characters, the most striking of which is, naturally, the central character himself. The dramatic technique for bringing the historic dead alive for the reader and for the member of the theater audience is the usual realistic-naturalistic one employed in the other plays. Basic are, of course, Strindberg's convictions that human beings are complex and dynamic, that heredity and particularly environment help shape their lives, and that though the Eternal One may control their destinies there is a measure of freedom of the will. There is again the use of material for purposes of characterization as much as for the development of themes, "which is . . . worked up, admitted, repeated, developed and built up, like the theme in a musical composition." [4] Gustav Adolf and the secondary characters are, in other words, revealed gradually and naturally through what they say and do and through what others do or say about them because of direct knowledge or hearsay. All these matters are used not according to a mechanically set pattern but according to the conceptions that Strindberg holds of the individuals. The result is a rich variety of dramatically alive characters.

Strindberg's extensive reading about Gustav Adolf and his time resulted, as we have already seen, in a quite new concept of the king. Gustav Adolf, he believed, was no saint but a very human being, "the blond man with the gentle spirit . . . very much a statesman, a little of the musketeer . . . a dreamer," as well as a military genius and a gifted leader, who seemed to Strindberg quite obviously one of the relatively few selected as instruments for changing the course of history. But the Gustav Adolf selected for performing great deeds in the seventeenth century was no duplicate of his grandfather, Gustav Vasa, with his one guiding principle—the unification and strengthening of Sweden. Nor was he another Magnus the Good, the last and sole pure instrument of the Lord among the "dirty instruments," the great Folkungs. Gustav Adolf was neither a man who made most of those about him cringe with fear nor a man who was a lamb at the mercy of the wolves and the shepherds about him. He was instead richly supplied with attractive qualities of personality as well as a rich endowment, including tenderness of conscience, firmness of purpose, and a capacity for intellectual growth that suited him remarkably well for playing his role as an instrument for curbing religious intolerance in large portions of Europe and for making bearable coexistence possible. Unlike his great predecessors on the Swedish throne, he played his designated role against a far broader background, a background that is epic in scope.

Strindberg thought of Gustav Adolf's life as king, and particularly of his last two decisive years as participant in the Thirty Years' War, as a pilgrimage in some ways not unlike his own as dramatized in *To Damascus* and somewhat similar to that of Magnus the Good in *The Saga of the Folkungs*. Gustav Adolf's pilgrimage is the pilgrimage from a bigotry that rests on limited idealism and ignorance to a genuine tolerance that embraces the racial and the nationalistic, as well as the religious. The pilgrimage ends with the king's death and, ironically, the achievement of the goals for which he ultimately fought.

In other words, Strindberg emphasizes the development of Gustav Adolf from the time he landed in Germany optimistic and naïve about his crusade until he gained the insight into and understanding of his mission. That development is presented by Strindberg not as simple and mechanical but as highly complex, delayed, interrupted, and changed because of factors such as the selfishness and ignorance of the king's allies, the limitations of the resources at his command, the bewildering religious and political facts of life on the continent, disaster and disease, well-meant interference by the people closest to him, his own past, and the gnawing conviction that he had a burden of blood guilt, and because of his human tendency to consider yielding to the temptation of seizing power for himself.

One factor which Strindberg emphasizes as a tragic motif is the blood guilt traceable to the cruel and unjustified acts of Gustav Adolf's father, Charles IX:

QUEEN: Was Banér's father beheaded in Linköping by your father?

KING: We don't like to talk about that but it's true. And Johan Banér's mother was Kristina Sture. But the saga of the Stures is so interwoven with the saga of the Vasas that I can't quite grasp it in what they call a natural way. As regents, the oldest Stures established the independence of the kingdom, but Gustav Vasa got the crown. Erik XIV had Stures killed for reasons that weren't fully clear. My father, Charles IX, beheaded the lords at Linköping and hit the Sture clan at the same time, probably without intending to . . . No fewer than six Stures got sorrow that day. Hogenskild Bielke was married to Anna Sture; Ture Nelsson Bielke to Margareta Sture; Ture Pederson Bielke to Sigrid Sture; Erik Stenbock to Malin Sture; Gustav Banér to Kristina Sture; and Krister Horn was the brother-in-law of Mauritz Sture. That's the blood guilt I've carried, and that's why I have put up with more from my friends Horn, Banér, and Stenbock than from any other human beings!

The motif is rewarding dramatically. Not only does the close and intimate relationship between Gustav Adolf and most of his leading Swedish advisers and commanders help characterize the king, but the variations in the closeness of that relationship provide an effective means of suggesting the tortuous development of his pilgrimage.

Strindberg's characterization of Gustav Adolf is an application of his conviction that, like Shakespeare, he had "to depict human beings both in their greatness and their triviality." Shown in action and inaction, in dealing with friends and enemies and many who are neither, in moments of deep despair and distress as well as exaltation and optimistic hope, in strength and weakness, in defeat and victory, with women and children as well as men, Strindberg's Gustav Adolf emerges as one of the greatest of his characterizations, decidedly human, dynamic, and complex, and, without question, tragic in stature.

Of the many other characters, more than twenty are secondary characters who are interpreted sufficiently to make them come alive as individuals. In keeping with what Strindberg says about supporting characters in the preface to *Lady Julie,* the following characters are thoroughly individualized and alive and play important roles in the characterization of Gustav Adolf and in the dramatic action: Queen Maria Eleonora, Gustav Horn, Johan Banér, Åke Tott, Lennart Torstensson, Fredrik Stenbock, Nils Brahe, Erik Rålamb, the Lutheran miller, his Catholic wife, the bailiff, the sergeant major, the quartermaster, the provost, the schoolmaster, Marcus the Jew, Rudolf, the cooper, his wife, his daughter, Gustav Adolf's illegitimate son (Gustav Gustavsson), the trumpeter Nils, Fredrik of Pfalz, and Leubelfing.

The rest of the many characters are minor or incidental ones of the kind discussed in the preface to *Lady Julie.* Fabricius, for example, is seen only as the king's personal chaplain and spiritual adviser; his character outside that professional role is not made clear nor is there any need for making it so. The Afghan Mohammedans, to take another example, are thoroughly static; they are present merely to help demonstrate the idea that the great monotheistic religions agree in their fundamental doctrine of a God who is the father of all mankind.

When the play was printed in 1900, most of the reviewers pounced as usual on historical inaccuracies and anachronisms and charged Strindberg with once again having aimed to destroy the Swedish concept of a great historical figure. Some of the reviewers, moreover, pointed out undramatic elements and underscored the difficulties any theater would have in attempting to stage the play. But friendly reviews appeared as well. In "Strindberg's Gustav Adolf," published in

Nordisk Tidskrift för Vetenskap, Konst och Industri, Volume VII, Erik Hedén had this to say:

When read Strindberg's *Gustav Adolf* is a masterpiece with many flaws. On the stage it will surely be simply a masterpiece. . . . One of the best artistic devices is the simple one of constantly repeating the same thing. That is true in his strangely gripping *Advent;* that is true, although naturally to a lesser degree, here. It is in this way, too, that he succeeds in creating the mood of the horror of war, of sympathy with everyone, all of it out of trembling before the strange ways of the Lord, which permeates and carries the whole play. He has skillfully raised its level by means of some elements of uniquely mystic glow such as the mirage over the Baltic and the crosses at Lützen. He has also raised it through his fashion of shaping the dialogue, with dignity and simplicity, mystically and naively.[5]

In the most significant of the more favorable reviews, the leading critic Oscar Levertin said, in part, that *Gustav Adolf* is

. . . a powerfully conceived and, if one disregards the author's usual and apparently incurable whims and sins against art, even a broadly and magnificently executed drama. . . . If one disregards its relation to reality and considers Gustav Adolf as wholly a dream figure the depiction is one of great beauty and a moving depth. Strindberg has not given many of his characters such an intense sincerity of feeling and noble agreeableness, and the scenes toward the end, in which one sees the hero offer himself as a sacrifice to fate, have a grandiose melancholy.[6]

It should be remembered, however, that these reviews as well as the others were largely products of one reading. A more deliberate and objective study of the play would probably have led to other conclusions about the historic validity of Strindberg's Gustav Adolf, for example.

The first real test of *Gustav Adolf* as a play for the stage was to have come in December, 1903, when the world *première* took place at the Berliner Theater in Germany. Unfortunate casting, lack of adequate rehearsals, and careless staging made the Berlin production almost a fiasco—undoubtedly, to judge from Swedish news items preserved in the Nylin collection, a fairly great satisfaction to Strindberg's enemies and opponents at home. Strindberg was not slow about replying to criticism. On December 7, 1903, in *Svenska Dagbladet,* his *"Gustav Adolf* föll?" appeared. This is called, in the catalogue of the Nylin Collection, "A Defense of the Play *Gustav Adolf* against both Swedish and German Criticism." Strindberg says that what irritates the Germans is that he has made the king a Saladin or a Nathan the Wise, still greater than Swedish historians had dreamed of doing. He asserts that the Germans consider Gustav Adolf an extremely ambitious man with a measure of sincere faith, an adventurer, and an opportunist: "So far as my characterization of Gustav Adolf goes, it is so faithful to all Swedish traditions that it nauseates the Germans. Fair, happy-natured, gallant but with this tragic element, the blood guilt from his father, with which I also motivate his intimacy with his generals, who are his relatives as well." [7]

The Swedish critics received their answers, too. Among them:

His [Gustav Adolf's] personal bravery I have revealed in several scenes. That he was excited and nervous the night and the morning before Lützen, on the other hand, is related in detail in the histories and is absolutely as it should be. He even went about as if beside himself before the battle, singing psalms. Now I should ask the Swedes, who have accused me of "pulling down" Gustav Adolf, what this pulling down consists of. If they were honest, they would answer, "because you did not make him a saint." "—But you don't believe in saints. Et cetera, endlessly, Amen!" [8]

But the near fiasco in Berlin, which even the German critics blamed at least partly on the directors and actors, left doubts and scars. On page 249 of the manuscript of *The Occult Diary (Ockulta Dagbok)* appear these statements: "Gustav Adolf has now been out and been condemned. I feel as if an unreasonable hate were discharging itself on me, and as if this hate threatened me with dangers, and still I wrote my drama in good faith with [the hope of] settling old controversies." [9] How hard he had been hit by Swedish criticism is clear from his correspondence with Emil Schering, his German translator. On November 15, 1903, for example, he warned Schering that *Gustav Adolf* would not be understood by Prussians. Seven days later, however, he wrote:

Today I reread *Gustav Adolf,* which I haven't looked at for three years—and I regained my bright, happy faith in the play of which they robbed me three years ago. I have decided—in the *Collected Dramatic Works* which are being printed—to eliminate the apotheosis. It is superfluous! And is Swedish boasting! This apotheosis reduces the play to a festival play or an occasional piece! Now it is a drama of character with development and a tragedy with guilt! [10]

In the following years he was to prepare or cooperate in preparing at least three acting versions, all with the feeling that his critics may have been partly right and all with his usual intense desire to get his plays produced and his conviction that he had written a great play.

A revision submitted before the *première* in Berlin to Director Ranft of the long-since defunct Swedish Theater and rejected by him was part of the library of that theater and may eventually be found. What is apparently a second revision is in the possession of Consul General Walter Ekman of Amsterdam. According to *Förteckning över Strindbergiana i Kungliga bibliotekets handskriftssamling* (A List of Strindbergiana in the Royal Library's Manuscript Collection): "In the copy [of the second] edition Strindberg has made cuttings and changes to shorten the play. This is presumably the copy that Landquist mentions on page 282 in Volume XXXII of *Strindberg's Collected Works.*" [11]

But in 1912 Bonners published August Strindberg's *Gustav Adolf, A Play in Five Acts Adapted for the Stage by the Author.* As early as May 30, 1911, Strindberg had announced in *Dagens Nyheter* and *Svenska Dagbladet* that *Gustav Adolf* would be produced at Cirkus, the large building in Djurgården: "The drama has been cut by half, half the characters have been eliminated, roles have been combined, and the dangerous Vasaborg [Gustav Adolf's illegitimate son] re-

moved although the Vasaborg crypt remains at the rear of Riddar-
holm Church [the burial place of royalty].[12]

The changes and the cuttings can be indicated by comparing the
following list of settings with that in the original version:

Act   I: Usedom—the landing.
Act II: Stettin at the cooper's. Outside Frankfurt an der Oder. In
     the camp there. In Spandau.
Act III: The churchyard at Breitenfeld. In Auerbachshof.
Act IV: The palace terrace outside Mainz. At Ingolstadt.
Act V: Alte Veste.
     At Lützen.

The version ends with the king's speech, "Have mercy on us all!"
and his drawing his sword to go into battle. The elimination of
Fabricius, Grubbe, the Danish ensign, the governor of Mecklenburg,
Schwarzenberg, Gustav Gustavsson (Vasaborg), Hrasan, Georg
Wilhelm, Johan Georg, the printer, the cantor, the grooms, and the
smith's boy, as well as many static characters, illustrates Strindberg's
willingness to make concessions to get the play produced. In addition, many speeches have been changed or reassigned.

In 1912, the year that the Olympic Games were held at Stockholm,
Oscar Wennersten of the People's House, the man primarily responsible for the production of *Gustav Adolf,* had first planned to
have the play put on at the Stadium; but, perhaps because Max Rein-
hardt had put on *Oedipus Rex* at the Cirkus the year before, it was
decided to stage *Gustav Adolf* there. The plans were ambitious and
the problems many. Difficulties and misunderstanding even led the
author, then dying of cancer, to send the following telegram to
Albert Ranft (quoted in *Aftonbladet* of April 24, 1912): "Surely you
don't want to ruin us; after all we are human beings. Wennersten
has risked capital, and I have once again put down work on adapting and producing [the play] in vain, and gratis at that! Say yes
to what is probably my last request."[13] On May 14, Strindberg died.

On June 4, the *première* took place. In the packed house, over
fifteen hundred people, dressed in mourning and headed by Crown

Prince Gustav (now Gustav VI Adolf), Crown Princess Margareta, and Prince Eugene, were present to see what amounted to a memorial performance. A "Hymn to August Strindberg," with words by Walter Hülphers and music by the great composer Petterson-Berger, was sung by several choruses to open the performances. (The music composed for the play by Strindberg's brother Axel was omitted.) The audience saw a performance played on two levels. The Stockholm correspondent of *Göteborgs Aftonblad* wrote on June 6:

Most of the spoken scenes are performed on the stage, and the silent scenes, consisting of refugees, marauders, starving crowds, men carrying occupied stretchers, symbolizing the horrors of the war, or war scenes, the marching in of troops on horseback or on foot, cavalrymen in armor, sharpshooters, mercenaries with halberds, feverish departures for battle to the accompaniment of the ring of trumpets and the thunder of drums, are performed on the arena.[14]

Even though the performance lasted from seven-thirty until close to midnight, the audience responded enthusiastically. (The correspondent of *Göteborgs Handels och Sjöfarts Tidning* did make a point of noting that the Crown Prince and the Crown Princess left early.)

The critical reception was mixed, with only John Landquist in *Dagens Nyheter* going so far as to say that the performance was

... a great victory both for the play and for the enthusiastic people who put it on.... The performance yesterday revealed completely [the play's] exceptional possibilities on the stage. *Gustaf Adolf* is without question Strindberg's most splendid, in terms of the theater most monumental, drama, and his theatrical imagination has never revealed itself more impressively than in this play's colorful and poetically suggestive scenes and processions.... *Gustav Adolf* is above all a drama about war, about the greatness of the victory, about the horrors of the vices, the sicknesses, and death which follow in its trail.... It was a memorable evening.[15]

The production closed after thirteen performances. Since then only the Lorensberg Theater of Göteborg has ventured to produce *Gustav Adolf* and then only in a cut version in honor of the tercentennial of the king's death, on November 11, 1932. Even twenty years after his death, Strindberg evoked strong and even violent opposition from his opponents. Dr. Per Pehrsson, Dean of Carl Johan's Parish in Göteborg, returned, according to news stories—among them one in *Dagens Nyheter* of November 11—from celebrating the tercentennial at Lützen in "proper" fashion, to find Göteborg—the city Gustav Adolf had founded—celebrating the tercentennial by means of "a repulsive lampoon"; he elaborates, in language strangely incompatible with his Master's, on Strindberg and his "lampoon." In reply, Torsten Hammarén, director of the theater, merely pointed out that the play is a monumental depiction of a human being.

Gustav Adolf has yet to receive its fair test as theater.

10

Charles XII: *Madman of the North*

IF THERE was any Swedish king for whom Strindberg felt genuine antipathy, it was Charles XII, the eighteenth-century ruler who had become one of the folk heroes of the Swedish people and had been exalted in Swedish literature as an ideal by, among others, the great romantic poets Esaias Tegnér and Erik Gustaf Geijer,[1] and who had become the object of attention on the part of foreign literary men, among them Voltaire and Samuel Johnson.[2] The general European opinion—that Charles XII was one of the greatest military geniuses in world history and a man who had risen to the very summit of greatness and then had been plunged to the very depths of tragic defeat—did not affect Strindberg's opinion of the king who had, he felt, destroyed Sweden's greatness as a world power and who had brought the Swedes more suffering and humiliation than any of his predecessors. In his pre-Inferno writing, Strindberg had made short shrift of the Swedish glorification of the king's military exploits, his simplicity of life, and, in general, the whole concept of Charles as a hero.

But Charles XII could not be disregarded in a cycle of dramas dealing with Swedish history from St. Erik in the middle ages to Gustav IV Adolf, who lost his throne in 1809. Strindberg's re-examination of the sources in 1901 did not lead to a change in his basic evaluation of Charles, but it did lead to a somewhat more sympathetic attitude toward him:

Charles XII, the man who ruined Sweden, the great criminal, the idol of the ruffians, and the counterfeiter, was the one I was going to present on the stage to my countrymen. . . . Well, everyone does have motives for his actions, every criminal has the right to defend himself, so I decided to plan my drama as a classical tragedy of fate and catastrophe. The end of a life that was a big mistake. A strong will that struggles against the course of historical development, forgivable because he did not understand what he was doing. Charles XII did not understand that Czar Peter of Russia was right when he wanted to Europeanize his country, just freed from the two-hundred-year domination by the Mongols; he did not understand that Europe needed Russia to defend its borders against the Turks and other Asiatics now that Poland had collapsed of itself. Charles XII is the barbarian when he allies himself with Asiatics; Charles XII is a *gengångare,* a ghost who walks the earth, who is given form by the smoke of powder, and who fades away as soon as the cannons are nailed down, the cannons with which he intended to keep world history from taking its course. Ruined even then by the revelation of his inner disharmonies and awakened doubt, he falls in his struggle against the powers. The problem of the bullet at Fredrikshald has not yet been solved; I let it come from "above," which Swedenborg, Charles XII's last friend, interprets in his elevated fashion, while the public believes it came from the fortress. Let that be as it may. It came when it should—and places the period after the last act of the tragedy.[3]

This passage reveals the essentials not only of Strindberg's concept of Charles XII but of the author's ideas about history in terms of God, man, and the universe. In his post-Inferno days he no longer even tried to subscribe to the deterministic concepts of naturalism. He judged Charles from a moral point of view, as a part of a world in which there is moral law; hence, his judgment of Charles as the man who ruined Sweden, the great criminal, the idol of the ruffians, and the counterfeiter. Charles, Strindberg believed, had freedom of the will, and that strong will of his had been in opposition to the Conscious Will that controls historical development and in opposition to the Powers who chastise human beings, who in their arrogance and unfortunate lack of understanding insist on acting in ways contrary to those approved by the Conscious Will. Such ideas are decidedly reminiscent of the classical tragedies of catastrophe and character. Inner disharmonies or conflicts and inner doubts must of necessity accompany a struggle of the kind implied.

Strindberg's classification of Charles XII as "a *gengångare,* a ghost who walks the earth, who is given form by the smoke of powder, and who fades away" as soon as the war is over suggests, moreover, that Strindberg's approach to his tragedy about Charles XII was primarily expressionistic, only secondarily realistic. Such an approach is in no way amazing: By 1901 Strindberg had composed some of his greatest expressionistic plays, notably the first two parts of his *To Damascus* trilogy (1898), and had used, in varying degrees, expressionistic techniques in such plays as *Advent* (1899) and *The Saga of the Folkungs* (1899). The whole dream-play technique, which he had made peculiarly his own, had stood him in good stead in several plays and was in *A Dream Play* (1902) to establish his claim as a revolutionary influence in the history of drama. His subjective treatment of his own life expressionistically in *To Damascus* undoubtedly suggested the approach to *Charles XII* that was to make this tragedy about that king an extremely original play.

No one can explain more effectively than Strindberg himself did his intentions in writing the tragedy and its structure:

My *Charles XII* is a drama of character and catastrophe, in other words the last acts of a long story, and it somewhat follows in this the tragedies of antiquity, in which everything has happened before [the play begins], and it resembles even the admired Dovre [Norwegian] dramas, which are merely the resolutions of dramas that are already over. In my Charles XII I begin with his return; show in vivid scenes the miserable state of the kingdom; present the half-mad despot, who doesn't condescend to say a word, and who doesn't receive the representatives of the four estates. In the second act he is in Lund doing nothing; is ashamed to return to Stockholm, seeks a war, anywhere at all, in order to regain his lost honor or—die. His problem is then to find an army. The tyrant's inner conflicts, when he has looked for support from a well-known adventurer (Görtz), who in his absence has tried to dethrone him, are highly dramatic; and at the end of the second act he succumbs to the Tempter, who promises to make gold out of brass.

In the third act you may see *the results* of the despot's wild actions. His victims try to get an audience, but the king is with Görtz *working*. Thus the drama has gone forward the whole time and therefore fulfills the requirements of drama, for only a drama that stands still is undramatic. But something else happens here, too. Horn and Gyllenborg, the men of the future, the men of the Age of Liberty, presented passively in the second act, have now gone actively to work and begin to sketch the perspective [of the future]. Thereupon something of worldwide historic consequence happens, allegorized by the raising of the flag at half mast: Louis XIV is dead. This means the end of Absolutism, of course—and Charles XII's impending finish.

That this act was omitted at the Dramatic Theater was a big mistake, which made my play even thinner, which was intentionally thin before, as a drama of catastrophe should be (compare *Antigone,* in which almost nothing happens but in which most is related).

In the fourth act suspense is sustained by waiting. Waiting for Görtz, who has been away. In the meanwhile Swedenborg and his Emerentia are brought on stage. This as a contribution to the characterization of Charles XII, for my drama is a drama of character, *too.* Charles XII's relationship to women (the girl and his sister) had to be included, of course.

Görtz returns from his mission. The adventurer was a good financier and a careful one, but Charles XII destroyed everything for him through his reckless choice of means. Görtz believed the kingdom could bear two million emergency coins, but the King on his own initiative had twenty million circulated. The kingdom is ruined and all that remains is an honorable suicide. So—to Norway! This is dramatic and it is the end of the act, too!

In the fifth act there is preparation for the bullet (at Fredrikshald). The suspense is sustained here, too: waiting for the storming or *the bullet.* The little device of having the dwarf return has the effect of a memento of better times and gives the king an opportunity to defend himself, at least from unjust accusations, and there were, of course, human qualities in him, too. Horn and Gyllenborg open completely perspectives of a new and better future, even if that, too, will be accompanied by new struggles. Swedenborg interprets the character of Charles XII, a character hard to explain; and when the bullet has been fired, everything is resolved—and thereby even the drama is resolved.[4]

It is a highly suggestive and justified summary of both intention and structure, but it does not explain why *Charles XII* is such a superb play.

Strindberg's analysis in retrospect does, however, establish certain facts. *Charles XII* is, as he says, a drama of catastrophe. It is not a chronicle play with representative episodes from the king's long career, stretching from 1697 to 1718. Instead of presenting episodes from the first eight years (1700 to 1708) of greatness as a military leader whose every move was accompanied by victory upon victory until his defeat at Poltava, or from the seven years of humiliating inaction in Turkey, Strindberg concentrates on and telescopes the period between his return to Sweden in 1715 and his death at Fredrikshald in 1718. What we learn about the events in the earlier period is conveyed by exposition or by implication through the effects of the events.

The play is limited in primary dramatic treatment to the twilight of a long career, to that time when the real tragedy of Charles XII became obvious to his people and, as Strindberg believed, to the king himself. Strindberg's Charles is not the young hero king of Tegnér but a weary defeated human being waiting in a state of frustration, indecision, and inner defeat for the outcome, whatever it is to be: "Against . . . the enemy . . . whoever wants to be . . . toward a victory . . . or certain defeat!" The catastrophe, as Strindberg saw it, has been prepared for during the long preceding years; only the end of "a career that was a big mistake" remains when the first curtain goes up.

The play is, moreover, a drama of character. As always, Strindberg is primarily interested in people, but in *Charles XII* the characterization differs radically from the technique of characterization used in all the earlier historical plays, with, to a limited degree, the exception of *The Saga of the Folkungs.* Instead of consistently applying his theory of the dynamic and complex (i.e., characterless) character, Strindberg in *Charles XII* uses a startlingly effective combination of the technique implicit in that theory (and explained in the preface to *Lady Julie*) and the expressionistic technique he had already applied in his autobiographical plays, *To Damascus,* I and II.

Strindberg's Charles XII is no longer a dynamic, developing human being; it is as if he had at some time in the past been frozen in a mold in all his complexity. The king we see is consequently characterized both analytically and synthetically. Charles XII has not always been the sort of person he is in this play, as Strindberg carefully makes clear time and again. It is Count Horn, the brilliant statesman, who provides a major key to Strindberg's concept of what Charles has been and what he has become. Note Horn's analysis of the king's career:

That man, who is lying there, waiting for his journey to the grave—for he is dead—was once the man of destiny . . . and success upon success attended him as long as he walked the paths of justice. But after that, when he wanted to walk his own paths eighteen years ago and to control the destinies of people and nations . . . then destiny took him by the ear and played blindman's buff with him! And now he stands . . . or lies divided against himself! He has wasted eighteen years to keep one vow— that Peter of Russia and August of Poland be exterminated from the earth! His whole life has revolved about these two poles! And now . . . now he's negotiating to get related by marriage to the Russians . . . one day, and for friendship with Poland, the next . . . all this while he has lain down in Norway! In Norway! . . . And this paradox that looks like a colossal hoax. He wanted to raise a strong Poland against Russia, but then he broke up Poland and did the work of Russia! Wanted one thing and did another! That is how destiny plays with those who want to play the part of destiny!

It is Horn, too, who in characterizing Görtz for the king ironically says that which everyone present finds applicable to the king and which helps identify the nature of the mold:

. . . that man is . . . an exceptionally unusual personality, and his desire to be unusual can only be measured . . . in its strength . . . by his desire for power. They say that he thinks he's the center of the world, that he looks in the papers every morning to see if the destinies of Europe have undergone any change while he has been sleeping, and the learned Swedenborg assures us that if Görtz died today, he'd set the kingdom of the dead against the heavenly powers. This overwhelming desire for honor he conceals . . . tries to conceal beneath a simple exterior, and a condescending manner towards his inferiors. Inferiors, whom he actually despises, just as he despises all humanity. These outstanding characteristics . . . coupled with his most exemplary insensibility to the sufferings of others, would seem incompatible with a religious spirit, but [he] is not without religion. One could say that he fears for God, without fearing God. The learned and pious Swedenborg believes [he] uses religion as a sort of magic, through which he secures support and power for himself, even in his purely criminal activities . . . for example, in extorting funds, in getting revenge on enemies . . . because he also has the peculiarity of never being able to forgive anyone. In a word, a great weakness . . . disguised so that it seems like a tremendous strength; a convulsive stubbornness that cannot break down his own willfulness . . .

Charles XII, in other words, is decidedly different from such great predecessors as Strindberg's Magnus the Good, Gustav Vasa, and Gustav Adolf.

The key to the difference lies primarily in Charles XII's relationship to God and the Powers or the Eternal One and the Powers. Strindberg's Magnus tried desperately to follow the wishes of God, even submitting to the interpretations of divine will by earthly representatives, to avoid pride and arrogance; Gustav Vasa through prayer and meditation tried to act in keeping with the will of God; Gustav Adolf was decidedly aware of his human limitations and anxious to serve God as He wished to be served. Charles XII, who believes in God as much as any of the three predecessors, has been incapable, Strindberg believes, of bowing in humility even before God. Hence, Horn's statement, "One could say that he fears for God, without fearing God." Charles XII is an "arrogant egotist who believes he is the man of destiny and the center of the world; who conceals his inordinate desire for honor beneath extremely simple speech, attire, tastes, and manner; who despises his fellow men to whose sufferings he is insensible . . . and who is willful and stubborn —basically, this is Strindberg's interpretation of Charles XII." [5]

As the above quotations suggest, Strindberg believed that Charles XII has finally been forced far down by the Powers who have been playing blindman's buff with the stubborn, willful king, so far down that he has lost his self-confidence and his will to live. In his bitterness, he acknowledges that his saga is over, that his people are hopefully waiting for his death, that he knows the position of the kingdom is hopelessly desperate, and that he wishes he were dead. But he is supremely confident that he is not alone, and the only request that he has to make of the deity who he thinks is always with him is, "Let this cup be taken from me!" The cup apparently implies draining the bitterness of life to the last dregs. The king who wishes for death has, however, come to terms neither with himself nor with the Eternal One.

Strindberg was well aware, moreover, that Charles XII was not fully to blame for all the disasters that struck Sweden during his time. Consequently, there are three places in the drama where Charles XII is permitted to enter his self-defense. In Act II, for example:

> FEIF: The country is impoverished . . . and the people!
> KING: And that is my fault! Did I cause the plague? Did I cause the crop failures? . . . Have I declared the wars? . . . No, I have only defended myself, my country, my royal inheritance!

and: "They thought I was impenetrable because I did not talk; and I did not talk because I did not drink; because I alone protected my senses among drunkards, they thought I was a fool. . . . There isn't an act I cannot defend."

In Act V, moreover, is his moving analysis of the letters he has received and of his whole life, which ends: "The whole of life is like this ball, a web of lies, mistakes, misunderstandings! To hell with it! . . . I cannot fight with lies and the father of lies. . . . Certainly I haven't been any angel, but so devilishly black I wasn't either!" His use of the past tense in that last revealing sentence shows clearly that Charles himself believes his saga has been over for some time, and only that which is better than sleep remains.

The testimony of the other characters must be noted, too, if one is to understand the full implication of Strindberg's interpretation of the strange king and his strange destiny. In Act I, the nameless Man implies that the king is a rotten apple clinging to the top of a leafless tree and, moreover, a rotten apple that, according to the coastguard, ought to be shaken down "by a man who has a heart in his body." The Man labels the king a villain whom, the coastguard says, neither the elements nor weapons can affect "until his time has come." The speaker of the House of the Clergy calls Charles a madman, the speaker of the House of the Burghers agrees, and the speaker of the House of the Yeomen, who has already called him a giant, calls the king a villain. But the king in his brief appearance in Act I brings them to their knees:

> LORD *(to Burgher)*: Why did we kneel?
> BURGHER: I don't know! Couldn't do anything else!
> FARMER: Was it the King? . . . So he does have something different from other people. Just as if someone had knocked my legs from under me . . . that is to say, it wasn't I who fell to my knees . . .
> LORD: So I imagine!
> COUNCILLOR: It's the conqueror and the Lord's anointed!

Hultman, the king's faithful steward, adds the final testimony in Act I: "My lord and King, the very greatest of men and conquerors, is the most perfect of all people born of woman." Even in Act I, the testimony and the reactions to the king are varied, often contradictory, and, above all, ambivalent.

Note that the king—pale, wet, freezing—makes only a brief appearance in Act I and that he does not speak audibly; he arbitrarily disregards the petition of the estates; he does not recognize, except through his adjutant, the representatives of the estates and of the royal council; and he has issued orders for his steward's carrying on his work and for the punishment of the skipper who, apparently for good reasons, failed to show up at the designated meeting place. It is the behavior of a despot who has come to believe he is the center of his world, not the reasonable behavior of a king returning to his kingdom after years of humiliation and defeat abroad.

In Act II, Horn says not only that the king is "a dead man, whose spirit is walking the earth" but that he is *"not* one person but a multitude . . . with twenty faces." The nameless Malcontent labels him a woman-hater. Horn analyzes the king, as we have already seen, and the act develops the testimony of the people about him so as to make clear that there are many conflicting reactions to the king who insists he is never alone.

The king we see in Act II is sickly ashen gray, serious, collected, dignified, secretive, inscrutable, uncertain. He is able to speak aloud only with difficulty; he is exhausted and ill. He is sure that there is only one doctor for his illness and knows that his people are angry with him because he is not dead. But grasping at any possible solution to his dilemma, he questions Horn about Görtz, only to be given the horrifying confirmation of his inner doubts and conflicts through Horn's unintentional analysis of Charles while characterizing Görtz. But the king "who despises all humanity" does not accept Horn's or anyone else's judgment of Görtz; he summons him, confers with him, and, after some hesitation, decides to make use of him and his services in an attempt at solving the problems posed by "the land of difficulties." Most moving of all the scenes in Act II, however, is the dreamlike episode in which the Man comes in with a bludgeon. The Man's accusations serve as a sort of indictment of the king as a criminal:

MAN: Can't you talk? . . . So you're the King of Sweden who lies in bed for seven years while the country is being ruined . . . you're a king, who leaves his capital and his government, who doesn't dare to return to his home and his people up in Stockholm, because he is ashamed of his fiasco! Had sworn, of course, that he would return with an arch of triumph at North Bridge, and have a conquered kingdom on every finger! . . . You're ashamed! . . .

But the Man who says this and more to the king who lies staring at him ends his indictment: "It has been marvelous to speak out for once! And now we can be just as good friends all the same . . ." The complexity of his people's feelings toward the king is illustrated by what the Man says, but for the king the experience becomes a dream-like experience which serves as a self-examination of his conscience. But that examination results, as we have already seen, in self-defense.

In Act III, Strindberg further clarifies his people's complex attitudes without having the king appear on stage at all. Shut up with Görtz in the latter's lodgings, the king confers with his new minister of finance but isolates himself from all the Swedes who have good reasons to consult him. Figuratively and literally, he has closed off all means of communication with them. But in Act III, Strindberg demonstrates the king's contemporaries' attitudes and explains their development into very complex matters. Take, for example, the Dwarf's statements: "You know, I have loved this king, worshipped him; once I kissed his boots . . . but now . . . If I had a barrel of powder, I'd stick it under that house!" and: "You may not say villain! Well, I just think it is sad to see a great man slowly come down in the world. . . . It is sad!" and:

DWARF: Sovereignty is dead! . . . God save the king! . . . in my case, though he tossed me aside!

MALCONTENT: In any case! . . . Think of it; I can't get really angry with that man!

DWARF: Is that really necessary?

MAN: Yes, it is absolutely necessary!

In Act IV, decidedly the most realistic in the play (yet set against the background of a steadily increasing crowd of shabby, horrible-looking people—of malcontents in the expressionistic manner), the major emphasis is placed on Charles XII's relationship with women, his rumored woman-hatred (already more than suggested in the earlier acts), and the king's self-examination and self-defense. The sick, sleepless, uneasy, and irritable king manages very well to hold his own in his contests with Emerentia Polhem, the teenager who has vowed to bring him to his knees; his sister Ulrika Eleonora, who would like to have him designate her husband as the heir to the throne; and Katarina of Poland, who wants him to understand how unjustly, in her opinion, he has treated her and her family.

It is in Act IV above all that the characterization of Charles XII finds its finest development—through the king's reactions to those about him and to himself and his destiny. With a silence as of death closing about him, Charles XII is in despair. He has at last reached that point where he admits that a higher power has the final say as to when and how his saga will end, but Charles XII is no Magnus the Good or Gustav Adolf who can bow in humility before such a power. Instead, as Strindberg conceives him, he is frozen in his stubbornness, self-will, and frustration. Knowing that his happy time —recalled by Emerentia Polhem as a tribute to the young hero-king of years ago—is over, he prays to escape the last cup, has lost his self-confidence and his desire to live, longs for death, and sets out on the futile campaign against Norway.

In the very brief fifth act, Horn, Swedenborg, and the Man sit in judgment on the king. Horn says, "It's not a secret that our king is physically and spiritually worn out—in a word, what they call . . . done for!" Everyone in the camp is waiting tensely for something to bring the whole story to an end:

SWEDENBORG: The king seems to wage this war as if he were trying to keep busy while he's waiting for something . . .

FEIF: . . . What is the king waiting for?

SWEDENBORG: Who knows! . . . See how he's lying staring into the fire! A great rich life is passing in review . . .

FEIF: Has passed by . . . a great man!

SWEDENBORG: Great, not great! Can we give the measure of a man with a few small words?

Charles, who has never identified his divine opponent as the Eternal One or the Conscious Will says, "I cannot fight with lies and the father of lies!" He defends himself and his life until he dies, but, once dead, he receives his people's judgment:

SAILOR: The greatest of all Sweden's kings is dead! God save us!
MAN: Is the villain dead?
MALCONTENT: He is dead! And now I forgive him!
MAN: Think of it, I couldn't get really angry with that fellow! A devil of a fellow all the same!

Strindberg's brilliant characterization of Charles XII is further proof of his gift for understanding people in terms of his interpretation of the historical evidence and of his own experience.

The effective blend of realistic and expressionistic techniques used in characterizing the king himself is just as rewarding in the depiction of the other characters. There are, first of all, the thoroughly realistic characters of the two great men of the future, Arvid Horn and Karl Gyllenborg; Feif, the king's secretary; Hultman, the king's steward; the adventurer Görtz; Luxembourg, the dwarf; Princess Ulrika Eleonora, the king's sister; Katarina Leczinska of Poland; Emerentia Polhem; and the genius Emanuel Swedenborg. They do not receive full attention of the kind given a central character, but they are sufficiently individualized to bring them alive as human beings.

Consider, for example, the characterization of Swedenborg. Strindberg presents him in a number of revealing situations and has some of his contemporaries comment on him and his qualities, as people will, but Strindberg makes no attempt to reveal Swedenborg as completely as possible. Strindberg does, to be sure, show Swedenborg as the fiancé of a coquettish young girl, being given advice by a king who does not admire women, and as an interpreter of the significance of Charles XII's person and destiny. But the treatment is confined to the matters designed to throw light on Charles, only secondarily on Swedenborg himself. There is very little said or demonstrated about Swedenborg as a scientific genius or as a religious mystic or, except for the episode with Emerentia Polhem, about him as a person. Yet, like the other secondary characters, he emerges as a living human being moving about in the dreamlike world surrounding Charles XII in the twilight of his career.

There are, moreover, the realistic supers who either have only a few words to say or are mute and stay on stage for brief intervals while they perform their function of helping reveal Charles XII's character or of advancing the dramatic development. Among these realistic types are the coastguard, the royal councillor, the speakers of the four estates, the adjutant, the skipper, and the guardsmen of Act I, the professor of Act II, the aristocratic "widows," the lords, the skipper's daughter, the sailor, the lackey, and the herald of Act III, and the officers and the soldiers of Act V. Strindberg felt rightly that there was no need for showing any of them from more than one side.

But there are expressionistic types who have a special function to perform. If one is to understand their function, it is necessary to examine the play further from the point of view of expressionism and thereby attempt to clarify the nature of a drama that as a historical play is startlingly original.

If one proceeds from the assumption that a Strindbergian expressionistic play—*To Damascus,* for example—has as its dominant characteristics a stress on subjectivity, a mixture of reality and dreamlike experience, symbolism, stress on the emotions and feelings, a predominantly melancholy mood, the use of music to set the mood, and synthesis as well as analysis for purposes of characterization, one may make further progress not only toward understanding *Charles XII* but toward the appreciation of its highly fascinating qualities.[6]

As we have seen, Strindberg was almost exclusively interested in the Charles XII of the last three years of a career that should have ended long before. The Charles XII who interested Strindberg is not a dynamic human being but rather one set and fixed or, as I have already said, a static human being frozen in a mold of his inner complexity. It is the relationship between Charles and an infinite being that interests Strindberg; it is the subjective inner state of Charles, rather than the external realistic events, that is of primary importance in his play. What relatively few external events there are in *Charles XII* fade into secondary significance when compared with those

presented in, say, *Gustav Adolf*. Strindberg's Charles XII is a synthetically conceived character, and the analytical elements are used
in throwing light on a human being who no longer is changing
essentially.

For the dramatization of the story of such a character Strindberg
emphasized with great care the basic melancholy mood. Note the
settings and the detailed care with which they are explained (here
quoted only in part):

Act I: A cold windy December morning on the southern Swedish
coast; a village almost completely in ruins as a result of war and plague;
one wind-ravaged apple tree with one lone apple shaking in the wind; a
dark sea; a pale gray ray of dawn; a man in rags searching among the
ruins.

Act II: An improvised audience room in Lund; two very low, soft,
and uncomfortable easy chairs. A room that is cold in spite of the fire in
the stove.

Act III: A square. . . . At the back ruins of burned houses. . . . Closed
green shutters [on Görtz's house, where the king is]. . . . A tavern with
tables and benches outside [where dissatisfied and disgruntled people are
gathered].

Act IV: A large garden. . . . A couple of high openwork iron gates
leading to an alley . . . [the king's temporary home].

Act V: The Swedish camp before Fredriksten Fortress. . . . The roof
resembles a large, black sarcophagus. Trenches . . . breast-works . . .
campfires . . . lighted torches. . . . Evening . . . moonlight and rapidly
moving clouds . . . chilly. [People either sitting still or moving about
but all waiting, waiting.]

The settings, supplemented by stage directions, and the behavior of
the characters throughout the play emphasize a mood that begins
as a melancholy one, deepens as such, and, ironically, ends with a note
of subdued relief as the play ends with the death of the king.

There can be no question about Strindberg's deliberately placing
emphasis on the emotions and the feelings. The king himself is no
longer the brilliant master of military strategy, who calmly and
objectively sizes up his situation, but a defeated shadow of himself,

who relies on primarily impulsive action to bring him "a victory . . . or certain defeat." Only at rare moments, such as in his contests with the three women, does he even begin to indicate an essentially analytic approach to an immediate problem, and then most of what he has to say is based on an old pattern of emotional reaction. The attitudes of the people about him are, moreover, definitely matters of emotional response to "that strange man" whose destiny even a brilliant Swedenborg cannot understand. Horn, who comes closest to understanding him, admits that his own attitude is partly emotional. From the opening curtain to the final one Strindberg has made the strange blend of respect and disrespect, liking and dislike, reliance and suspicion, blind admiration and fear, one of the most striking aspects of the whole play.

As if to underline all this emphasis on mood through setting and stress on emotions and feelings, Strindberg uses a saraband by Bach in the play. The men of the future, Horn and Gyllenborg, who tend to look upon the king's last period as a ghastly travesty on reality, comment:

GYLLENBORG: What is that infernal music that I've been hearing all morning?
HORN: It sounds like a grasshopper . . .
GYLLENBORG: I think it sounds like the autumn wind blowing between the double windows, or like the crying of children.

But the Dwarf knows its value:

MAN: Why do you always play that sad piece?
DWARF: Because I used to play it for my king when he was sorely afflicted.
MAN: Listen to that fellow!
DWARF: And a king composed this song of sorrow—Sebastian Bach, the king of the Land of Sorrows and Pain . . .

Just as he used music in *To Damascus,* Strindberg has accentuated the mood in *Charles XII* by means of the stately but melancholy saraband. There is, furthermore, a debt to music even in the structure of the play; as in *The Ghost Sonata* later, Strindberg has in Act I given a preliminary exposition of his themes, given them varied development in the second, third, and fourth acts, and recapitulated them in the final act: a ruined Sweden that looks like a wasteland, a long-suffering but no longer patient people, and an absolute monarch who pays attention to the needs of neither.

Symbolism permeates *Charles XII* much in the manner of the expressionistic autobiographical *To Damascus*. The ruined Sweden that looks like a wasteland is symbolized, of course, by the one wind-ravaged apple tree in Act I; the lone apple that clings stubbornly to its top and that should be shaken down represents Charles XII himself. But the tree itself is not dead in the cold gray December beside the dark sea; the tree itself may sprout new leaves and bear sound fruit when light and warmth return. The pale gray ray of dawn on the eastern horizon represents no doubt the hope of a long-suffering people that a brighter day will dawn when the crippling effects of absolutism need no longer deter them from getting rid of the rotten fruit. In concrete human terms, the hope is given form in Horn and Gyllenborg, the men who are waiting only for the apple to fall.

Symbolic of Sweden's suffering millions are the Man in rags who calls himself Hunger and who searches among the ruins of his home for some of the things that gave meaning to his life; the nameless Malcontent; the poverty-stricken Woman with the petition, and the ghostlike people. Note in Act IV: "At the iron-grill gate people now gather; among them are the Man from Act I, the Malcontent, and the Woman from Act III. They are all silent, but horrible to look upon." And a moment later: "Shabby-looking men and boys begin to gather by the wall at the back. They appear silently, unnoticeably, and sit there one, two, three, but are not noticed yet by the people on the stage." And at the very end of the act: "Now the iron-grill gate is opened, and shabby figures steal in, ghostlike, curious, and fingering everything; the figures by the wall silently join them." Symbolically conceived and symbolically used, these, like the Man, who confronts the king in Act II with a bludgeon and an indictment, are in appearance and behavior deliberately subtly distorted in the manner of the dream experience and subtly underscore the play's predominantly expressionistic nature. They serve along with the "widows" in their generally silent but clear protest against the actions of a man who despises humanity and is insensible to the sufferings of his fellow human beings; the nonrealistic types serve as one expressionistic equivalent of a chorus of lamentation and foreboding.

In *Charles XII,* Strindberg composed a historical drama which demonstrated once again his genius for adapting his technique to his subject. Although there are obviously parallel matters in all his historical plays, each one of the major plays is composed in such a way that there is no mechanical repetition but, instead, a highly suitable and appropriate fitting of the dramatic composition to Strindberg's concept of each central character as a human individual. Strindberg did not forget that though all human beings are very much alike in their human qualities each is different in various ways from all his fellows, past or present.

For the presentation of Charles XII on the stage for his countrymen, Strindberg chose, then, the happy blend of realism and expressionism that provides a deeper insight into the essential nature of the enigmatic king toward the end of his days than all the preceding romanticized interpretations of the young king and the military genius who made all Europe tremble. Strindberg's basically sympathetic and poetic interpretation of the great king at the end of "a great rich life" in final isolation and inner defeat is a tragedy of great merit and a drama with challenging possibilities for the theater when presented in keeping with Strindberg's intention.

When the Swedish Theater refused to put on *Charles XII* in 1901, the Berlin correspondent of *Svenska Dagbladet* wrote (September 6, 1901):

The king is revealed in a highly sympathetic light in Strindberg's drama. In it is depicted the human being, who because of events and circumstances, hence fate, is led along his way, and not only a historical personage, who interests mainly biographers and historians. That which is great in Strindberg's writing lately is that he has gone over to depicting human beings, human characters that are valid for all times. . . . Is it presumptuous to prophesy . . . that the *Charles XII* that has now been refused will some day become one of the best liked of all Strindberg's dramas about Swedish history? [7]

On February 13, 1902, the first production had its *première* at the Dramatic Theater. The reception by the audience was friendly, that by the drama critics mixed. Typical of those who felt that the play was hardly an apotheosis of Charles XII is the critic in *Varia* (Volume III, March, 1902) who, while he acknowledges that there are individual scenes and lines that are superbly effective, condemns the play as a work of dramatic art definitely below standard and laments that there is little of the historical Charles in the play: "[Strindberg's Charles XII] is the vacillating, weak man who is guided by the Powers, not by his own absolutely firm will and character, a despot basically but between the explosions of this temperament affected by both people and circumstances. And Mr. Strindberg makes him *cowardly!!*" [8] Tor Hedberg, in *Svenska Dagbladet* on February 14, 1902, was much more favorable. Although he, too, objected to what he called flaws, he acknowledges the tragic greatness of Strindberg's Charles "presented in a few brief, suggestive strokes." [9] The production consisted only of fourteen performances in the 1902-3 season and three the following fall.

Since then there have been a number of notable productions in Swedish cities in addition to a few productions abroad and to tours of the provinces, notably the tour by Oscar Winge's company from Norrland to Skåne in 1912-13. Aside from a production in Göteborg *(Stora teatern)* in 1904, the second major production came in 1918-19 at the Dramatic Theater. Apparently that production, designed for the two-hundredth anniversary of Charles XII's death, was unimaginative and thoroughly realistic. The drama critic who understood the play and the flaws in the 1918 production best was Pär Lagerkvist, who in *Svenska Dagbladet* (December 1, 1918) wrote:

A drama like this must not be played with disregard of all the loose, impressionistic elements in the way it is composed, with any efforts to try to cover up as well as possible these "flaws." It should be played faithfully with retention of the special mood, which this looseness, awkwardness, and improvisation give to the scenes and the characters. . . . Through the feeling or mood of uncertainty which is thereby created Strindberg has certainly intended to give the whole play something disjointed and unreal in a ghostlike fashion.[10]

Lagerkvist was right, as highly successful productions at the City Theater in Hälsingborg in 1938 and at the Dramatic Theater in 1940 demonstrated. There can be little question that *Charles XII,* presented in keeping with Strindberg's intentions, can be great theater and for the reader a superb interpretation of the king who presided over the end of Sweden's period of greatness. Strindberg's own comment is indeed justified: "The man who wrote . . . that my *Charles XII* is not a drama does not know what a drama of character and catastrophe is." [11]

11

Engelbrekt: *A Most Beautiful Memory*

ALWAYS keenly aware of issues of immediate interest and pressing concern to his fellow countrymen, Strindberg capitalized in 1901 on the increased bitterness in both Sweden and Norway about the uneasy union effected in 1814 and rapidly drawing to a close. Feelings on both sides of the border stemmed particularly from the facts that the union had been arranged at a conference table, that it did not result from any particular desire for union on the part of either the Swedish or the Norwegian people, that the Norwegians were convinced that they had a subordinate role in the union, and that the vast majority of Swedes had never been personally concerned with the implications of the union as it had been set up. Like many other Swedes who were aware of how most Norwegians felt about the union, Strindberg himself favored full independence for Norway and did not hesitate to say so in print. His personal awareness of the whole complex problem was heightened, moreover, by the fact that he was then married to the actress Harriet Bosse, who, in spite of a mixed background, considered herself Norwegian.

The contemporary situation illumined without question a similar problem that the Swedes themselves had faced intermittently between 1397, when the Kalmar Union of all Scandinavia had been loosely and inadequately formed, and 1523, when the Swedes under the leadership of Gustav Vasa definitely and finally broke away from a union that they had never enthusiastically and unanimously favored and that they had at no time found fully satisfactory. The historical sources indicated, moreover, that the perplexing problems resulting from an unequal union of closely related peoples involved dramatic possibilities ranging from political struggles for power to the distressing difficulties facing both supporters of such a union and opponents of it. Certainly the Swedish efforts to free themselves from the Kalmar Union had produced heroic leaders—most notably Engelbrekt, Karl Knutsson Bonde, the Stures, and the Vasas—and for many of these the whole problem was complicated because of intermarriages with Danes or Norwegians and other ties that went beyond the Swedish borders.

In Engelbrekt, who was assassinated in 1436, Strindberg had a superb illustration of the liberator of a people from foreign oppression and bondage. Swedish dramatists (notably Per Ling in 1819 and August Blanche in 1846), poets, and novelists had already exalted Engelbrekt as a folk hero; scholarly historians—as well as the popular ones Strindberg favored—conceded that Engelbrekt's achievements included the preservation of national liberty through laying the foundation of a distinctly national point of view, protecting the Swedish people from the system of serfdom, and laying a solid foundation for parliamentary government based on native Swedish concepts of law and human rights. Even the skeptical historians of recent times have found no good reason for belittling either the man or his achievements, although, like Strindberg, they have treated him as a human being rather than an untouchable saint.

Strindberg had no inclination to depart sharply from the accepted interpretation of Engelbrekt: "Engelbrekt is one of Sweden's most beautiful memories, and I felt I should keep his character as high and pure as Schiller kept his William Tell." [1] Even so, Strindberg, thwarted by the usually fragmentary and always inadequate historical documents and historical accounts of the early fifteenth-century hero, felt it necessary to eke out through his own imagination and experience the slim records so as to have a concept of a leader that could be seen and observed from more points of view than his literary predecessors had presented him. Engelbrekt, Strindberg knew, must have been a being of flesh and blood involved in many kinds of human relationships and in many kinds of situations, trivial as well as important in varying degrees to himself, his family, neighbors, friends, enemies, opponents, and followers. The real Engelbrekt must have been as dynamic and complex as Master Olof, for example, even though as a *good* man he resembled King Magnus the Good in *The Saga of the Folkungs* and Svante Sture in the later *The Last of the Knights* far more than he resembled, say, Gustav Vasa.

For dramatizing the story of such a hero for the stage, Strindberg chose a form that is decidedly that of the folk drama. But that it is much more than a folk drama of the kind Blanche had written two generations earlier is revealed by Strindberg's preliminary notes and plans preserved in the manuscript division of the Royal Library. Too numerous and too long to be quoted at length here, these notes and plans demonstrate Strindberg's careful planning. One apparently early comment helps clarify his intention: "ENGELBREKT. A drama of character. A drama of ideas. Miniature scenes, intimate. Engelbrekt's private life is depicted as this is influenced by the great historic events." [2] In the collection are also notes on background reading, brief hints about the relationships and conflicts of the various characters, and notes on various ideas as they occurred to him.

Most important of all are the unfortunately undated outlines of his plot. Two brief preliminary ones and one longer—almost final—one will help to show that Strindberg speculated on many possibilities (all from Carton 1, Number 6):

A [3]	B (fragment) [4]
I: In the forest by the charcoal huts: Saturday evening. Margaret's Day. Miners come up from the mine opening with lanterns. Farm-	Scene III: In Dalarna. In Engelbrekt's home. His wife leaves. His daughter's love affair with Måns Natt-och-Dag's son is discovered.

ers with scythes and rakes. A memorial of spruce branches with the coats of arms of the three kingdoms. In Engelbrekt's home.

II: With King Erik.

III: At the meeting of the lords. Engelbrekt has to do it all over.

IV: Engelbrekt passed over.

V: Engelbrekt is murdered.

The son is already gone. The house empty.

Scene IV: The meeting of the lords. Engelbrekt's doubt. The king breaks his promises. Engelbrekt has to do everything over.

Scene V: Karl Knutsson Bonde is elected.

Scene VI: Engelbrekt is murdered. The children have to be parted. Göksholm Castle burns.

C⁵

Act I: Engelbrekt has taken Måns Natt-och-Dag's fiancée. *The mile-post on a highway in Dalarna.* Engelbrekt's son Karl and his daughter. Poles to which farmers have been tied can be seen. . . . *In Engelbrekt's home.* Bishop Styrbjörn; the children tell about foreign countries. Måns Natt-och-Dag's son Harald and Engelbrekt's daughter.

Act II: *At Jösse Eriksson's.* Elk—bear hunting. Orgy: the bishop misbehaves. One hears farmers screaming. Bishop Arnold Clementson, Måns Natt-och-Dag, Karl Knutsson Bonde, Erik Puke, Cristiern Nilsson Vasa visiting. Engelbrekt with his children and wife come. The law of domicile —Margaret's vs. Magnus Erikson's. Jens Erikson engages Karl Engelbrekt in his following. Break between Engelbrekt and Måns Natt-och-Dag. The omen: the man who broke his leg. The conspiracy. The golden helmets. Bishop Styrbjörn.

Act III: The royal councillors. Engelbrekt has negotiated with Erik XIII; then the people become suspicious. Engelbrekt elected head of state. Thinks he has arrived. Hybris. The four estates. *In Engelbrekt's home.* All desert him.

Act IV: The election of regent. Engelbrekt passed by. Has to start again.

Act V: *Engelbrekt is murdered.* Alone on the pier.

Plan C is remarkably close to the final plan as the final settings will indicate:

Act I: At the barricade on the highway; Engelbrekt's home.

Act II: In Jens Eriksen's quarters in the castle; in the mine.

Act III: Engelbrekt's home.

Act IV: Outside St. Gertrude's Guild Hall [the election of regent]; at the ferry crossing [Engelbrekt's death].

These are all representative scenes, all of which link closely, in the Strindberg manner, episodes in Engelbrekt's private life as they are influenced by historic events. But the major emphasis falls on Engelbrekt as an individual, not on the events.

Although the play is a folk drama, it is sharply different from earlier Swedish folk dramas. Instead of loosely related representative scenes from Engelbrekt's period of leadership with the outstanding events emphasized as in chronicle plays, *Engelbrekt* has a form based on the techniques of the Scribean type of well-made play with a development that can perhaps best be called impressionistic. Certainly there are few loose ends; motivation, exposition, and foreshadowing are furnished with a care and naturalness that are typical of the better well-made play. Even the highly theatrical endings of two of the acts (the archbishop's voluntary death in the fire in Act II and the death of Engelbrekt at the end of the play) are in keeping with the pre-*Master Olof* traditions of the Swedish theater and the practices of foreign writers of well-made plays.

It is as if Strindberg were deliberately trying to meet the Swedish criticism that came without fail every time a new Strindbergian historical play was published or produced by presenting the Swedes with a play that met all objections, among them the charges that he had reduced the great heroes of the past to ordinary human beings, that he was guilty of anachronisms and did not know his history well enough, and that he somehow failed to understand the heroes of the past and their times as well as the average Swedish reviewer and critic. But in writing *Engelbrekt,* Strindberg did much more than write a conventional well-made historical folk drama.

His play has as its unifying theme the whole complex of problems involved in an unequal union of closely related peoples. Basic to an understanding of Strindberg's treatment of the central idea involved is his clear-cut emphasis of the idealistic merits of a union of all Scandinavians:

ENGELBREKT: It's the day of the union today. Margaret's Day.

GERTRUDE: Blessed be her memory!

ENGELBREKT: Yes, indeed! Forty years of peace after a century of Folkung wars. That's worth something!

BISHOP: It's worth a lot!

ENGELBREKT: The borders between the three sister nations have been eliminated, and everyone's as much at home in either of the other two . . .

BISHOP: That's a great thing . . .

ENGELBREKT: There have been so many intermarriages that our descendants will have a hard time distinguishing Danes, Norwegians, and Swedes!

BISHOP: That *is* fine!

There are no chauvinistic elements; instead, there is a clear statement that Denmark is "a wonderful country . . . a charming and a lovely country" and a clearly expressed view that the particular Scandinavian group a man belongs to is not in itself the factor which determines his moral worth or virtue.

The problems are rather the results of the egotism and selfishness characteristic of human nature. The union which theoretically began as a union of three *equal* partners—Sweden, Norway, and Denmark —under Margaret of Denmark degenerated very quickly after her death into the reduction of Norway to centuries of subjugation to Danish rule, and Sweden was threatened with a similar fate. The efforts of Erik XIII and the Danes and Germans about him to grasp complete control over all Scandinavia and to make it a sort of greater Denmark with German overlords, the human tendency to get as much personal power as possible and to use it without much regard for others, the feeling on the part of most Scandinavians that they were individually Danish, Norwegian, or Swedish, *not* Scandinavian, the very human tendency to defend what the individual regards as his own, the divided loyalties, the personal obsessions and resentments, and personal ambitions and frustrations are all dealt with in Strindberg's play.

To illustrate his ideas about what happens to a country that discovers quickly that the union it has entered is not an idealistic union of equality but an arrangement by means of which its people may lose their human rights, every means of protecting them, and those things that it has learned to appreciate through many centuries of trial and error, Strindberg uses the story of a man who as an idealist has believed in the union and who as a practical man still believes in it. The story as both history and Strindberg understand it is of a man who is forced by visible proof to re-examine his ideas about the union, to try as long as possible to do what he can to set it right, to turn against it in part and then fully in order to protect his fellow countrymen's rights, and to lay the basic foundation for the ultimate destruction of such a union.

In keeping with his conviction that most people are complex, Strindberg presents the middle-aged practical idealist as an individual, as a husband, as a father, as a citizen, as a friend, as an opponent, as a son of the church, as a leader, as a man of action, as a man dedicated to thought, and as a sensitive good man in an imperfect world.

Strindberg himself has explained how he has supplemented the relatively meager historical and semihistorical accounts and has explained why he did so:

Since I begin with the last act in constructing a drama, I proceeded from Engelbrekt's murder, which is a fact. History does not make clear the motive for the murder. Engelbrekt had had a quarrel with the murderer's father, but they had been reconciled. Since no one knows what the quarrel was about, I had the right to make Måns Natt-och-Dag the envious man in whose way Engelbrekt was unfortunate enough to get. It certainly is true that ingratitude is often, though not always, the reward of the world, of course, but a person probably does not have the right to toss out one-sidedly such a comfortless and half-true idea, so I tried to give the great man something of an appearance of tragic guilt. In the manner of the Greek tragedies, I took the liberty of foisting upon him the very human sin, which almost regularly follows great success, that is, arrogance, *hybris,* which the gods hate above everything else. When the hero has then come as far as the election of a regent and considers himself the obvious and only possibility, it is not at all strange that he becomes emotionally intoxicated, particularly since he is sick enough to run a temperature. And, in the intoxication of victory, he sees the prospect of both the royal crown and the power—the power to oppress enemies, to trample under foot, to humiliate. Then come his reverses when he is rejected in the election, and everything collapses!

This final scene is tragic and could be called Swedenborgian. My *Engelbrekt* is a tragedy, and as such it should be judged, without regard to the latest fashions in literary journals.

But strong inner conflicts also belong to tragedy. The first conflict is that he has made the idea of the union one of his youthful ideals and has made his son accept it as well. When he now, like the prophet Jonah, does not want to step forward to prophesy, a man is sent to him and that man takes him by the ears and pulls him forward. That is Erik Puke. But now the hero stands between the vow of his youth and his oppressed country. He finally breaks his vow, comes into disharmony with himself, and goes to pieces when his own son, representing his former self, rises against him as he is *now* imbued with a new ideal. That is tragic conflict.

But, to increase the suspense, I had to introduce still more intimate conflicts, so I let him suffer in his marriage all the horrors of disunity. And when no one knows to whom Engelbrekt was married, I had the right to make his wife a Dane, which I thought was a very fine device for making the disunity concrete.

When Engelbrekt is forced to imprison his own son, the tragedy has reached its highest point. That is Brutus the Elder, but with a plus, since the Swedish Brutus thereby passes judgment on himself as having deserted the idea of his youth, but for a higher goal, one more than equally justified for the time being.

The tragedy therefore has no points of contact with Blanche's play, which was based on inadequate knowledge. Since 1846 new information about Erik XIII has appeared, and Erslev in his study *Erik of Pomerania* (1901) presents three motives for the Swedes' dissatisfaction with the Danish union king, who was not so bad as he has been pictured. First is emphasized Erik's unforgivable way of forcing bad bishops upon the Swedes. Then he is accused, and rightly so, of using and ruining Swedish servicemen in the pointless war against Slesvig.

Last comes the matter of the bailiffs. The king had accepted complaints and removed Danish bailiffs, but, when complaints continued against the Swedish bailiffs, he got weary and did not find time to straighten out that matter. Since he was least defendable on the matter of bishops, I made that the major item, and I was right.[6]

Interesting and helpful as these comments are, they do not fully explain how by means of a broad simplicity of characterization Strindberg manages to give us a memorable portrayal of the middle-aged leader at the same time that he gives us a vivid interpretation of the Swedes' first crucial attempt to break away from an unhappy union.

The "calm, dignified, straightforward, somewhat reserved . . . serious" Engelbrekt who comes on stage first in scene 2 of Act I is a man who is small only in physical stature. He is, moreover, a middle-aged man who feels, "When a person like me has never molested anyone, it would seem only fair to be left in peace." But as Strindberg quickly makes clear, Engelbrekt is the sort of man who will not be left in peace. One of the Strindbergian instruments of the Lord, he faces problems which break into three groups—personal, family, and public matters. He has something particularly painful on his conscience ("a secret sorrow"); he is a Swede by birth and loyalty but a unionist by conviction; he has a Danish wife whose loyalties go to Denmark; he has a son who not only has disregarded his father's wishes but who has gone into the union king's service and considers himself a Dane; he has a daughter who is obviously emotionally involved with the son of Engelbrekt's most bitter enemy. The head of an attractive family with the seeds of disunity in it, Engelbrekt is inwardly tortured by all of them as well as by Swedish visitors' tendency to make anti-Danish comments in the presence of his Danishborn wife.

Yet even more disturbing are the external events by means of which anti-Danish Erik Puke brings external pressure on Engelbrekt —the appointment of incompetent non-Swedes as bishops, the appointment of German and Danish bailiffs, and the king's failure to appoint either a Swedish chancellor or a Swedish marshal. The implications of the arbitrary actions of the royal agent in converting a free public road into a toll highway without consulting the Swedes and of the illegal torture of Swedish smiths are that if the German king and his non-Swedish representatives can proceed without being effectively curbed by the Swedes, they may reduce Swedes to serfdom.

It is that threat and the oppression of the Swedish smiths that make Engelbrekt act, not to destroy the union but to remove abuses against it. In the very moment when he has decided to act, however, he makes the very human mistake of making his son vow that he will never be a traitor to the union.

A revealing behavior pattern becomes clear in Act I. A practical idealist convinced that a union based on equality is sound, Engelbrekt gives all the indications of being slow to anger, of giving thoughtful consideration to the problems facing him, of assuming that no problem is either black or white, of carefully investigating and then acting on the basis of what he thinks is best for both his fellow countrymen and the union. Still more is revealed in Act I about Engelbrekt, including, for example, his love for his wife and his children, his tactful treatment of them and others, his friendly but not subservient treatment of the old bishop, and his capacity for judging people pretty much for what they are.

While Act I primarily tells about flaws in the union, Act II demonstrates what is wrong with it. Scene 1 not only is a highly dramatic presentation of the behavior and attitudes of the German-Wendish union King Erik XIII through the actions and frank talk of his henchmen but also reveals the disunity among the Swedes themselves. The Danish bailiff, the Danish archbishop of Sweden and their Danish and German companions in the course of their orgy make it clear that they have no regard for the rights or the sensitivities of the Swedes; their behavior is that of conquerors and masters, not that of fellows and equals. But no less striking is the behavior and talk of the Swedish leaders who are present not as participants in the "celebration" of Margaret's Day but as outsiders looking in, as it were, on a union in which they had been promised equality. Aside from Engelbrekt and to a degree Puke and the bishop, the Swedish leaders are men dedicated neither to the union nor to Sweden; they are instead personally ambitious rivals interested in seeing to it that no one among their fellows gains anything. Even Engelbrekt, who *sees* what is happening to the union, does not see clearly enough that principles as high as his will hardly guide the thinking or the conduct of non-Swedish or even Swedish leaders:

It isn't a question whether the archbishop's a fool or not, for he can be sent away; it isn't a question either of whether you make people pay tolls on the highway, tie other people's men to poles, or tax Swedes' mines. All that the national council will settle. But it's a question of this . . . about the union coat of arms, whether the Pomeranian griffin is to put his claws into the lions, and if the three crowns of Sweden shall be placed below the Danish lions instead of at their side! . . . No, Jens Eriksen, the great thought of the union has been twisted; you have stolen in like foxes with lies and trickery upon honest unsuspicious Swedish men who keep their word . . .

Engelbrekt acts only when his man Varg is threatened and when he learns that Swedish girls have been forced to come to the castle. But he does not break with the union.

Scene 2 presents through exposition the progress of Engelbrekt's efforts to set the union right, demonstrates Swedish pressures on Engelbrekt to break with the union and to lead his countrymen in an all-out effort to make all Swedes free of foreigners, and explains why Engelbrekt made the decision to do so. In keeping with the historical and traditional accounts, Strindberg's Engelbrekt is not willing to be forced into a course of action advocated by other leaders but depends on his conscience, his own observations, and the common people's testimony to make his final decision. The motivations for his decision as Strindberg saw them are Engelbrekt's sense of human decency, his integrity, and his sense of responsibility to "Sweden's patient, faithful, good people." But Strindberg's Engelbrekt is not merely a well-behaved aristocrat who looks after his underlings; he is a leader with an exceedingly active and sensitive conscience who knows his motives have not been completely pure:

ENGELBREKT: I am not the man you seek. I am no Gideon . . .
BISHOP: You are Joshua, the Lord's Joshua, for whom the walls fell . . .
ENGELBREKT: I have sinned . . .

BISHOP: We all have.

ENGELBREKT: I have worked only with the thought of gaining praise.

Strindberg's Engelbrekt is a Joshua forced unwillingly by his conscience and by events to lead his people against the union.

Act III is a highly moving depiction of the victorious Engelbrekt, who returns from his victories to find his beloved Danish wife gone, his daughter ready to follow the man she loves into the camp of her father's enemies, and his son faithful to the vow of loyalty to the union Engelbrekt had urged him to take. The act presents, moreover, Engelbrekt's being forced to take up arms again, this time both against the union king and against the ambitious Swedish leaders who have defected from the Swedish cause. In this act Strindberg illustrates his conviction that no situation in which human beings are involved is likely to be simple and clear-cut. For example:

KARL: You once made me swear I'd never be a traitor to my king, never harm the union to which you had devoted your life . . . I've kept my vow.

ENGELBREKT: You have done the right thing. And you are right! *(Gets up)* But I am not wrong, God knows! Destiny has tied my hands—wound the snare about my throat—and I've been forced to rebel against the past—against myself—tear down what I've built; but I have freed my country from tyrants and fools.

Strindberg's Engelbrekt understands that his wife's sympathies are natural, he understands that his daughter's loyalty to the man she loves is right, and that his son has the right to prefer his mother's country. It is this sort of material that Strindberg uses to make Engelbrekt far more than an apotheosis of a folk leader; Strindberg's Engelbrekt is no exultant victor but a man plunged into anguish and inner despair as he leads his people in their fight for freedom.

Act IV presents Engelbrekt after his final victory, when he brought his fellow countrymen to the point of agreeing to elect a Swedish regent free of all ties with the union. To convey his understanding of Engelbrekt, Strindberg first presents him when he thinks he will be elected regent in spite of the conniving of Karl Knutsson Bonde and others and the envy of some of his fellow aristocrats:

ENGELBREKT: Styrbjörn, you're my witness I never sought power; I preferred to live in the quiet valley for my own work and for my own people. But, when what little I had has been taken away from me and I'm now without a goal in life, I'll take what is given me. Well, then, you have given me power; I'll accept it! It will give meaning to my life; it will take the place of my home and family.

BISHOP: Now the ruler came into being! Hail, anointed of the Lord, chosen of God. . . .

ENGELBREKT *(softly)*: But power mustn't be divided . . . you see, *one* must do it, or nothing gets done . . . A difficult people must be ruled with an iron hand, and lords and commons must be disciplined alike . . . *(whispers)* . . . justice must not give way to mercy . . . I shall make my enemies my footstool . . . my Father has disciplined them with switches, but I come with scorpions!

This self-analysis presents, among other things, the nature of Engelbrekt's tragic guilt—his admittedly slender arrogance and pride. Contrasted most effectively is Engelbrekt's reaction when he knows that he has lost what, in a moment of temptation, he coveted:

ENGELBREKT: Come with me anyway . . . to find a roof and a bed so I may die. The Lord has punished me.

BISHOP: Engelbrekt, your work is rewarded by your own knowledge of deeds well done and by the people's love and blessing, which will follow you all the days of your life and longer still.

ENGELBREKT: Better to die than to live without honor!

It is a "splendid instrument of the Lord" who in defeat and humiliation and anguish goes to his death in the final scene. That final scene is an extremely theatrical one, and as such is in keeping with the spirit of the traditional accounts of Engelbrekt's assassination, and with Strindberg's intention of presenting one of Sweden's most beautiful memories in a well-made folk drama "as high and pure as Schiller had kept his William Tell."

Strindberg's characterization of Engelbrekt is, however, a far more convincing and more well-rounded characterization than one can find in any other Swedish literary work. Presenting him in the roles that history and legend had given him in the meager accounts, and supplying through his own insight and experiences many of the other roles Engelbrekt must have had, Strindberg gave Engelbrekt dimensions not given him elsewhere. Strindberg's Engelbrekt has a stature reduced, to be sure, from the traditional apotheosis but still kept high and made humanly believable.

Strindberg's insistence that his *Engelbrekt* is a tragedy and should so be judged is certainly justified by an examination of the play from the traditional point of view of tragedy. Engelbrekt has individuality; is keenly aware of himself as an individual; is fundamentally alone; has clearcut values; takes the responsibility for what he does; has the capacity to observe, choose, and act for himself; struggles for mastery over life; and functions within an atmosphere of freedom and responsibility.

But in frankly admitting (see the long passage quoted from *Open Letters to the Intimate Theater*) that he has given Engelbrekt "an appearance of tragic guilt" and "the very human sin, which almost regularly follows great success, that is, arrogance, *hybris,*" Strindberg suggests a fact about *Engelbrekt* that he was to make even clearer in a letter to August Falck on June 19, 1909:

I have reread *Engelbrekt;* it is only 66 pages long; does not need to be cut, for it is already intimate. But you may not imitate big theater. Produce it with columns and background scenes. We shall have to convert Engelbrekt's room to a stone house; take the tower room of *The Dance of Death,* which will fit in with the columns. And don't concoct. No poles and no watchman's cottage in Act I. No griffin and no view of the banquet. Pretend they are in the wings. No folk scenes: only *one* archer. No smiths, only *one* smith. No singing, only recitation by one smith. The host of young men is represented by *one,* who can be seen in the wing, pretending that the others stand in back of him. Don't try the impossible, and fail! Don't interrupt the program: Intimate.[7]

Although most of these suggestions stem from Strindberg's desire to have the play receive a friendly production at his and Falck's Intimate Theater, the emphasis on the play's being "already intimate" suggests that Strindberg in writing *Engelbrekt* had deliberately employed techniques that can perhaps best be labeled impressionistic.

With the exception of Engelbrekt himself, all the characters are presented with broad simplicity and a minimum of detail. But the details are chosen and presented in such a telling and evocative fashion that no sympathetic reader can have any serious difficulty in grasping the secondary characters—the members of Engelbrekt's family, the Danish bailiff, the Danish-born archbishop, Bishop Styrbjörn, Varg, Erik Puke, the Natt-och-Dags, Karl Knutsson, and Vasa, for example—as living, breathing human beings. Even such minor characters as Nigel, the archer, are so effectively sketched that the reader's imagination stimulated by Strindberg's impressionistic technique can have little difficulty in giving them their share of individuality and life.

The sources of information about the historical Engelbrekt are slight and thin, but the very meagerness of detail has not prevented some Swedish writers and Swedes in general from interpreting Engelbrekt and the people about him in thoroughly individualized fashion. Anyone who has read the sources will have to admit, moreover, that such matters as Engelbrekt's death have been conceived as highly theatrical in what could justifiably be called symbolic fashion.

It is precisely this sort of thing that Strindberg has exploited in his well-made folk drama and impressionistic experiment. The traditional background of Dalarna-Västmanland (see the detailed descriptions of the settings); the traditional role of Englebrekt as a good man, a folk leader, and a liberator from oppression; and the simple but clear lines of development in the struggle for freedom are all in this play. Nor, in his post-Inferno conviction that the theatrical need not be avoided in the theater if it is based on a genuine mood and sincerity of feeling, has Strindberg neglected the theatrical. Only for those who insist that a historical play must restrict itself to what the canons of realism and naturalism approve can these theatrical elements be disturbing.

Engelbrekt has never received a sympathetic test on any stage. Its one production—at the Swedish Theater in December, 1901—was a failure. The reviews imply that the play was presented as if it were a thoroughly realistic play like, say, the prose *Master Olof*. Although the audience applauded enthusiastically and frequently at the three performances, the drama critics centered their attacks on Strindberg's concept of Engelbrekt and, significantly, on what Sven Söderman in *Stockholms Dagblad* called "the loose and confused dramatic composition." [8] Tor Hedberg, who could have been expected to have grasped the discrepancy between the play as Strindberg wrote it and the play as the Swedish Theater produced it, joined in the attack on the play as a dramatic composition but qualified his criticism, in *Svenska Dagbladet* as applied to Act IV, scene 1:

> There was a tragic greatness about the figure of Engelbrekt. He is, moreover, conceived well in his big all-inclusive features. He is the calm, quiet, fair-minded man, who at a late time and almost against his will is driven to great and determined action, who sees his personal happiness crushed and instead grasps for the phantom of honor and power, which he himself does not believe in and which glides away from his grasp and disappears.[9]

If *Engelbrekt* is ever to have a fair test as theater, it will have to be presented in keeping with Strindberg's intention, and the production cannot be like that of *Gustav Vasa* or *Master Olof*. It will have to be produced imaginatively, so that what seemed to the critics in 1901 a loose and confused dramatic composition will, as in fairly recent productions of *Charles XII,* come into its right as an impressionistic composition designed to give the Swedes an interpretation of Engelbrekt "as high and pure as Schiller kept his William Tell." Swedish theaters will then have added another effective historical play to their repertory.

12

Queen Christina
The Strangest Creature God Ever Created

As ONE considers the historical plays through *Engelbrekt,* one is struck by the amazingly effective characterizations of women of the Swedish past. They are brought alive as dynamic and complex human beings and are not twisted because of prejudices Strindberg allegedly had against women as such. There is, to be sure, the not always saintly Birgitta in *The Saga of the Folkungs,* but, even in interpreting her, Strindberg strictly refrains from denigrating her because she is a woman; instead, as he explains in *Open Letters to the Intimate Theater,* he sees her, like many of the men in his plays, as a human being egotistically striving for power and, in the attempt, being false to her nature as a woman.[1] Not only are the vast majority of the women characters in the historical plays individuals in their own right but they are women, sympathetically and penetratingly seen and interpreted, neither idealized nor denigrated because they were women. But all of them through *Engelbrekt* are, because of the very facts of history, either secondary or minor characters.

In 1901, Strindberg composed *Queen Christina,* a play in which the queen had to be the central character, just as in the seventeenth century the reigning queen had managed to occupy the center of the stage wherever and whenever she was present. In his search for material about Queen Christina, Strindberg had what one might call a whole literature at his disposal. In addition to the large number of historical and semihistorical, scholarly and semischolarly, books and articles about the queen and her time, there was a considerable number of documents that can be classified as contemporary accounts largely based on gossip at home and abroad. Even in the accounts published after her day there was no single interpretation of the queen that was universally accepted. Queen Christina had been in her lifetime a controversial and contradictory figure and has pretty much remained so since.

What Strindberg's study of the sources led to by way of his own concept of the queen he has explained in part:

Christina. A woman reared to be a man, fighting for her self-existence, against her feminine nature and succumbing to it. The favorites—translated lovers, frankly speaking—but with forebearance for the daughter of the great Gustav Adolf. Stjernhjelm includes among her lovers even Holm the tailor, but I did not want to do that. Charge that to my credit, Quiriter! Christina was so genuine a woman that she was a woman-hater. In her memoirs she says frankly that women should never be permitted to rule. That she did not want to get married I think natural, and that she who had played with love was caught in her own net, is, of course, highly dramatic.[2]

Illuminating as these statements are, they do not center their attention on what was the very core of his concept of the queen, nor do they fully suggest what interpretation he gives the queen in his four-act play.

Almost every one of the sources available to him mentions either in passing or at length Christina's great interest in theater and comments on the artificiality of her behavior on most occasions. That such brief comments and detailed accounts gave Strindberg the unifying idea for his play cannot be doubted by anyone who studies the play carefully and objectively. If one recalls, moreover, Strindberg's admitted practice of infusing life into historic characters by drawing upon his own observations and experiences, the point is even clearer.

The dramatist and student of the theater had been married to Siri von Essen, the willowy blonde whose ambition to become a great actress had to some degree been realized, partially through Strindberg's efforts, and whose sources of income, after their divorce in the early 1890's, had included activities that were primarily dramatic and theatrical.[3] In May, 1901, Strindberg was married to Harriet Bosse, the relatively petite brunette who was a great actress and who, to judge from all accounts, rarely let Strindberg forget it. The memories of the first marriage and Harriet Bosse's pattern of behavior in the present fitted in nicely with what the sources said about Queen Christina's interest in the theater and her generally artificial or, if one will, theatrical behavior.

The very core of his concept of Queen Christina is that of an actress who happened to be the reigning queen. That she plays the role of queen not only on public occasions but on most private ones as well did not strike Strindberg as unusual. That she had actually developed to the point where she saw playing roles as *the* necessary and central activity as queen Strindberg considered unfortunate. His concept gave him not only a dramatically rewarding insight into the character of the queen but a plan for putting her story into dramatic form.

Faithful as usual to his conviction that human beings are many-sided and constantly changing, Strindberg scrupulously avoided making Queen Christina a mere type. In deciding on a form that would effectively present a complex and dynamic queen addicted to playing roles Strindberg chose what strikes many students of the theater as perhaps the most artificial of all forms in modern drama—the well-made play. But, as we shall see, he proceeded to fill the frame of the well-made play with vitalizing techniques from his own realistic-naturalistic dramas and a few touches from his own post-Inferno expressionistic plays.

Limiting his action to the last few months up to and including her abdication in 1654, Strindberg chose four representative and revealing settings:

> Act I: Riddarholm Church: the queen, her court, and others there to commemorate the death of her great father, Gustav Adolf.
> Act II: The National Treasury: the unfortunate state of the kingdom and the role the queen has played in making it so.
> Act III: The Tailor Shop: Queen Christina and her ballet costume.
> Act IV: A Pavilion in the Palace Gardens: her performance for Tott and her abdication.

The list of settings and the brief explanations merely hint at their rich implications. A detailed examination of Strindberg's central character and of the dramatic structure, act by act, will reveal them.

Queen Christina differs from all the other historical dramas in its presentation of a woman as the central character, surrounded by men and only incidentally affected by other women. The center of a masculine world, insisting that she herself is no woman, Strindberg's Christina is a product of her heredity and her environment. Brilliant by endowment, Christina has by circumstances beyond her control become, as Allert says, "the strangest creature God ever created." Note what the queen mother says: "But then they tore my child from me . . . God forgive them, if He can! . . . and they reared you to be a man. . . . Now they have what they have!" Christina has never been allowed to develop normally and naturally as a woman; in fact, she has been trained to look upon women as inferior creatures and believes that she is a woman-hater. Forced to pretend that she is something she is not, she has become a strange creature and, in Strindbergian terms, a sleepwalker who is not fully conscious of either herself or the world about her. She has not been trained to be honest with herself or with others. She has become a human being who is both fascinating and repulsive, a human being who while "fighting for her existence" has early learned to play innumerable roles, all designed to protect herself and to give herself satisfaction. For Queen Christina is surrounded by men, men who have to do their work through her, with her if possible, or in spite of her if need be; men who want to use her; men whom she wants to use for her own generally whimsical purposes; and at a distance the little men—her resentful subjects, who, she has been led to believe, love her.

If it is remembered that power ultimately rests with the reigning queen, Strindberg's interpretation is clear. Only six when she ascended the throne, Strindberg's Christina has been trained more for the observation of the outward forms than for understanding of, and devotion to, her duties as reigning queen; in the process of that training she has acquired, as a child queen, an amazing notion of her position and has retained it even at the age of twenty-seven. The "little Kerstin," center of attention at court and even nationally during her formative years, learned early to get her way by playing on the sympathies and masculine attitudes toward little girls to a degree far beyond any implication of Shakespeare's lines in *As You Like It*: "All the world's a stage, And all the men and women merely players." Even Oxenstjerna, the great statesman more than any one else responsible for her training, senses part of what is basically wrong:

OXENSTJERNA: Christina, little child, get up! . . . I will help you, but you must never do this again! . . . You see, to rule nations, one has to be an everyday sort of person. Why, there are farmers and businessmen in parliament! . . . And you are not an ordinary person. You are like an artist—just as careless, just as carefree, just as thoughtless . . . and this . . . does not suit you!

CHRISTINA: It does, no doubt, but it's so boring!

OXENSTJERNA *(smiles)*: Yes, it is boring . . . and you want to have a good time above all else . . .

What Oxenstjerna does not understand is that he and the other members of the regency during her minority are primarily responsible for making her what she is and for giving her a strange notion of her position.

Forced to act the role of queen in her childhood and teens, both in ritualistic and nonritualistic situations, Strindberg's Christina has come to the conclusion that her position is basically a series of games or plays, each of which permits her to use her brilliant endowment to keep herself the center of attention and the dominant figure in every move and gives her a great deal of egotistic satisfaction in controlling the men about her. In talking with Magnus De la Gardie, the one man who dares on occasion to be frank with her, Queen Christina frankly admits what her concept is, only to have De la Gardie classify it beyond doubt as to its basic nature:

DE LA GARDIE: Poor Kerstin, you're involved in . . . something that does not befit you!
CHRISTINA: Yes, it is too binding. *(Changes her manner)* But it is interesting! *(Childishly)* And it's fun at times!
DE LA GARDIE: Playing with dolls!
CHRISTINA: Exactly! Big dolls!

and

CHRISTINA: What have I done to make everyone hate me?
DE LA GARDIE: You have played with the destinies of men as if you had been playing with dolls.
CHRISTINA *(amazed)*: Have I?
DE LA GARDIE: See, you didn't know! . . . You do not know what you are doing, so God forgive you!
CHRISTINA: You are kind, Magnus!
DE LA GARDIE: Always kind to little Kerstin. Always unkind to the big, nasty Christina!

Nominally queen until she was eighteen and reigning queen after that, Strindberg's Christina thinks then of her position as roles to be acted and as roles, moreover, in a comedy, not in a serious drama. She says to Holm, her tailor: "Holm, I'm tired of this whole comedy! . . . *(as if to herself)* I suspect this is the last act that's on . . ."

As Strindberg makes clear, Queen Christina has during her nine years of actual reign ruled largely by whim and impulse. Oxenstjerna's speech to Magnus De la Gardie summarizes her whimsical behavior as a ruler:

Reverence, deference, loyalty to the royal house, everything that I have respected I shall have to throw overboard! I have closed my eyes out of reverence; I have closed my ears out of deference and I have finally become false from pure loyalty. I have become cowardly; I have become a servile toady at court; I have respected meanness; and I am beginning to despise myself. . . . The kingdom is ruled by a crazy woman, the accounts look as if a mad child had kept them! All the possessions of the crown have been ruined for foreigners, ballets are presented at thirty thousand crowns a night; the army exists only on paper; and the navy is rotting outside Karlskrona; the estates of parliament are treated as a parish council; the national council is recruited with second lieutenants; the palace chapel is a Jesuit meeting place; and the palace is a dance hall.

To be sure, the queen has the impression that she has been a very good queen indeed:

> CHRISTINA: Why do they hate me? *(Childishly)* What have I done? Am I not kind to everyone? Haven't I supported the lower estates against the arrogance of the lords? Haven't I . . .
> DE LA GARDIE: Child, you have been playing . . . but you mustn't any more. Little Kerstin died long ago, but you insist on reviving her.

It is the crowned actress who impulsively has the Messeniuses, who have summarized the hard cold facts about her whimsical reign in a pamphlet, arrested and brought to trial without any forethought about the practical consequences for her. It is the crowned actress who impulsively gets Sweden involved in a war with Bremen and its allies. It is the crowned actress who offends both France and Portugal because of her whimsical behavior. It is the crowned actress who considers the crown possessions her personal belongings and brings her country to the verge of financial ruin.

Strindberg's Queen Christina has indeed mastered the art of acting in an amazingly broad range. She is usually only slightly interested in content and almost always intensely interested in effect, and she sees each situation as a dramatic challenge and rises to the occasion not as ruler but as an actress by adapting herself to the situation to protect herself, to keep the center of the stage, and to gain as much selfish satisfaction as possible; these are some of the most basic elements in "the strangest creature God ever created." As Swedish actresses who have played the role have discovered, Strindberg's Queen Christina has a wide range of the nuances of voice, manner, gesture, and diction.

The Christina of the many faces has to deal primarily with the men about her—Pimentelli, the Spanish ambassador and one of her intimate favorites; Bourdelot, the French physician; Oxenstjerna, her former tutor and the great statesman with high ideals and a realistic program; Prince Carl Gustav, once her leading suitor and now heir apparent to the throne; Magnus De la Gardie, a former favorite and the one man who dares to be frank with her even before her abdication; Holm, the tailor who lends her money and gives her good advice; von Steinberg, who worships the queen whose life he once saved; and her subjects who look at her with open eyes and whom she despises. There is, moreover, Tott, who loves her. Note well that in the whole play there are only three other women—Queen Mother Maria Eleonora, Lady Ebba Sparre (Christina's one woman friend), and Countess Ebba Brahe De la Gardie, Magnus' mother and the woman Christina's father loved and wanted to marry. Even these three have minor roles; the last two appear only once. It is a man's world in which the crowned actress has her place, and it is a man's world in which she schemes, poses, and intrigues to keep the show going with herself as the center of it all. And each of these men gets, the queen insists, "the Christina he deserves."

Six of the men are sharply individualized, and we learn what she thinks of each of them, what each one thinks of her, how they individually behave toward her, and how she behaves toward each of them. Three of them—Oxenstjerna, Magnus De la Gardie, and Prince Carl Gustav—are in varying degrees men dedicated to the welfare of Sweden and forced consequently to work through Queen Christina or, that failing, in spite of her. Holm is interested in the prosperity of his own business and has no objection to benefiting socially as well from her patronage, but he has a friendly loyalty to her. Von Steinberg is simply a devoted follower with neither selfish nor national goals in view. Tott, as we shall see later, is a man in love.

Yet these six men and the less sharply individualized Pimentelli and Bourdelot are the men against whom the queen plays her "comedy." It is in the occasional presence, too, of the little men whom she despises that she acts the innumerable roles that she selects for herself and, while so doing, ultimately reveals herself as far more than a crowned actress.

The testimony of the little men who look on as tribute is paid to the great Gustav Adolf on the anniversary of his death at Lützen emphasizes the queen's addiction on occasion to stooping to un-queenly behavior, Bourdelot's teaching her to sneer at everything, the Jesuit Pimentelli's influence on and intimacy with the nominally Lutheran queen, her envy of her father's reputation and the great men about him, her favorites, and her unusual pattern of behavior. Note what Allerts, the keeper of the Golden Peace, and the farmer say:

ALLERTS: Now the Queen's coming! . . . No suite . . . no chamberlains . . . no guards. Doesn't fear her loyal subjects . . . believes everybody loves her, because she loves herself!

KEEPER: Does she believe that?

ALLERTS: She believes only what she wants to!

FARMER: But she is majestic, little as she is!

ALLERTS: At the moment, yes, but in the next she's a shopgirl . . . Now you're going to see the strangest creature God ever created . . .

In one act after the other, Strindberg makes it clear that his Queen Christina had no objective reason for believing that her subjects loved her.

In dealing with each of the men most significant to her, she employs a variety of techniques subtly adapted, she feels, to the particular man and the particular occasion. Oxenstjerna, the chancellor, has not only supervised her training but still, as the most powerful man in the country, has her, as the Keeper of the Golden Peace says, under his thumb. As Act I makes clear, she has long since become used to having to wait for the chancellor:

MARIA ELEONORA: Whom are we waiting for, my child?

CHRISTINA: The chancellor, Mother! Little Kerstin always has to wait for the great Oxenstjerna!

She conceals both her impatience and her resentment when he comes, brushes aside his important news, and, a little later when talking with Magnus De la Gardie, finds compensation through belittling him. Strindberg has employed an effective device in the last three acts for clarifying the relations between the queen and her powerful chancellor. In Act II as long as she feels secure, she deals coldly with him, even lashing out and glaring at him. In fact she dares to engage in a duel of words with him until he suddenly levels his most serious charge against her and wins. Having lost, Christina instantly resorts to another technique:

> CHRISTINA *(coquettish and friendly, pats Oxenstjerna on the hand that holds the papers)*: Thank you very much, good friend. I take Axel Oxenstjerna's word; no papers are needed with little Kerstin! *(Oxenstjerna remains cold.)* Are you angry with Kerstin, old fellow? Do you remember when you used to pull my hair during my history lessons . . . *(Takes his hand and puts it on her head)* Caress me a little; I am so spoiled . . . and I had neither a father nor a mother . . .

In Act III, she tries in vain to bribe him; that having failed, she engages in another duel with him which he instantly wins by asking her searching questions about her correspondence with Königsmarck. Frightened and embarrassed, she quickly changes her approach to what one might call her "little Kerstin routine," announces her desire to abdicate, and gives in. It is made curiously clear that Oxenstjerna likes the child Kerstin but detests the adult actress Christina. In Act IV, it is Oxenstjerna who asks for reassurance about her possible change of faith and what little victory there is goes to the queen, who at last is "out of his claws" and as a queen without a throne is in a position to be as frank and honest as her nature permits her to be.

Even more revealing of the nature of the queen and of her behavior are the scenes with Count Magnus De la Gardie, formerly her special favorite and intermittently in disfavor. In his way, Magnus loves her, but he knows her very well, has been her intimate companion, and dares to be frank with her and to challenge her in a number of contests of wit. He knows her for the actress she is, he knows that she has shown no real evidence of having a heart, but whenever she appeals to him for help he demonstrates that he is "always kind to little Kerstin. Always unkind to the big, nasty Christina!" Note in Act III, for example, Christina's response to his frank appraisal of her character and of her old concept of love as a game, her repertory of reactions—anger, haughtiness, humiliation, shame, scorn, derision, brutality, threatening, gentleness, pathos, sadness, fury, and cold anger. But it is Magnus who wins the contest in wits:

DE LA GARDIE *(caressingly)*: Little Kerstin! . . . Poor little Kerstin, you are the one who is on trial and who is being investigated . . .
CHRISTINA: How stupid . . . it is to do stupid things!
DE LA GARDIE: Of course! I certainly know, I who am being whipped for my . . . let us say stupidities!
CHRISTINA *(sadly)*: Why are you always superior to me?
DE LA GARDIE: Am I? . . . Perhaps I am!
CHRISTINA *(furious, flashes out)*: Don't be impudent!

But it is Magnus, whom she has favored, put into disfavor, and played with—falsely and crudely on occasion—to whom she frankly and honestly confesses her love for Klas Tott:

CHRISTINA: Yes, I do love him; I am in love for the first time in my life, and . . . for ever!
DE LA GARDIE: You played with him, lured him, and now you're caught!
CHRISTINA: Yes, I am caught, and I love the dear bonds! He alone can lift me out of this filth!

It is Magnus who sees Christina the woman as she might have been —beautiful, charming, feminine—as she is awakened from her sleepwalking. It is Magnus, too, who makes the telling Strindbergian remark:

CHRISTINA: Do you believe that it . . . is . . . the Queen he loves . . . the Queen alone?
DE LA GARDIE: I don't know! We are just as strange as you!

Important in her life is Prince Carl Gustav, her heir apparent and the one she had promised to marry. When he appears on stage for the first time in Act III, he is, says Strindberg, "fat, sweaty, soft, bourgeois, good-natured, a little roosterlike but always dignified," a cousin and rejected suitor whom she has "in her claws." Note how she uses baby talk to him condescendingly, puts her finger in her mouth when she uses him to get information about government finance, how she feels free to yawn in his presence, how she brings pressure to bear on him, how she sees him as a kind, well-informed dear who is too dull and serious to be fun. As long as she has power, she can control him by cajoling, by threat of public exposure of his affair with Allerts' daughter, and by bribing him with the crown. Carl Gustav treats her as a relative who happens to have power, who is ignorant and careless in wielding it, and who is touched and disturbed by what she has done. But in Act IV, Carl Gustav, about to ascend the throne, no longer has to guard his tongue and most succinctly tells her the bill of complaints against her:

CARL GUSTAV: Yes, you should have read Swedish history a little better before you set out to make Swedish history!

CHRISTINA: Don't you have any shame?

CARL GUSTAV: And the pages you have written ought to be torn out . . . for they deal only with unlawful acts, embezzlements, scandals, and favorites!

CHRISTINA: And *you* dare say that?

CARL GUSTAV: Yes, I dare! . . . And I add . . . your nursery politics have plunged the nation into adventures that I'm to inherit . . .

Having listed them, he gives her the opportunity to present her well-known defense. Then:

CARL GUSTAV: Have you really had any meaning in your meaningless actions, or are you improvising?

CHRISTINA: It's possible that now when I'm first attacked my need for self-defense helps clear up the darkness in my intentions . . .

CARL GUSTAV: Perhaps this country was too limited for you?

CHRISTINA: Who knows? Perhaps that's it!

CARL GUSTAV: And what do you intend to do now?

CHRISTINA: That does not concern you! And no other mortal, either!

Holm, the master tailor, who not only supervises the preparation of her wardrobe and her ballet costumes but is always ready to lend her money, too, knows the queen and understands the impossible situation in which she has become involved. Respectful to a degree, not always completely courteous to her, he nevertheless is loyal to her and warns her both about the little men and about the Messenius trial. She sees him as a faithful servant, praises him on occasions, and condescends to call him "my friend." But his compliments (her beautiful eyes, her willowy figure) arouse her anger and her disgust, both of which she attempts to conceal. But Holm, whom she has ennobled as Lejoncrona considers her abdication realistically, and even he does not play merely the simple role the crowned actress has assigned him:

HOLM: Is . . . Your Majesty leaving? . . . May I ask you for something in writing?

CHRISTINA: Shame! You have my word!

HOLM: Words are words, but writing is money!

CHRISTINA: You speak of money now . . . at this moment . . . Shall I think about money now? . . . And you whom I raised from the dust and placed in the House of Lords! . . . Churl! Go!

Steinberg, the good, simple-hearted young man who had saved her from drowning regards her unselfishly. Not a little naïve and not very bright, he thinks "the queen is an angel." Christina uses him as a faithful servant, ordinarily speaks to him "in a friendly tone as if she were speaking to a harmless person," lashes out in rebuke on one occasion without cause, but has the grace to apologize to him. Note this passage:

CHRISTINA: Steinberg, don't desert me, even though I have been ungrateful! Go away with me!

STEINBERG: Wherever Your Majesty commands! Around the whole world!

CHRISTINA: Come with me! But don't demand any reward . . . like the others . . .

STEINBERG: That is my reward . . . that I may go with you!

Even Steinberg in the sincerity of his feelings and the purity of his motives proves superior to the queen.

But Axel Oxenstjerna, Magnus De la Gardie, Prince Carl Gustav, Holm, and Steinberg are not the only sharply individualized men about Queen Christina. A brief look at Strindberg's plot stripped to its bare outline will indicate as much:

> The queen, a sleepwalker both as woman and ruler, acquires an unfortunate and unsavory record.
> Klas Tott awakens her as a woman.
> Her past, both as woman and ruler, is exposed.
> She loses both her throne and the man she loves.

Klas Tott, her handsome twenty-three-year-old distant relative, is exceedingly important to Strindberg's interpretation of Queen Christina. In Act I Strindberg presents the young descendant of Erik XIV as the object of the queen's close and speculative scrutiny; he is another young man she finds attractive and, because of his antecedents, someone she can use in her struggle with Oxenstjerna. In Strindbergian terms she plays with him and, in doing so, runs through an amazing range of emotions from indignation to affection. Tott does not appear in Act II, but Magnus De la Gardie reveals that she is showering Tott with favors. In Act III—apparently some weeks later in time—Tott does appear, this time as the romantic lover, who adores, worships, idealizes the queen:

TOTT: . . . Do you think she's playing with me?
DE LA GARDIE: Playing? Can a woman do anything else? Why, love is a game!
TOTT: To play with heaven and hell—that's a dangerous game!
DE LA GARDIE: There are people who die!
TOTT: I love her as a youngster would; I worship her like a higher being, and I call her my first love!
DE LA GARDIE: A higher being?
TOTT: Yes, exactly! Don't you see how she hovers above life, how everything is insignificant to her? The crown, which kings place on their

heads, she tramples under her feet. I'm almost sure that she'll throw it away some fine day!

The queen, still assuming that love is a game, is amazed by his expression of his romantic love:

> CHRISTINA: Dear child, keep your feet on the ground . . . Kerstin cannot fly! . . . Alas! I shall bring you misfortune . . . Epimetheus!
> TOTT: Pandora! You who have given me the first inkling that there is such a thing as happiness. . . . You . . . pure, snow-white . . . in your innermost being you are that, even if . . .
> CHRISTINA: Even if?
> TOTT: Even if the little earth spirit which sets your beautiful figure going . . .

It is Tott who awakens the woman latent in Christina; in Strindberg's own words: as a woman sincerely in love, she becomes "a graceful woman with a gentle manner and languorous movements," a person who can begin to forget her own ego for the sake of the person she loves.

But it is highly significant that for Strindberg's Christina even her love for Tott must be staged—hence the Roman feast for just the two of them. Note in Act IV, the set stage with its backdrops, carefully selected stage properties, the background music, the beautiful costuming of Queen Christina as Pandora, the role of Prometheus—Epimetheus assigned to Klas Tott, the exact timing of stage effects (the rain of flowers at Tott's feet, for example), the tableau planned at the back, and the carefully worded and spoken lines. It is a love scene, an "act" played as much for effect as for sincere expression of feeling. Note the theatrical and symbolic sacrifice of her royal crown. But "when the wall in the section at the back is drawn up":

> *One sees instead of the expected tableau a crowd of strange people, all of them motionless, silent, pale-faced. . . . Christina screams—prolonged. Tott comes down from the throne and puts his arm about her waist.*

> CHRISTINA: Are they specters from Hell?
> TOTT: I don't know! But I feel as if I were awakening from a long sleep! *(Looks about)* What sort of game is all this?

CHRISTINA: What did I hear? Klas Tott!
TOTT: Yes, my Queen!
CHRISTINA: I am no longer the Queen! I am only your . . .
TOTT: What?
CHRISTINA: Your queen of hearts!
TOTT: Whore, you mean!
CHRISTINA (*staggers backward*): Good God, now you really hurt me!

Ironically, the awakened sleepwalker is rejected by the sleepwalker who has awakened her. Strindberg is quite right in asserting, "that she who had played with love was caught in her own net, is, of course, highly dramatic." By means of the expressionistic effect of the sudden startling appearance of the crowd of motionless, silent, pale-faced, strange people and the Strindbergian hate-love mutual recriminations following the awakening of Tott, Strindberg has underscored aspects of Queen Christina as he saw her in a manner decidedly reminiscent of the well-made play.

The realism, the careful preparation, the logical development of motivations, the effects, the denouements, the intrigues, and even what Strindberg in the preface to *Lady Julie* calls the symmetrical French dialogue are all there. But all of these devices are used deliberately to make his serious drama about Queen Christina highly theatrical or, if you will, dramatic in its effects. For his stage interpretation of a woman who was fascinated by the theater and who, according to the sources, behaved theatrically on innumerable occasions, the form of the well-made play was eminently suitable.

Strindberg himself emphasized this when on March 27, 1908, he sent Falck a long series of suggestions for the production of the play at the Intimate Theater. One suggestion reads: "Christina must not neglect the big scene at the Treasury, where every word is a knife: and she is to watch if it cuts. . . . Oxenstjerna and De la Gardie exchange glances throughout the whole scene." [4] But what Strindberg apparently felt no need to emphasize is that his interpretation of Queen Christina is not restricted to that of the crowned actress but is extended to the revelation as well of the real Christina with her core of basic individuality and naturalness, which an unfortunate training and a trying environment have, intentionally or unintentionally, done much to conceal and cripple. The Christina who walks off stage just as the final curtain is about to fall is a woman who no longer believes that either ruling a nation or being in love is merely a game.

Queen Christina has shared the fate of many Strindberg plays. It was thoroughly damned by the reviewers when it was published in 1903, and the theaters without exception refused it. In 1908 it was presented in Falck's and Strindberg's own Intimate Theater. The dramatic critics were almost as brutal in their criticism as the reviewers had been some years earlier. But staged with the well-known substitution of drapes for wings and the use of furniture, other stage properties, and costumes to suggest the period, and by a sympathetic cast, *Queen Christina* won the audience so that it could be presented sixty-five times between 1908 and 1910.

Since then *Queen Christina* has slowly but surely won recognition both at home and abroad as theater and drama. The play has been successfully performed in both Austria and Germany from 1910 on and has been praised by both critics and audiences. There have been memorable Swedish productions—in 1926, Harriet Bosse played Christina in a brilliant staging at Lorensberg Theater, in 1941, Karin Kavli played the role in the successful Hälsingborg City Theater production, and in 1941-42 Per-Axel Branner staged *Queen Christina* in what was a brilliant confirmation of Strindberg's faith in *Queen Christina,* expressed on March 29, 1908: "My finest work with perfect technique, characters developed in detail, the greatest feminine role in Swedish, the most beautiful of declarations of love, played as reality itself. . . ." [5] Proceeding from the belief that Queen Christina is both poetry and theater, Per-Axel Branner studied the play as both and produced it with Karin Kavli as the queen.[6] Both critics and the twenty-eight audiences at the New Theater were enthusiastic about the imaginative and creative production. A more recent major Stockholm production with Inga Tidblad as the queen has confirmed the theatrical effectiveness of *Queen Christina.*

13

Gustav III

A Hero and a Dancing Master

Much of what sets Stockholm off from the other capitals of Europe and gives it a great deal of its own peculiar charm and color can be directly traced to Gustav III, who in his twenty-year reign (1771-92) deliberately attempted to make the city a cultural center comparable to any on the continent. Intensely interested in literature and the arts in general, Gustav III's long list of achievements include the founding of the Swedish Academy in 1786, the encouragement of the royal opera and the royal theaters, the stimulation of a national literary awakening, and a substantial influence on Swedish taste in many areas from art and architecture to furniture and dress. An avowed disciple of Voltaire, the king tried heroically to raise his country and his people to a level of greatness they had apparently been about to achieve back in the days of Gustav Vasa, Gustav Adolf, Queen Christina, Charles X Gustav, Charles XI, and the early Charles XII.

Following the traditional practice of many of his great predecessors on the throne, he deliberately enlisted the aid of the three lower estates—the farmers, the burghers, and the clergy—against the privileged lords; through the revolution of 1772, he freed his country from humiliating subservience to foreign powers, liberalized the laws in ways that Voltaire could applaud, and gave his people a program that only because of lack of material and human resources and his own incapacity for sustained planning and effort could not be realized. In the ensuing struggle for power with his opponents, Gustav III found it necessary to compromise both his ideals and the programs more or less hurriedly put together to realize them; in fact, his compromises went so far that toward the end of his reign he successfully made himself absolute monarch, without, however, discarding many of his basic goals.

Confronted with all the contradictions about Gustav III both as a king and as a person, his contemporaries and people in later generations have never reached any generally acceptable judgment of either the man or his reign except in a number of cultural areas. The scholars, the writers, and all other Swedes have, for example, agreed that Gustav III was intensely interested in the theater and in drama. All Swedes beyond early childhood are aware of the Drottningholm and Gripsholm court theaters, the royal theater, and the royal opera, and in varying degrees know what they represent in the cultural history of Stockholm and the nation. Most Swedes think of Gustav III as the king who above all others not only liked the theater but did much for its development in Sweden. Apparently all of those Swedes who are actively interested in theater and drama know, as Strindberg did, that Gustav III was a playwright who either alone or in collaboration with other dramatists wrote some of the best Swedish plays of his time, that he managed the production of plays at his court theaters, that he produced impressive open air spectacles, and that he was interested in and devoted his attention to every other phase of theatrical activity besides: theories and practices of acting, dramatic theory, casting, costuming, stage design, rehearsals, even the setting up and printing of programs for performances. Above all, most Swedes—if one can judge by what has been written about the king —think of him as the king who above all others made living and acting almost synonymous terms.

It is that Swedish idea of Gustav III that Strindberg has used in his *Gustav III*:

Gustav III. The enlightened despot, who carries through the French Revolution at home in Sweden—that is to say, crushes the aristocrats with the aid of the third estate. That is a paradox that is hard to deal with. And as a character, he is full of contradictions, a tragedian who plays comedy in life, a hero and a dancing master, an absolute monarch who is a friend of liberty, a man who strives for humanitarian [reforms], a disciple of Fredrik the Great, Joseph II, and Voltaire. Almost sympathetic [i.e., likable], he, the Revolutionist, falls at the hands of the Revolutionists. Anckarström [the assassin of Gustav III] was, namely, a man of the revolution who has had his story written by the Swedish court of appeals *(Svea Hovrätt)*.[1]

As this brief explanation indicates, Strindberg's concept of Gustav III is not limited to the actor king or, if you will, the actor on the throne; he is as much a hero as a dancing master.

Strindberg knew that the king, who had written plays about his two great predecessors who had shared his name, had sincere ambitions to emulate them in terms, of course, of his own time. But the eighteenth-century king who admired French culture and would have liked to have Sweden achieve an equal culture of its own was no Gustav Vasa stubbornly dedicated to building a Sweden from foundation to rafters without much regard for the reactions of his people or of foreigners; nor was he a Gustav Adolf dedicated to achieving great goals for Sweden and its people without any striking desire to gain the applause of his fellows. As Strindberg understood Gustav III, the king had the desire to be a hero not only for Swedes but for humanity, he had a genuine program for achieving heroic goals and stature, but he had no intention of becoming a hero in privacy or obscurity. Instead, he wanted to play his role as a hero—based, to be sure, on genuinely heroic achievement—on the stage of the world and in so doing to gain the resounding applause of mankind.

To bring such a man alive on the stage for his countrymen, Strindberg again selected the dramatic form most suitable for such a crowned actor—the well-made play of the Scribean tradition. A brief look at the settings will suggest as much:

Act I: Holmberg's Book Store: the case against King Gustav.
Act II: The king's reception room at Haga Palace: the king's problems; his dealing with his enemies and the people about him.
Act III: A room at Huvudsta Manor House: the conspirators; King Gustav's unannounced appearance amidst the conspirators.
Act IV: In China Castle at Drottningholm: the king's moves toward absolutism and the conspirators' countermoves; the king saved at the last minute by Badin—the Negro—and the queen.

Even the settings and the brief summaries of the contents of the acts suggest that the play about Gustav III was deliberately designed to bring out the theatrical and artificial elements in a monarch and a court permeated by both. None of the other dramatic forms used by Strindberg in his historical plays can be so eminently fitting as the well-made play to bring either a crowned actress or a crowned actor alive on the stage—in keeping with the national traditions. Both *Queen Christina* and *Gustav III* are proofs of that.

While the two plays are closely related both in form and content, there are basic differences that distinguish them from each other as well as similarities that make them companion plays. While both of the central characters have become actors largely because of the influence of their early environment, Queen Christina is a sleepwalker who must be awakened; Gustav III is not. While both have mastered the art of acting to the point where it has become almost as natural to them as breathing, Christina acts largely to gain attention and to get her way without having any clear idea of the important implications of either her position or her role. Gustav III, on the other hand, knows very well indeed what he is, what he wants to do, and why he does what he does. Strindberg's Gustav III, unlike Christina, knows that he is involved in a struggle for power, the results of which will signify a great deal not only for himself but for his country. Christina is, to be sure, involved in a struggle for power, but the objects of that struggle are pretty much limited to slight personal gains—for herself. But both are consummate actors.

Even more than in *Queen Christina,* Strindberg has exploited the setting, the manners, the ideas, and the leading personalities of a particular period. Haga and China Castle at Drottningholm; Bellman and his songs; Thorild the idealist, who dreamed of a Utopia that would come into being as a result of the realization of the ideas of liberty, equality, and brotherhood; Kellgren, the advocate of reason and common sense and on occasion King Gustav's literary collaborator; the close ties with France; the enthusiasm about Voltaire, Rousseau, Washington, and Franklin; the colorful rich apparel of the Gustavian courtiers; Holmberg's book store, representative of an intellectual awakening that was to make the Gustavian period one of the most interesting in Swedish history; the emphasis on ritual and form—all these are more than suggested and must give all Stockholmers the pleasure of recognition of affinities between the present and a period that has long since passed but that still plays an important basic role in the Stockholm and the Sweden of today. Strindberg is indeed a master at providing atmosphere of time and place both effectively and economically.

Every Swede who knows his country's history will appreciate Strindberg's effective use of the traditions about Gustav's appearance, manners, and mannerisms. The king is handsome, but it is the handsomeness of a slight, delicate man who is somewhat effeminate in his walk, his gestures, his speech, and his embroidering. Strindberg's Gustav III is an actor who checks on both his appearance and his manner in the mirror whenever he has the occasion; he is an actor who feels that costume, gestures, movements, and speech must be right for the occasion, the situation, and the particular person. But behind all these artificial and even superficial matters is a brilliant mind, handicapped, as Strindberg believed, by lack of staying power, by a tendency to confuse the goal with the means, and by a tendency not to restrict his activities to what can be realized.

Act I, in which King Gustav does not appear, is largely devoted to presenting the case against the king, his major adversaries, the intellectual and the political setting, the conspiracy of the lords, who plan either to depose or liquidate him, and Anckarström's intense personal hatred of the king. It is an act that at once provides the basic exposition, preparation, and motivation for much of the action that is to come. There are, for example, the slim but necessary details about the king's revolution of 1772, when he not only had freed his country from humiliating foreign intervention but had taken his stand for the commons against the lords; his liquor law drawn up with good intentions but without careful consideration of its inevitably evil effects; his guaranteeing freedom of the press and his later limitation of it; his diversionary and formally illegal war against Russia; his printing of counterfeit Russian rubles for use in the war; corruption in his government; his challenge of the lords by granting the lower estates privileges earlier reserved for the nobility.

Act II is designed to reveal how the king plans and tries to realize his plans in terms of his favorites, his partisans, his officials, and his enemies. Skillfully, and in keeping with the theatrical qualities of the Scribean play, Strindberg makes it clear that Gustav plots his actions as if they were parts of a play and suits his action as far as possible to the person he is dealing with. Note his easy intimacy with his favorite, Armfelt; his brusque treatment of Taube, the young aristocrat whom he cynically has made the court chaplain, partly to help Taube out of financial difficulties, partly to be able to use him for his own purposes; his blend of friendly familiarity, flattery, and condescension to Olsson, speaker of the house of farmers; his direct and frank treatment of Schröderheim when they discuss anything of no pressing concern to Schröderheim personally and his diabolically devious preparation of Schröderheim for the latter's divorce; his matter-of-fact attitude and slight hint of threat in dealing with the chief of police; his frank, rational, and not unkind refusal of the queen's request for a divorce.

But it is the sharp exchanges with his avowed adversaries, Baron Pechlin and Lady Schröderheim, that most clearly suggest his keenness of wit and his mastery of the art of acting as well as his inner conflicts. The exchange between Gustav III and Pechlin is a duel of words in which one master of tactics meets another, all of this happily related in the Gustavian manner to the fable of the fox and the goose. The king, who tries never to be caught unaware and can, if not caught at a loss, demonstrate sharpness of cut and thrust, finds Lady Schröderheim only a little inferior to Pechlin as a worthy opponent in a duel of words. Strindberg more than suggests, however, in this act that Gustav is not sure that he controls his environment, that he has sore points—note the effects on him of any mention of either Munck or Anckarström—and that he is not merely a male counterpart of Queen Christina. Strindberg's Gustav III is well aware of his position and of what the people about him think of him.

Act III presents the conspirators at Huvudsta Manor, reveals the qualities of each of them, and clarifies the motives of their opposition to the king, ranging from the relatively simple idealism of Ribbing, through the complex motives of most of them, to Anckarström's mysterious personal and bitter hatred of the king. The act does more, however, than emphasize that most of these men are engaged in a far from selfish struggle for power. It underscores their keen awareness of the king and their respect for him as an antagonist even if they do not respect him as a man and as a king. They have thought about him and his actions, but their analyses have led to no one completely firm conclusion. Pechlin, for example, admits Gustav is "a pretty good player. . . . Just because he never follows the rules, he's very difficult . . . and besides he learns so easily." In keeping with Scribean practice, a few moments after Pechlin has said, "I believe he's capable of coming over here!" the king theatrically appears unannounced among the conspirators, engages in a sharp duel of words, fails to get the better of Pechlin, and makes an exit far less effective than his entrance. But he leaves only after having invited all the conspirators he sees to his fête at Drottningholm, a challenge and a display of bravado rather than an act of courage.

Act IV is, with the exception of the scene between Schröderheim and his wife, the most thoroughly Scribean of all the acts. As the king plans to gain absolute power and his opponents plan either to depose him or to assassinate him, the whole act becomes a series of moves and countermoves. Strindberg happily uses fencing and chess as symbols of the duels of the words and actions that bring the king close to the semblance of achievement of his goal but do not bring to a definite and final close the struggle for power between the king and his enemies. In a series of little vignettelike scenes between the king and the queen, the king and Armfelt, the king and Taube, the king and Liljensparre, the king and Thorild, the king and Bellman, the king and Pechlin, the king and Anckarström, Fersen and De Geer, the king and Fersen and De Geer, and Schröderheim and Badin, the crowned actor is shown both while planning and while putting on his performances.

Aside from the highly realistic scene between the Schröderheims, the whole act is deliberately designed to give the effect of action that is taking place on a stage and not of action off stage in a room with one wall removed. In heightening the theatrical elements in the final act, Strindberg has skillfully succeeded in conveying the artificiality of a highly formalized court and the artificiality of the king's behavior. The whole play with only a few brief exceptions exploits the Scribean techniques of contrivance, intrigue, neatly resolved plot, melodramatic devices, and what Strindberg called symmetrical French dialogue.

But Strindberg was neither a Scribe nor a Sardou. Like *Queen Christina, Gustav III* has the form of the Scribean well-made play, but in spite of the artificial and theatrical form the play is not a superficial treatment of a dancing master who happens to occupy a throne. To be sure, everyone at court is well aware that the king is an actor; being so aware, Armfelt says, "Yes, people admire you, though they despise you!" His enemies consider his reign a comedy, Horn testifies to his success as an actor in Dalarna, Anckarström labels him "a faithless, infamous comedian," who is "acting Mirabeau and blinding" his opponents, and Pechlin comments: "The exit was not quite as happy as the entrance! But that happens to even the best of actors!" What is even more important: the king himself not only knows he is an actor through and through but enjoys acting and uses it to achieve his goals. Almost all of his appearances with other characters are as carefully plotted and staged as possible, and the king himself looks upon his professional activities as not a little like a drama:

ARMFELT: That's not badly put together! Considered as a play!
KING: Who knows? Perhaps the whole thing is a play!
ARMFELT: But the last act. Do you have that?
KING: It will come of itself!

But the king, who can on the spur of the moment collaborate with Lady Schröderheim in putting on a little scene, can protest gently against Armfelt's comments on the theatrical nature of the royal plans:

KING: I had a plan . . .
ARMFELT: For a play?
KING: Shame on you!
ARMFELT: The one with the Dalesmen!
KING: Yes!
ARMFELT: That's a play, if it's anything . . . In costume? Eh? As Gustav Vasa? . . . That's a masquerade.

It is the king as "dancing master," expert at embroidering, fencer with his tongue, and actor, that makes the primary impression when one reads the play without careful attention to what Strindberg has amply provided by way of telling information about Gustav the human being and Gustav the hero.

The first impression is inadequate and partly false. Strindberg's Gustav III is not merely a Scribean hero, for Strindberg has given his characterization of the king whom he calls "a hero and a dancing master" anything but a superficial treatment. Close reading of the play reveals a study in depth of the hero and the dancing master which his behavior as a dancing master may easily conceal. The play is, in fact, a case report in terms of heredity and primarily environment, set in the theatrical framework of the Scribean play but transcending it through a scrupulously maintained attention to the whole individual somewhat concealed by his superficial behavior. Including information about the king's formative environment, his education, his marriage, his family life, his positive programs, his accomplishments, his contradictory pursuit of his goals, and his personal problems, the play is a full characterization of a human being who is far more than a crowned actor.

There is not the slightest question on the part of a single person about him as to the king's remarkably rich natural endowment intellectually, although some of the people at court may wonder about the completeness of his physical endowment. The latter suspicion rests largely on the general curiosity about the paternity of the young crown prince, who never appears on stage, but, faithful to the uncertainty both in Gustav's time and later, Strindberg leaves unanswered the question as to whether Baron Munck or the king is the father. (Strindberg does not avoid the issue, which has fascinated gossips from the Gustavian period on, but uses it most effectively as a means of clarifying the background and of characterizing the king.) About Gustav's intellectual gifts there is not the slightest doubt, however.

Anckarström, who hates him, testifies that the king is "a diabolically clever schemer," and Pechlin, who enjoys matching wits with the king and on occasion holds his own in so doing, frankly admits that the king is a difficult opponent. There is no question on the part of the conspirators but that Gustav III, in planning the revolution of 1772 and in giving Sweden independence from foreign interference and a liberal constitution, has well deserved the praise of Voltaire:

HORN (*reading the freedom of the press law*): Those are proud words, worthy of a great king. "Freedom of the press informs the general public about its true welfare and does not permit the ruler to be ignorant of what the people think."

HOLMBERG: And this . . . I know it by heart: "If freedom of the press had been permitted in the last century, King Charles XI would perhaps not have taken such measures at the cost of public security as to make the royal power detestable."

HORN: Or this: "Through freedom of the press a king learns the truth, which people frequently with much effort and unfortunately often enough with much success conceal from him."

HOLMBERG: Our gracious King wrote that himself, and at the time he was so proud of his generosity that he sent a French copy to Voltaire, who graciously approved and complimented the author, which didn't prevent His Majesty from having Halldin there condemned to death, because he wrote against the liquor law.

The people about Gustav who are capable of judging such matters have no doubt about King Gustav's genuinely great gifts of mind and wit; they do not doubt that he understands clearly contemporary events in America and in France; they know he is quite capable not only of understanding them but of exploiting them for his own purposes. His enemies' objections to the king are not based on the king's lack of intellectual endowment. Their reasons for opposing him have to do with morality, politics, personal hatred, selfish interests, or a combination of these.

Well aware that these objections could not be understood without information about many other matters, Strindberg has briefly but effectively supplied the basic information about them. Consider, for example, the information given about the early environment that helped to shape the king. Here is Count von Fersen's speech: "And the King! He was taught to lie as a child—especially during the unsuccessful coups d'état. . . . I was along then! And since then he has lied so much he doesn't know who he is himself, and as he jokes about everything he can't tell the difference between a joke and what's serious." The coups d'état, as all Swedes know, were the unsuccessful attempts on the part of Gustav's gifted mother, Queen Lovisa Ulrika, to seize more than a semblance of royal power for herself and her husband in the 1750's and 1760's, when Sweden was in the depths of its most humiliating period—at the mercy of foreign interference and domestic corruption. In such a period, young Prince Gustav had been taught to lie, to dissemble, to act, and to develop his charm as a means of survival in a corrupt and chaotic world. Note what the king tells his queen: "No, the time is past when the Russian ambassador and the English chose the members of our parliament, appointed the secret committee, and named our national council; yes, it was Russia that gave my father, the prince-bishop of Lübeck, the throne of Sweden and me a consort."

Strindberg amply demonstrates that Gustav's early environment, for all its intellectual and social brilliance, was essentially one of corruption, dishonesty, and never-ending intrigues—hardly the sort of environment to permit a gifted, attractive, and sensitive young prince to develop into a normal, well-balanced adult, but an environment decidedly suited to produce an adult who takes refuge behind appearance and acting.

But Queen Lovisa Ulrika and the tutors did not restrict Gustav's education to the mastery of the arts of intrigue, acting, and charm. The king acquired, for example, one feminine occupation:

KING: Tell me, how many cross stitches are equivalent to a diamond stitch?
QUEEN: I don't understand that sort of thing! . . . How did you ever get started embroidering, sire?
KING: My mother taught me, and afterwards I got pleasure out of it! I think very clearly when I embroider, and then I feel that I have the strings in my hand. You despise handiwork, don't you?
QUEEN: Pretty much!
KING: And *I* learned it primarily to lend respect to woman's work! Making sacrifices is rewarding.

The prince was exposed to an education designed to permit him "to have the strings in his hand" in a figurative sense, too. Strindberg's Gustav knows literature and can compose it himself; he knows Swedish and European history and understands what is happening both at home and abroad; he has learned to conceive of the role of a monarch as that of a patriot king who lines up the commons against the lords (a traditional role for many a Swedish king) in the struggle for power and who must strive in many ways to rebuild his country—politically, intellectually, culturally. The education Strindberg illustrates through impressionistically presented details, in passing as it were, is indeed a well-rounded one, but it has the Machiavellian implication that the end will have to justify the means. Strindberg emphasizes not only that the education has taken hold but that it is continuing: Gustav adjusts himself to changing conditions without, unfortunately, much regard for either consistency or morality. The idealism of the patriot king has by no means been destroyed, but what faith he may have had in the natural goodness of man has given way to cynicism.

Interested as always in the family and its problems, Strindberg has provided illuminating and detailed consideration of Gustav as a husband and a family man. The unequal marriage, arranged because of foreign insistence, between the gifted Swedish prince and the dull foreign princess has brought happiness to neither, and it has led to difficulties that in no way have made Gustav's lot either as a human being or as a king free of embarrassment, isolation, and humiliation. By means of carefully selected episodes—the give-and-take between incompatible mates, usually but not always within the limits of courtly politeness, and the highly realistic parallel of the Schröderheim marriage—Strindberg approaches the searching analysis of marriage that characterized the plays from *The Father* to *The Dance of Death,* and, in so doing, he reveals aspects of the highly complex king who is far more than "a diabolically clever schemer":

I suppose you, no doubt, know as well as I that our marriage was arranged by the secret committee in its day and by the empress of Russia at the time of the peace treaty; in other words, the government at that time was forced to select a bride for me without the slightest regard for our personal feelings. That time when we both yielded to the powerful interests of two nations, we made a sacrifice that has cost us our personal happiness. . . . The concept *sacrifice* implies giving up happiness. . . . Can't then the knowledge that we have suffered together for others, for many others, keep up our courage until the cup has been drained? Aren't there other reasons than the political for our bearing the burden all the way? Hasn't our son the first right to be reared by parents, by his father and his mother . . .

I remember that you wept when I sent my chamberlain to Ekolsund to tell you that my revolution had succeeded . . . when I played Brutus and destroyed the Caesars in homespun . . . In a tender moment you admitted that they were tears of miscalculation as you had not believed me capable of a manly act. . . . From that moment you hated me, because it was my feminine qualities you loved, and I had become feminine because I had been reared too long among women and at the embroidery hoop—that was not my fault! You loved, but despised me; because you received my tactfulness as a sign of respect, which you nevertheless despised, and when I acted as I should . . . as a man . . . you called it coarseness and hated me! . . . So I had to choose between your contempt and your hatred, and I finally chose your hatred!

These quotations illustrate the relationship, expanded in detail by Strindberg, the whole unhappy story of the royal couple's marriage, with its frustrations, misunderstandings, and vain attempts to conceal the truth from a curious and cruelly gossiping court, and the very real possibility that their son may be King Gustav's only in name. It is that whole complex of details that makes even the sophisticated Count De Geer protest against the scurrilous brochure:

DE GEER: Yes, it's the old story with new additions.
FERSEN: About . . . the Queen?
DE GEER: And the prince! (*Throws the brochure into the fire*) But he is a human being with human feelings, all the same . . . that is ugly!

In his illuminating analysis of the royal marriage, Strindberg shows us the king both as an actor and as a human being. Note particularly the king's moving and sincere plea: "Out of consideration for our son, have a little respect for my name and my reputation. . . . I do not ask much, because I don't deserve it!"

Strindberg's king, who married because it was his duty, has been educated to be a benevolent ruler interested in the great ideas that were causing great changes abroad, dedicated to his country, and determined to raise his country and his subjects in terms of those ideas. Exposed to the ideas of the enlightenment, Gustav has learned from Voltaire, has become keenly aware of what was happening in the contemporary world (most notably, in the American colonies and France), has acquired as a result humane ideals of tolerance and liberalism, and has achieved great things for his people. Speaking of the days when Sweden was at the mercy of its enemies and Swedish politicians vied for the financial favors of its enemies, he tells the queen:

Those times are past, and that is my modest achievement, which people have forgotten, and to the degree that they haven't understood my last war against Russia which they call treason. Recently a court poet compared me with Gustav Vasa, the liberator from foreign oppression; I smiled when I read it, but there may be a grain of truth in the flattery.

Neatly and generally impressionistically present in the play, but somewhat obscured by the deliberately theatrical elements, are the details of Gustav III's far from modest achievements: his revolution of 1772, which saved Sweden from foreign interference and domestic anarchy, his new constitution, which extended the rights of the commons, his encouragement of a genuinely Swedish culture. There are, moreover, hints about the weaknesses in his program: the liquor law, for example; his unfortunate lack of the power of sustained effort; the gradual heightening of his struggle with dissident lords; his gradual evolution from a young king who has at least a measure of faith in the natural goodness of man to an experienced king who finds Voltaire's cynical view of the nature of man far more accurate in an environment of acting, pretense, intrigue.

It is the Gustav III who has become cynical about the means he uses in attempting to achieve his not always clear-cut goals that Strindberg presents. Presented as Strindberg's central characters always are against the background of contemporary events at home in Sweden and abroad as well, the Gustav who emerges is both complex and dynamic. The king concealed behind the actor's mask is inwardly insecure, uncertain, sensitive, and afraid; he is basically an idealist who has been subjected to pressures until he has difficulty at times distinguishing between the values of ends and means. While he has become cynical about many things, he has not become cynical about one basic goal—making Sweden great, culturally and politically. He has come to the point where if one method will not work he is willing to try another, even if its moral implications are questionable. If, for example, his revolution of 1772, through which he tried to make Sweden a strong nation in which parliament worked with a patriot king for the welfare of the country and its people, cannot lead to the desired goal, then he must turn to his revolution of 1789, through which he hopes to make the nation strong through parliament's granting him, the patriot king, absolute power.

As I have said elsewhere:

Strindberg emphasizes and illustrates a fundamental contradiction in Gustav again and again: the man who wants to accomplish great things, wants consciously or unconsciously to accomplish them *as* an actor who will secure the applause of an audience, who will be the center of attention and the dominant actor while on the stage and the director of the action when he is not. For Gustav, Strindberg felt, the major facts became the effect he was making, the applause he was getting, and the pleasure he personally received from intriguing to achieve his ends. The goals themselves became subordinate, for their attainment too frequently involved planning and detail work that could not be accomplished on the lighted stage either of an actual theater or the greater one of the world.

Strindberg's interpretation then is first of all that of the actor on the throne, an actor who shares with many of his fellow actors a superficiality that does not involve much more than the mastery of the lines, the development of a technique of improvisation when necessary, the delivery of the lines in a fashion that will impress the audience—both seen and unseen, an attention to the details that concern effects, and, briefly put, the performance of a role rather than the performance of deeds and the realization of a program. Included in this interpretation [are] the charm of manner, the elegance of dress, and the emphasis on appropriate gesture, walk and speech. That sort of thing has become the important factor; *playing* Gustav III as a hero in worthy succession to the earlier heroic Gustavs has become, for the most part unconsciously, far more important to the king than *being* Gustav III the hero.[2]

When this play, with its fascinating characterization of the charming crowned actor and its richly rewarding interpretation of the brilliant Gustavian period, appeared in print in 1903, the reviewers were unkind as usual and the theater people uninterested.

Strindberg himself did not live to see the play presented or to have his conviction that *Gustav III* is great theater confirmed. His hope that the play in a somewhat revised version could be presented at the Intimate Theater was not realized. But almost four years after Strindberg's death, in 1916, Gustaf Collijn at the New Intimate Theater produced it with Lars Hansson as the king in what became one of the most successful productions in Swedish theater history. In spite of the enthusiastic response of the audiences through the theater season from January 25 to May 5 and at ten guest performances at the New Theater in Copenhagen after that, almost all the drama critics indulged in typical response to a new Strindberg *première*. One of the less unfavorable critics, Nils Erdmann, wrote the following in *Nya Dagligt Allehanda* on May 5, 1916:

Today . . . *Gustav III* is being presented for the hundredth time at the Intimate Theater. The direction is praiseworthy, the staging good, the actors flawless. Mr. Hansson's interpretation of the charmer-king is frequently interesting, a personally unique creation, which richly deserves praise, even if one cannot share the public and critical delight about everything [in the creation of the role]. But the play—and Gustav III? [3]

After conceding Strindberg's brilliance, extraordinary dramatic ability, the power of the dialogue, the skill with which the acts are constructed, his psychological intuition, the life with which he has infused his characters, and his right to adapt history, Erdmann added, "Many a person who will applaud August Strindberg's strange monstrosity tonight, probably would benefit from recalling what the real Gustav was like!" Four days later, John Landquist replied at length to such criticism in *Dagens Nyheter*. Two passages are highly apropos: "Some of the Stockholm critics have not been able to forgive Strindberg for the brilliant success of *Gustav III*," and:

The public has with unbiased sense pronounced its judgment. But this Strindberg play has as many of his others, too strong a spontaneity, too powerful a wealth of life, not to disturb minds as feeble as the gentlemen mentioned above [i.e., the critics], who year after year patiently fill columns with their rhetorical nonsense but have never looked a beautiful reality in the eye.[4]

Even as late as January 23, 1928, *Stockholms Dagblad* recalled that *Gustav III* was presented "150 times in 1916 in spite of sour criticism." [5]

Since 1916, *Gustav III* has been successfully produced in the provinces, Stockholm, Göteborg, Helsingfors, Åbo, and Berlin from time to time. A highly significant observation on the merits of the play was made by Gustaf Collijn in *Intiman: Historien om en teater* (Stockholm: Wahlström & Widstrand, 1943) when he recalled:

My thought of producing Strindberg's *Gustav III*, which had never been presented, grew even stronger. I knew, of course, what people thought about the play but I believed that it would have the wonderful Strindbergian quality of getting an unsuspected life when actually presented. There was in Strindberg's *Gustav III*, I thought, so very much that would then come into its own.[6]

Theater people have invariably had the same experience since 1916, and the Swedish critics have gradually learned to appreciate the merits of the play.

14

The Nightingale of Wittenberg

The Trojan Horse and Germany's Biggest Voice

As WAS pointed out in Chapter 1, Strindberg in 1902 "read right through world history" and, as one result, wrote *The Mysticism of World History,* the essay which contains the core of his post-Inferno philosophy of history and which was published in *Svenska Dagbladet* the following summer. The essay is highly significant to our present purposes, for in it Strindberg discusses at some length Martin Luther and his significance in world history.

Note particularly these passages:

Luther was a man who caused schisms, who began by denying and ended with asserting, and it is quite unbearable to follow him in all his self-contradictions. At any event, he says that his goal in life was to crusade against papism and he kept that up to the very end. But both Julius II and Leo X were humanists and renaissance men representative of the liberating tendencies of the time, and in that way Luther was in conflict with the spirit of the age at the same time that he was borne along by its undercurrent. . . .

Luther went back to the Christianity of the apostles which was in the process of being humanized, and he was more orthodox than the popes and the councils. One ought just imagine him at the disputation about the doctrine of communion when he writes with chalk on the table: "This *is* my body and my blood." "This is!" That is literal faith without meaning, without interpretation, without explanation; it is blind faith, submission, without appeal. People have called Luther a Ghibelline, sympathetic to the emperor, in contrast to the papal Guelphs, and in that he is akin to Dante. But in the pope's place he put the infallibility of the Bible, and that was a greater misfortune, because with that book one can prove everything and nothing. . . .

If Luther's mission was the destruction of papism, one certainly can not say he succeeded. . . .

And, to repeat one brief passage quoted in the first chapter: "A man of Providence, a man in the ranks who goes blindly ahead without knowing the commander's intentions, a great instrument, a symbol of contradiction and a rock of irritation, a human being filled with pride and humility, with sound ideas and obscure purposes—that was Luther." [1] Strindberg obviously considered Luther another instrument of the Conscious Will called upon to perform a task assigned to him without ever quite understanding what that task was exactly. Then, too, Strindberg considered Luther a highly gifted human being and, as such, a complex and dynamic character.

Näktergalen i Wittenberg, the play that he wrote in 1903 about the great reformer, is in some important respects different from the twelve major plays about great Swedes. Act I reveals young Martin Luther in his formative environment. Set as the act is in his childhood home in 1492, it places Luther as the product of an extremely unfortunate family situation and of a heredity that is at once both fortunate and unfortunate. The act goes beyond all this, however, in its fairly detailed clarification of the broader environment of the school, the church, the community, and, in fact, Europe. That environment includes almost every conceivable aspect of both the little and the big communities—intellectual, religious, moral, economic, physical, and social.

The Luther family life is decidedly reminiscent of Strindberg's own as he relates it in *The Son of a Servant*. A stern father and a harsh mother—all too keenly aware of the practical economic results of having ungrateful children—enforce, without much regard for justice, the idea "Listen, keep still and obey! That's right for children!" But while the discipline in Strindberg's childhood home produced (as he apparently believed or at least asserted) a young adult whose major feelings were those of fear and hunger, Luther's parents have a son who may fear to be disciplined by the schoolmaster in front of girls but one who has never been driven by fear to any real sense of inadequacy. In fact, Strindberg's young Martin Luther, exposed to his environment, big and little, by means of a curiously and artificially contrived set of visits from an apprentice, a soldier, a Dominican monk, and a wanderer—who turns out to be Dr. Faust—is a remarkably fearless rebel and questioner, a self-confident egotist who questions everything and is anything but frightened. He has a tongue and a free will, as he says, and will question and talk as he pleases. He is a genuinely curious young rebel, fascinated by what the visitors have to tell him about a corrupt Rome, a corrupt Roman Church, an inadequate and corrupt empire, and a world newly discovered. He is, moreover, a son who, in contrast to his gentle, obedient brother Jacob, is a good match for a harsh and blunt father and a mother who frankly prefers Jacob and dislikes Martin. Act I, in which a ghastly family scene ends with the schoolmaster's news that Martin may leave home in order to study at Eisenach, is an effective introduction to a reformer whom Strindberg labels "Germany's biggest voice." It is effective, too, in making clear the nature of the time and its problems and in preparing the reader or audience for what will follow. But, aside from Martin and, to some degree, the members of his family, the characters are merely introduced, not characterized.

In three scenes, Act II presents Luther, now a doctor studying law, in the presence of some of the most famous or infamous men of his time—Diezel or Tezel, the notorious pardoner; the gifted Ulrich von Hutten; Dr. Faust; the Augustinian Staupitz; Spalatin;

and the elector of Saxony. In scene 1, they discuss the bad conditions in the cloisters, the corruption in Rome, the spread of venereal disease in Germany (the evil pardoner knows von Hutten is afflicted), the discovery of America, the theory that the earth is round, and the founding of the new University of Wittenberg. Perhaps the most significant matters in terms of Luther are the hint that the Church of Rome may have a Trojan horse within its walls and Dr. Faust's exposing Luther for the first time to the complete Bible and getting him to read it. If the scene does nothing else for the characterization of Luther, it does establish his extreme intellectual curiosity and his brusque, even brutal, disregard for others when he is intensely concerned with himself. He reads the Bible with avidity. His friend Alexius appeals in vain to him for help.

Scene 2 establishes the profound effect on Luther of reading the Bible—he finds it a terrible book that he wishes he had never seen and a book that has something personal for every individual. Uncertain, restless as a result, Luther learns to his horror that his friend Alexius has either committed suicide or been murdered. The man who has been studying law because his father wanted him to finds himself inwardly convicted of guilt.

Scene 3, set in Luther's student home, presents a festive dinner at which the guests eat in the absence of their host. A strange love song is recited by von Hutten; it becomes a complaint against the corruption stemming from Rome (oddly enough, a song about *morbus gallicus!*). When Luther comes, he announces that he will become an Augustinian monk:

Therefore, noble patrons and friends, I have come to say farewell. *(Lifts his glass)* My childhood was no bed of roses, nor was my youth. If this is what life has to offer, I shall reject it; I take my glass in my hand, but I don't empty it, I pour it out as a toast to your well-being; as an expression of gratitude for your friendship! And I break this glass as I break with this uncertain life and its frail happiness! *(He breaks the glass)* Farewell, my friends; we shall never meet again, for tomorrow Dr. Martin will be buried, and the day after I shall be merely Brother Augustine.

Reminiscent as it is of a memorable scene in *To Damascus,* III, this confident announcement of a firm decision by the inwardly certain Luther is followed by Dr. Faust's significant comment: "Fellow doctors, our friend Martin has a greater grasp of the art of besieging; he goes into the fortress and opens the gates from within!"

Act III is intended to illustrate Martin Luther's crucial experiences from his days in the monastery to the ending of his disputations without any clear-cut victory for either Luther or his opponents. Again the episodic construction leads to no impression of well-rounded, carefully planned dramatic composition of the kind that dominates in the major plays about figures of the Swedish past. But it does give information about Martin Luther's difficulties in adapting himself to a life of obedience in the monastery, the struggle between the emperor and the pope, Luther's acceptance of a professorship, his personal witnessing of degradation in Rome, his inspection of cloisters, his preaching against the pardoner Tizel, his nailing the ninety-five theses to the door of the castle church at Wittenberg, his refusal to recant, the spread of Lutheranism (like that of *morbus gallicus,* we are told!), and his expulsion from the order. The five scenes present also information about Ulrich von Hutten's breaking with the lovely Constantia Peutinger because of his disease.

Two matters stand out in Strindberg's attempt to clarify Luther's character and development: Dr. Faust's continuing role of spur and guide, and Luther's reactions to his experiences and the resulting changes in his thinking. The proud, self-confident monk who has a hard time being either obedient or silent is called by his friend Staupitz "the proudest human being I've ever run across." Erasmus speaks of Luther's growing fame by saying, "But there are people who get a reputation without cause." Spalatin calls him "the biggest voice in Germany," and, when he is released from his vows, Luther himself utters the telling words, "Thou strong, living God, it's only Thou and I! Art Thou going to fail, too? I certainly will not!" To keep the continuing family situation clear, Strindberg has Luther reject both parents when they arrive to berate him and to try to make him behave as they want him to.

Act IV, with its one relatively brief scene (outside the Elster Gate at Wittenberg), presents an assembly of distinguished contemporaries—von Hutten, Cranach, Amsdorff, Schurff, Melanchthon, and several doctors—witnessing a little Hans Sachs play, like the *Epilogue* to *Master Olof,* in which there are allusions to "the nightingale," who has "squeezed the Holy Father, the holy fathers, and us respectable worthy gentlemen." Then follows an extemporaneous and brief contest in poetic composition between Ulrich von Hutten and Hans Sachs; their subject is Luther and what he has done to set the Germans free, religiously and morally. After university students have lighted a bonfire and burned Catholic theological and legal books and documents, Luther enters with the ban of excommunication in his hand. The most significant speech is Luther's own, "I never forgive an enemy—before I've broken his arms and legs." When one of those present protests that Luther in spite of what he says has comforted his enemies, including the notorious pardoner, Luther says, "Well, Satan's to be pitied, too, and we are human beings after all."

Scene 1 of the final act presents Luther in the waiting room outside the courtroom in Worms, with the soldiers and the people looking at him as a curiosity and making him the butt of their ridicule; Papal Legate Alexander's attempt to get a stubborn Luther to cooperate and subsequent threat to have him executed; and Luther's refusal to recant.

Scene 2—in Luther's parental home in Möhra—is a typically Strindbergian family scene reminiscent of many in earlier plays, both historical and nonhistorical:

MARTIN LUTHER: Do you recognize me, father?
FATHER: Yes, but I don't acknowledge you!
MARTIN: Thank you for that!
FATHER: That's how my child answers his father!

MARTIN: I am not your child, because I am not a child, but I am your son, and that's why you have to take me in!
FATHER: You haven't changed!
MARTIN: You haven't changed!
FATHER: The tongue of a serpent! If I had a red hot iron I'd burn it out!

And, after some blunt exchanges:

FATHER: Jacob, do you think this ruined person has any feelings?
MARTIN: Jacob knows that I had feelings once, but you beat them out of me, and that didn't harm me, for I've got along best without feelings. Now I'm absolutely without them, and that's a blessed thing, because now no blows really hit me.

Finally after more ugly exchanges:

FATHER: Beast! You *forgive;* but I never forgive!
MARTIN: Then you're a heathen! *(Father silent)* But you're a man and I admire you! *(Father says nothing)* I could swear you don't despise me, me, the only person who has dared to look you in the eye! . . . Now I'm going, out into the night, the rain, the darkness of the forest, to the emperor's soldiers!
FATHER: Yes, go to hell, from which you came!
MARTIN: Fine!—But I'd like to shake your hand!
FATHER: Shame!
MARTIN: Like father, like son!
FATHER *(smiles)*: My word, you are my son.—Put it there!
MARTIN *(shakes his hand)*: Hard against hard like Saxon steel.

Scene 3 (at Wartburg nine months later) presents Martin Luther, a semiprisoner, as he believes, but, as Dr. Faust reveals, really having been kept in protective custody so he could finish his translation of the Bible. It is Dr. Faust, his mentor and his guide, who informs him, too, that the new pope Adrian VI has set out to reform the Church of Rome from within and who tells him how much he— Martin Luther—has accomplished and what he must do.

This fairly detailed analysis should indicate that *The Nightingale of Wittenberg* is a chronicle play, episodic in nature, and not, like most of the other historical plays, composed with scrupulous attention to background, exposition, and foreshadowing. It is probable that Strindberg gave it such a form partly because he was not personally so engaged with Luther as he had been with the great Swedes and partly because he may have felt that such a dramatic form suited the very nature of Luther himself.

For the characterization of Luther that emerges from this serious drama with an ending that is neither victory nor defeat is a characterization of an extremely energetic and dynamic man who rushes through life without permitting others to see clearly many of the nuances of his complexity. Strindberg's Luther is no attractive young idealist like the Master Olof of 1872; he is much more like the Swedish reformer of the so-called verse *Master Olof*: he is self-confident; reveals no sense of inferiority or inadequacy; is usually blunt, brusque, and even brutal in dealing with friend and foe, equals, inferiors, and superiors. He is not self-dependent intellectually, however; Dr. Faust plays much the same role for Strindberg's Luther that Lars Andersson and Gert had played for Master Olof in the prose play of 1872. In that way, Luther resembles Strindberg's first Master Olof.

Strindberg's Luther is arrogant and proud, hard and harsh—in brief, except on a few occasions, a far from pleasant man. It is an interesting characterization, but one completes a searching examination and scrutiny of the play with the wish that Strindberg had given far greater attention to the complexity of his central character and a bit less to his dynamic qualities. Instead of being overwhelmed by the vast literature about Gustav Vasa, Strindberg, as we have seen, selected one episode for dramatic treatment and composed a masterpiece unsurpassed at least since Shakespeare's day. He succumbed to the temptations of treating too many episodes of the last two years of Gustav Adolf's life and of presenting too much information about the background, and, as a result, his *Gustav Adolf* is an unwieldy play. Regrettably, he not only succumbed again to both temptations in writing his play about Luther but failed to do what he had done admirably in *Gustav Adolf,* i.e., give a remarkably rich characterization of his central character in its many nuances.

Curiously, too, many of the other characters in *The Nightingale of Wittenberg* do not come alive but remain mere names whose major significance comes from the reader's knowledge of them rather than from what is revealed about them in the play. Exceptions to such a conclusion are Luther's parents, his brother Jacob, Ulrich von Hutten, and Dr. Johannes (Faust). The others are so lightly sketched that without previous knowledge of the historical models the reader is left with little more than impressive names.

Three other matters in the play need to be emphasized: the Trojan horse, the expression "Germany's biggest voice," and, what has not been mentioned in the analysis, the presence in some scenes of reproductions of the famous Laocoön group. Of the three, the first has a symbolic significance that is obvious: Luther began his work as a reformer as a monk within the Church of Rome. The second expression, "Germany's biggest voice," is an inadequate translation of the Swedish *"Tysklands största trut."* Cognate of "throat," "trut" refers to Luther's capacity to use his vocal organs effectively and loudly, overwhelmingly and bluntly; *"största trut"* does not have the dignified and gentle connotation of "greatest voice" but has the connotation of "the biggest loud-mouth" or "the biggest gab." The reproductions of the Laocoön group, quietly, almost unobtrusively in the background, are evidently used to symbolize Luther's struggles and far from clear inner agony.

There is, moreover, the title of the play itself. A quotation from the play will explain that:

SPALATIN: Your Grace, I have at my disposal the biggest voice in Germany.

ELECTOR: That's the monk Augustine or Dr. Luther as he used to be called. Let me see that strange and rare bird that everyone is talking about.

SPALATIN: His speech is a bit unpolished so Your Grace . . .

ELECTOR: That doesn't matter—on the contrary let him in.

Strindberg's "nightingale" could sing sweetly, too, but Strindberg rarely illustrates that sweetness.

In 1903, Strindberg himself was in no mood to detect weaknesses in his play about Luther. Excerpts from two of his letters to Emil Schering will illustrate that fact. On October 13, he wrote, "I love the play and consider it among my best." [2] On November 15, he wrote about both *Gustav Adolf* and *The Nightingale of Wittenberg:*

I have warned you about Gustav Adolf; the Prussian can't understand it, and it must be unpleasant for him. What does the German know about Gustav Adolf's blood guilt [inherited] from Charles IX and the lords at Linköping? That is my tragic motif! though! That's why I wrote: Take Luther instead! You people know him! Yesterday I reread my Luther! It gave me strength and light! It is the strongest and the most youthful [play] I've written! No doubts as Master Olof [has], no scruples, no women about his neck, no parents in his way, no compromises with friends. And the historic traditional Luther was like that.[3]

While many readers will no doubt agree that Martin Luther was like that, it will be hard to find anyone who will agree to Strindberg's impulsive statement that his play is among the best he ever wrote. It is far from that!

The Nightingale of Wittenberg has not enjoyed successful productions in either Swedish or non-Swedish theaters. As far as I have yet been able to determine, there have been these very few productions —at the Deutsches Künstlertheater in Berlin in 1914, at the Swedish Theater in Stockholm in 1917, in an off-Broadway German production in New York in 1917, and at the Lorensberg Theater in Göteborg in 1927. All of them were quickly taken off the program. A review that is typical, although in error in its assertion about successful productions in Germany, appeared in *Stockholms-Tidningen* on January 27, 1917:

Strindberg's Luther play which has been put on with rather great public success in Germany, has now been made part of the Swedish repertory. It is not a dramatic work Strindberg has produced; so far as I know he has never insisted that it should be considered a work with dramatic suspense. It lacks completely the unities of place, time, and action. The whole play is a series of tableaux, fourteen in all, in which Luther and several of his noted contemporaries play their more or less characteristic roles. The only more dramatic figure in the play is Dr. Johannes Faust, but he appears as a sort of *deus ex machina*.[4]

The truth of it is that Swedish critics have not been particularly interested in *The Nightingale of Wittenberg*. The general Swedish scholarly and critical opinion that Strindberg was at his best as a historical dramatist when he composed plays about the Swedish past is indeed sound.

15

Moses, Socrates, *and* Christ
Instruments of the Conscious Will

As WE have seen in Chapter 2, "Plans and Fulfillment," Strindberg not only toyed with the idea of composing a cycle of plays about world history, but he actually did write four of them—a trilogy about Moses, Socrates, and Christ and the play about Martin Luther, *The Nightingale of Wittenberg.* Of the four, only the last received a form fairly close to those of Strindberg's plays about Swedish history.

On December 6, 1902, Strindberg wrote to Emil Schering:

The question will be if I can get my synoptic point of view into a series of worthwhile dramas and if I can get sufficiently many living characters without repeating myself—which I doubt. My discovery is, of course, "the Conscious Will" which reveals itself at the same time in several places in the world, and in literature one may not serve up discoveries but only work with and refer to known matters.[1]

On the fifteenth of September, 1903, Strindberg announced to Schering: "Now comes the series! Twenty plays, *independent,* but with the invisible thread, which makes the necklace!"[2]

Two of Strindberg's notes clarify what he had in mind when he wrote the three plays:

> This trilogy, which has also been called *Moses-Socrates-Christ,* are the first three parts of a larger, as yet unfinished, cycle of dramas about the history of the world, in which *The Nightingale of Wittenberg* is the eleventh.—A treatment of the same subjects appears in my *Historical Miniatures* in the following stories: "The Egyptian Bondage," "The Hemicycle in Athens," "Alcibiades," "Socrates," "Leontopolis," "The Lamb," and "The Wild Beast."
>
> The three parts here presented were written in 1905 [actually 1903] and their presentation was considered in 1908 in the simplified theater or drapery stage [of his and Falck's Intimate Theater] with movable backdrops and *barrière* emblems on the stage. To simplify them still more, several of the backdrops for the fifty-five tableaux could be used again and again so that in all only fifteen different backdrops need to be used. See the disposition of backdrops listed in an appendix.[3]

The appendix reads:

Moses	*Socrates*	*Christ*
The arch: palms and sphinxes	Columns and statues with cypresses	A. Olive trees and a well
		B. Columns, statues, rostra, pines
Backdrops:	Backdrops:	Backdrops:
1. Temples	1. The Parthenon	A
2. Pyramids	2. Curtain	1. Bethlehem
3. Sinai	3. Curtain	2. The same
4. See Number 1	4. See Number 1	3. Number 1 from
5. The desert	5. See Number 1	*Moses* The Temple
6. See Number 5	6. Curtain	of the Sun
7. Ditto	7. Curtain	4. Curtain
8. Ditto	8. See Number 1	5. Number 15 from
9. See Number 3	9. Curtain	*Moses* The forecourt
10. Ditto	10. Number 1	6. The Temple in
11. Ditto	11. Curtain	Jerusalem
12. Ditto	12. Curtain	7. The same
13. See Number 3	13. Number 1	8. The same
14. The tabernacle	14. Ditto	9. Curtain
15. Its forecourt	15. Curtain	10. Golgotha

16. See Number 5	16. Number 6	B
17. Ditto	17. Curtain	11. Curtain
18. Ditto	18. Temple	12. Curtain
19. Ditto	19. Prison	13. Curtain
20. Ditto		14. The catacombs
21. Nebo and Canaan		Curtain
		15. Rome and fore-ground

7 backdrops	3 backdrops	5 backdrops

Total   15 backdrops [4]

It must be said about all three of these plays that they are not conventional dramas, nor do they resemble the other plays that have been considered in this volume in structure or composition. What they are will perhaps become clear from a look at the content of each of them.

Moses, or *Through the Wilderness to the Promised Land,* consists of twenty-one brief tableaux:

1. A prologue in which Pharaoh and his high priest talk about the Hebrews and their role in Egypt; 2. Pharaoh's daughter, taking Moses as her son; 3. Moses and the burning bush (Moses given his assignment); 4. Moses before Pharaoh, persuading him to let the Hebrews go; 5. The crossing of the Red Sea; 6. The miracle of water in the wilderness; 7. The holding up of Moses' arms to assure the Hebrews victory; 8. Moses and his father-in-law; 9. Jehovah, giving Moses the regulations by which the Hebrews are to live; 13. The episode of the Golden Calf; 14. The sanctuary in the tabernacle; 15. The return of the spies from Canaan; 16. The wandering in the wilderness; 17. Moses' doubt; 18. The death of Aaron; 19. The Copper Serpent and Bileam; 20. Moses and the twelve elders; 21. Moses' death as he sees the Promised Land.

Socrates, or *Hellas,* consists of nineteen longer tableaux:

1. Below the Acropolis, Pericles, Phidias, Euripides, Socrates, Plato, Alcibiades, and Protagoras converse about the gods, man, and the state (Cleon and Kartafilos, a Hebrew, hear their talk; Anytos and Cleon discuss government by the few as opposed to

government by the people); 2. Most of the men first listed discuss women, woman-hatred, the gods, and the state at a dinner at Alcibiades'; 3. Aspasia and Pericles at the deathbed of his son; 4. The death of Pericles; 5. The "democratic" election of Cleon as commander of the armed forces against Sparta; 6. Xanthippe and Socrates (in a domestic scene) are joined by Alcibiades, who informs them about Cleon's defeat in battle; Anytos, Socrates' enemy, comes to tell of Cleon's victory; 7. The Roman Lucillus and the Hebrew shoemaker talk about conditions in Athens and the roles of the Romans and the Hebrews; Cleon has been defeated in a second battle; 8. Alcibiades' proposal to make Sicily the Athenian base of operations approved by the people; 9. The death of Phidias, the exile of Protagoras as blasphemer, the defeat of Alcibiades in Sicily and his flight to Sparta; 10. Thrasybulos' and Anytos' discussion of need to appeal to Persians for help; 11. Alcibiades at Sparta, his plotting with Queen Timäa, with whom he has slept, his flight; 12. Alcibiades at the Persian court; 13. Socrates and Plato; the recall of Alcibiades to Athens; 14. The Athenians' rejection of Alcibiades; 15. Euripides' departure from Athens; 16. Socrates' and Aspasia's discussion of Xanthippe and the official order that Socrates cease teaching; 17. The death of Alcibiades; 18. Discussion of the gods; the testimony of the Hebrews about the one God; Socrates' sentence of death; 19. Socrates and Xanthippe in his prison; the death of Socrates.

Christ, or *The Lamb and the Wild Beast,* has fifteen tableaux:

1. The shepherds near Bethlehem, the angel, the three wise men; 2. Outside the stable in Bethlehem; 3. Outside the Temple of the Sun at Leontopolis (Lucillus' and the Hebrew Kartaphilos' discussion of the Messiah); 4. Pilate's talk with Simon Peter about the Galilean and about John the Baptist; 5. Pilate and the Younger Herod's discussion of Jesus; 6. The priestly decision that Jesus die; 7. John, Judas, Zacheus, Peter; 8. Gethsemane; 9. The release of Barabbas; 10. Golgotha; 11. The Temple of Caligula, the wild beast, in Rome; Lucillus now a Christian and with his fellows in the catacombs; the frightened Caligula as Jupiter; death of Caligula; 12. Emperor Claudius, the second wild beast; 13. Emperor Nero, the third wild beast, trying to have the blame for the burning of Rome placed on the Christians; 14. Crucifixion of Peter,

persecution of Christians, flight of Nero; 15. Death of Nero, the victory of the Galilean.

An examination of the above list of tableaux might make any reader agree with Martin Lamm's summary condemnation of the whole trilogy:

He has never perpetrated anything more miserable than this trilogy. The first drama, *From the Wilderness to the Promised Land,* is a dramatization of the story of Moses from his birth on with a faithful and wooden reliance on the Bible, which makes the work remind us most of all of the naïve Biblical dramas of our reformation period. In the second play, *Hellas,* we meet all the great men from Greece's time of flowering, talking with each other in the manner of the Platonic dialogues. The interest is soon concentrated on Socrates' marital sufferings, which Strindberg presents with much sympathy. In the third drama, *The Lamb and the Wild Beast,* a complete Offenbach mood prevails.[5]

Judged from much the same point of view as the plays from *Master Olof* to *The Nightingale of Wittenberg,* the trilogy, as Lamm suggests facetiously and perhaps a bit maliciously, is downright miserable, not to say silly. The three plays simply are not dramas constructed in the manner of a *Gustav Vasa;* Lamm sensed that when he mentioned the Platonic dialogue and the Biblical dramas of the Reformation. What he did not do was to determine what Strindberg was attempting and to judge the results accordingly.

That Lamm did not do so is all the more amazing since he is the scholar who above all others has emphasized Strindberg's role as the greatest experimentalist in the modern theater.[6] That Strindberg was experimenting with his own version of a genre going back to the Platonic dialogue and the reformation dramas is obvious. The three plays are in fact dialogues by a master of the dramatic art. They are Strindbergian imaginary conversations with specific backgrounds; they re-create the historic dead in situations which permit them self-expression, call up around each person a setting, and reveal history and its significance through some of its major actors; and they are designed primarily for reading aloud in the theater.

In other words, these are plays composed for simplified theatrical productions, in which conversation is of primary importance and acting as such decidedly secondary. In these psychological conversations, Strindberg has aimed, through what are basically sketches of historical dramas, to provide his own insights into the significance and contributions of three major eras and civilizations—the Hebrew, the Hellenic of Socrates' time, and the early Christian. Judged from that point of view, the trilogy becomes interesting in its own right and highly informative in terms of Strindberg's thinking about history.

Moses deals with the Hebrews from the last years of their bondage in Eygpt to their entrance into the Promised Land, or from shortly before Moses' birth until his death after he has seen Canaan. Knowing the Bible as few other major authors have, Strindberg has selected with scrupulous care episodes that illustrate the story and tie it up with happenings elsewhere for an audience or reader fairly well acquainted with the Old Testament account, and he also manages to clarify the role of the Hebrews in world history as he understood it.

It is the Hebraic emphasis on law, order, and obedience to a stern but just deity that emerges as the most striking aspect of the little play. In keeping with his own early conditioning at home and in church and with his own post-Inferno concept of deity, Strindberg presents God as a dictator who deals surely and usually harshly with any offender against any of His many regulations. It is, moreover, a deity who deals with a stubborn and recalcitrant people to whom has been granted a measure of freedom of will. Fear instilled by harsh discipline and promises of rewards for obedience are the means by which He makes His people walk a path that will lead to the fulfillment of their mission: the establishment of law and order in a key portion of the world at a crucial point in time.

A Strindbergian touch becomes clear in that Moses, the major instrument of the Lord, and the more important men who surround him do not emerge as highly individualized human beings in such an authoritarian community with its strict discipline. It is rather the concept of the whole mass of the chosen people that stands out, not the individuals. Strindberg's depiction of that people is hardly a flattering one, but it is faithful to the Old Testament concept. Little of the complex and dynamic qualities of Moses and the men closest to him ever becomes clear.

Moses, or *From the Wilderness to the Promised Land,* is certainly unlikely to warrant a regular production in a conventional theater, but it would be eminently suitable for production, in America at least, by church groups, readers' workshops, and perhaps even in "little theaters." With the aid of lighting effects and such equipment as the Clavilux, the play would, I suspect, make a rewarding show. By means of a few carefully selected and decidedly provocative stage directions, Strindberg has suggested stage effects and bits of acting that could be quite effective. Those directions range from the conversion of the pillar of cloud into a form that resembles an enormous old man to a view of Canaan in the distance. In addition to the brief statements of setting in terms of time and place and indications of entrances and exits, there are occasional directions for the emotional states of characters and their movements and other actions, some hints about stage properties, and, above all else, fairly scrupulous attention to lighting and sound effects.

In *Socrates,* on the other hand, stage directions are reduced to the minimum. The emphasis is placed completely on the conversations, which have a verve and vivacity that is anything but wooden. Strindberg's interest in, and enthusiasm about, a civilization in which the intellect was respected as it was in neither the Hebrew nor the Christian worlds may account at least partially for that fact.

As a result, Socrates and the prominent men about him, as well as Aspasia and Xanthippe, become far more highly individualized than any of the characters in *Moses.* Through the self-expression of their ideas and through their fellows' comments about them they stand out as distinct human beings in both their strengths and weaknesses, not, as in *Moses,* almost completely reduced to standardized behavior in an authoritarian community.

The Greeks talk about almost every conceivable aspect of deity, mankind, and the universe. They talk as free men in a community in which freedom of speech is still permitted though there are those among them who would restrict speech and practice thought control. They talk in a brilliant era of Hellenic civilization, with all its glory of spontaneity of thought and free inquiry as well as of considered intellectual discussion about such matters as the gods, the state, beauty and art, drama and the theater, morality and immorality, men and women, domestic matters and foreign; and they discuss from many points of view. In the course of the many tableaux there emerges Strindberg's concept of the role of the Greeks in world history—the civilization of man through the development of all his faculties. In keeping with what he had had to say in the preface to *Lady Julie,* the conversation flows freely without assuming mechanical form.

Lamm is quite right in saying that Strindberg pays a great deal of sympathetic attention to Socrates' marital difficulties. He might have mentioned, too, the attention given Euripides and his wives and their relationships. What he would have noticed if he had examined more closely the sections devoted to marriages, is that Strindberg has dealt with them not only with sympathy but with good humor.

As a play to be read in public rather than acted, *Socrates* should do even better than *Moses.* It is not suitable for the regular stage: it has only the slimmest of plots, the elements of suspense are few, and, for the theatergoer used to movement and action, it has very little. But for an audience interested in the exposition of ideas through conversation, it has much.

The weakest of the three plays is undoubtedly *Christ.* Divided into three parts (I: Tableaux 1-3; II: 4-10; III: 11-15), it illustrates the Christian account in the New Testament supplemented by selected episodes from the days of the three wild beasts in Rome—Caligula,

Claudius, and Nero. It ends, as the outline indicates, with the death of Nero and the impending victory of the Christians. The tableaux are far more fragmentary than those in *Socrates,* the stage directions are, except in certain scenes, reduced to very little or nothing, and the characters are merely sketched. There are tableaux that could easily give what Lamm calls Offenbach effects. Note, for example:

CALIGULA *(enters, dressed as Jupiter, frightened, steals along the walls)*: Is the priest here? —Priest! *(The priest enters)* Priest, little priest, I'm so afraid; I can't sleep!

PRIEST *(on his knees)*: Jupiter, Optimus Maximus, frighten thine enemies!

CALIGULA: So I do have enemies—that's why I'm so afraid! Do you think I am God?

PRIEST: You are! Let your lightning flash and your thunder roll, then your enemies will flee!

CALIGULA: Are the works in order?

PRIEST: I'll pull the string and the thunder will roll! Sit down on the throne!

CALIGULA *(sits down)*: Let it thunder! *(The priest pulls a string; it thunders. The emperor laughs)* Now I'm frightening them! *(Laughs)* Priest! Sacrifice to me so I may feel my might!

A couple of minutes later, when the emperor wants the thunder to crash again, the priest reports the string is broken. Such an episode could obviously be made ridiculous, but, on the other hand, read with restraint, it could do what Strindberg was apparently trying to achieve in the episode—illustrate the degradation of one of the wild beasts.

Strindberg does get his synoptic view of history into the three plays, he does illustrate his view of the role of the Conscious Will, and he does relate the three plays to each other. The "thread" which was to go through the whole "necklace" is there, although it is not altogether invisible, as Strindberg claimed it would be. In terms of his total contribution to the historical drama, the trilogy must be judged as among his slightest. But as experiments in the imaginary conversation, certainly a minor form of the drama, the three plays deserve consideration. For those who have been fortunate enough to hear and see Pär Lagerkvist's *Let Man Live* performed, *Moses, Christ,* and particularly *Socrates* might well be a rewarding experience.

16

The Last of the Knights
and The Regent

Coping with Evil

In the summer of 1908, Strindberg set out to fill two gaps in his Swedish historical cycle: first, the regency of Sten Sture (1512-20), which culminated with the death of the last Sture regent, the Danish invasion led by Christian II, and his series of bloodbaths; and, second, the Swedish war, under the leadership of Gustav Vasa, for total independence from the unfortunate union. *Master Olof* had, to be sure, dealt with Gustav Vasa as king in the earlier years of his reign, and *Gustav Vasa* portrayed him at the height of his power. Neither play had, however, paid primary attention to the problems of the Swedes in the closing years of the union, nor had they concentrated very much on Gustav as a very young man or as the maturing but youthful leader in the war for national liberty.

In his re-examination of his sources of historical information about both the regency of Sten Sture and Gustav Vasa's activities in the war for independence, Strindberg found in the person of Gustav Trolle, long called "the Judas Iscariot of Sweden," the basic idea

for companion plays about the two major figures in the struggle for
national survival. The popular historians classified Archbishop
Trolle as well-nigh the embodiment of evil, and even the more
scholarly historians recognized the archbishop as an anything but
saintly major opponent and antagonist of both Sten Sture and Gustav Vasa.

The two leaders' relations with the archbishop, each one's struggle
with him for power, and particularly the striking differences between
their attempts to cope with him provided Strindberg with the basic
material for two companion folk dramas which are essentially
studies in ways of dealing with an opponent who is a dedicated
egotist set on acquiring prestige, possessions, position, and power,
for the sake of neither the nation nor a Scandinavian union but for
his own personal satisfaction.

Consider this typical excerpt from Anders Fryxell's account of
Sten Sture:

Lord Sten Sture the Younger, like his father, was a very noble and
distinguished man in many respects. Upright but humble before God,
honest and loyal toward his fellow men, wise and sharp-witted in counsel, brave and unafraid in battle: like his father, he was all this, but in
addition, he was much more gentle, friendly, and goodhearted than
Lord Svante. As a young boy he was often seen, his eyes filled with
tears, kneeling to propitiate his father when the latter's violent temper
lashed out against cowardly, false, or negligent servants; and in that
way, he saved many from the severest of punishments. When he
grew up, he retained the same gentle, conciliatory turn of mind, and the
people loved him for it warmly. But his best friends, who loved him
for this very quality, complained that his gentleness misled him to the
point of gullibility and altogether too much forbearance for his enemies. . . . He traveled regularly throughout the country to learn about
the circumstances of the people, and both his ears and heart were
open to the complaints the people had to offer; for he wanted to protect
everyone, the learned as well as the layman, the powerful as well as the
humble, so that no one would have to suffer injustice under his admin-
istration. Without hypocrisy, he considered himself the father of his
countrymen; he did not seek his own pleasure and his own advantage,

but sacrificed for the welfare of the people his time and his energies, yes, eventually his life itself.[1]

The account is typical of those in all the popular histories Strindberg regularly used for his historical information and differs only in detail from standard scholarly accounts he consulted.

Contrast this brief excerpt from the Starbäck-Bäckström account of the archbishop:

He did not return in the least as Sten Sture's friend, but as his enemy. Hate dwelt in his heart and other ties determined his actions. Besides, his state of mind was exactly the same as that with which we saw him force his mother to let him have his way. The goal that he once had made his own, he never deviated from; for its attainment he sacrificed everything. And this goal was now revenge, even if its attainment would lead to the destruction of his fatherland.[2]

The popular histories supply plenty of details that supplement and complement the suggestions in the brief excerpt.

A keen observer of human nature, Strindberg could hardly have found better illustrations of the uses to which men put their dual capacities for good and evil. With his customary awareness that no man is likely to be a perfect or complete embodiment of either good or evil, Strindberg accepted the traditional accounts of the two men, qualifying his personal interpretations only by the realistic assumptions that Sten Sture had essential human imperfections and Gustav Trolle had at least slight saving qualities and that both of them were essentially products of their heredity and particularly their environments.

Strindberg's Sten Sture is a highly gifted and very young product of a training implicit in the ideals of chivalry and of the church. The code of knightly honor has become Sten Sture's own code of conduct; the church with its emphasis on ethical conduct and on brotherly love has complemented what chivalry has come to mean for him. In other words, Strindberg's Sten Sture believes that it is his duty to fight openly and honestly for what is just and good: his country, the church, the defenseless, and the oppressed; he has, moreover, learned to respect women. As I have said elsewhere:

> The knight who, theoretically, was to dedicate himself to an enthusiastic love of good and to hatred of evil was exposed to a training designed to develop him physically, socially, and, above all, morally. Strindberg's Sten Sture has not only been exposed to all this but *it has taken*: physically, the training has developed his body which is to serve the spirit by means of military skills (the desire for military prowess and glory was considered highly justified); socially, the ideals of courtesy, gallantry, and romantic love have made him a model of social conduct; morally, he has developed those traits of chivalric (and Christian) conduct that make him a good man, constantly aware of his own weaknesses and ever struggling against them, and applying the doctrine, "Do unto others as you would have others do unto you." He has been imbued with the ideals of self-sacrifice, service as a goal, liberality and generosity toward friend and foe alike, opposition to injustice, promotion of peace, and defence of law and order.[3]

To present on the stage the story of the struggle for power between the knightly regent and the Machiavellian archbishop, Strindberg chose the folk drama as his form and used a primarily realistic technique.

A brief summary of the play will suggest as much:

Act I (one scene): The preparations for celebrating the election of the regent: either Erik Trolle—Gustav Trolle's father—or nineteen-year-old Sture. The election of Sten Sture. The introduction of the two candidates, their supporters, and their ideas. Preparation of the audience for the role Gustav Trolle will play in Sten Sture's regency. The clarification of the conflict between nationalists and unionists.

Act II (one scene): The young archbishop's defiance of the young regent and Trolle's refusal to cooperate with Sten Sture. The latter's refusal of the crown.

Act III (one scene): The archbishop's thwarting of every attempt on the regent's part to secure cooperation for the good of the nation.

Act IV (one scene): Sten Sture's wasting his great opportunity to achieve his goal by behaving like a knight toward his captive antagonist.

Act V (two scenes): Sten Sture's knightly treatment of Trolle's supporter, Danish Christian II, and the resulting loss of his best men.

Scene 2: Sten Sture now dead; Trolle among the besiegers of Stockholm's Castle.

Strindberg has effectively used a device that had been decidedly successful in *Gustav Vasa*. Just as he delays the appearance of the king until the third act in that play, he postpones the appearance of Archbishop Trolle until the third act of *The Last of the Knights*. Again Strindberg uses the first two acts to make the audience keenly aware of the man who has not yet appeared and to anticipate his eventual coming on stage. Strindberg has used the device to fit the character, however. There is in Acts I and II of *The Last of the Knights* an emphasis, on the part of every one (but Sten Sture) who mentions Gustav Trolle, on a distrust and dread of him as of someone who is evil. Trolle's own father admits that he and his son are not friends. Lejonhuvud, who is no model of integrity himself, does not hesitate to imply that the archbishop is evil. Bishop-elect Heming Gad, the brilliant and wily supporter of Sten Sture, calls the archbishop an ugly fish and expresses genuine dismay over his election as a result of Sten Sture's recommendation and puts the matter clearly:

GAD: And you've invited him here! Your enemy!

STURE: I'm no one's enemy ...

GAD: But all are yours! You want to talk with him; he never talks; he only hears, listens, steals every word and converts it into a promise, which he'll force you to keep later ...

Very young Gustav Vasa, loyal follower of Sture, bluntly calls the archbishop both a robber and a devil. Least partisan of all the judges of Trolle is Herman Israel, representative of Lübeck:

BREMS: Who is Gustav Trolle?

ISRAEL: He's a French, no, an Italian bandit, like Alexander VI Borgia, a fat fish like the eel. If you try to seize his head, you get hold of his tail, if you manage to get hold of him at all.

It is only Sten Sture who, giving the archbishop every knightly benefit of doubt, can speak of the archbishop's great gifts and his learning, who can consider him as the worthiest candidate for the archbishop's throne, and who at most, while labeling Trolle on occasions of Trolle's decidedly unchristian and unknightly behavior as "discourteous," "shameless," "hard," "unruly," and "unkind," insists "I'll not say anything bad . . . and he'll most likely become good."

The archbishop who then appears when the curtain for Act III goes up is what all but Sten Sture have said and implied in the first two acts. The tall dark archbishop nervously tapping on a window-pane of the sacristy of Uppsala Cathedral a moment after the curtain goes up on Act III may have the priestly garb of a Christian arch-bishop, but he has neither the inner tranquillity nor the outward manner of a servant of the Lord. Bluntly and brutally frank with his father, the former regent of Sweden, Archbishop Trolle quickly reveals himself:

ERIK TROLLE: And it's the custom to say: Sit down. I've taught you that.

GUSTAV TROLLE: You have taught me a great deal!

ERIK TROLLE: If I could only teach you to forget the evil I've taught you!

GUSTAV TROLLE: Don't say that. What you call evil has benefited me most in life!

ERIK TROLLE: What have you gained in life, really?

GUSTAV TROLLE: I'm the archbishop of Sweden . . .

ERIK TROLLE: Even if you won the crown, and your soul were injured, what would be gained by that?

GUSTAV TROLLE: *Soul!*

ERIK TROLLE: That's Rome, that's Borgia, that's heathendom, that's Johanna of Naples and Lucrezia, the *Decameron* and Leo, who paid five thousand ducats for the manuscript of Plato . . .

GUSTAV TROLLE: Won't you sit down? Sit down!

ERIK TROLLE: Soul? You most likely don't have any.

GUSTAV TROLLE: You must have had such a little one there wasn't enough to give me one.

The Machiavellian product of an evil environment, Archbishop Trolle simply cannot understand the knightly and Christian behavior of Sten Sture, whom he considers a stupid sheep, whom he labels a child, a perjurer, a thief, and a rebel—to his face—and, when he hears that Sten Sture has rejected the royal crown, a hypocrite, a wolf, and a monster.

In an intensely dramatic fashion, Strindberg places the two diametrically opposite antagonists face-to-face in both Act III and Act IV. In Act III, the archbishop, who has become a priest not because he believes in Christ but because the church can lead to the attainment of his ambitious goals, and the regent, who is dedicated to serve his people and his church, meet under circumstances that are highly advantageous to the unscrupulous egotist. In Act IV, the archbishop is a prisoner at the mercy of the regent. In both acts the major emphasis is placed on the futility of chivalrous and Christian acts as a means of coping with evil. Condescension, familiarity, and rudeness characterize the archbishop's behavior when he is in a position of vantage, silent speculation and watchful waiting when he is not.

It is an amazingly admirable (idealistically considered) series of acts by means of which Sten Sture attempts to secure the welfare of Sweden and his fellow Swedes—welcoming his defeated enemy Erik Trolle to the banquet, recommending Gustav Trolle for the archbishop's chair, taking the word of other people at face value, inviting the archbishop to be his guest at Stockholm Castle, refusing to believe that Trolle and Christian II are not men of integrity, attempting to win the archbishop's cooperation, refusing to dispose of the archbishop when he is a defenseless prisoner, providing his enemies —Christian II and his starving Danes—with supplies, and allowing his best men to row out to negotiate with Christian with no substantial assurance that Christian will keep his word. All these are

admirable acts but, as the archbishop knows, quixotic in a realistic
and semibarbaric world in which chivalry and Christianity are little
more than convenient labels.

Contrasted with both the evil of Gustav Trolle and the chivalric
honor and Christian goodness of Sten Sture is the realistic idealism
of Sture's supporters, notably the very old Heming Gad and the very
young Gustav Vasa.

It is Heming Gad, the eighty-year-old supporter of the church and
a loyal Swede who has acquired the wisdom that experience, observation, and thought can give, who understands the situation Sten
Sture faces:

HEMING GAD *(to Gustav Vasa)*: Believe me, this isn't over; there's a
lot left. Prince Christian is a devil from hell, and now he's the brother-
in-law of the emperor; the emperor is the friend of the pope—at times.
You who are young will see a lot; it's no art to prophesy when one's
eighty, because everything's alike, repeats itself, and the same cause has
almost the same effect. If those of us here could see our future . . . You,
Gustav, are gifted, and you're realistic about the evil in people. Sten's
too soft-hearted and believes they're better than they are; that's why he's
always deceived. You're too frank, on the other hand, and impatient,
too. You should be something of a fox, Gustav, a fox!

GUSTAV VASA: A wolf, rather, but not a fox. I can't!

A man dedicated to the causes of his people and of the church, the
priestly vows of which he has taken, Heming Gad knows people and
the society in which they live. He can only protest against Sten
Sture's unpractical acts, which ironically are right from a Christian
point of view but which can only lead to defeat and disaster in a
turbulent age. Ironically, too, Gad can succumb to the deceitful but
apparently logical arguments of a Christian II and, in so doing, un-
wittingly help to betray the cause of his own people.

Young Gustav Vasa, vehement and enthusiastic, on occasion crude
and even distressingly forthright, may be at the Sture court to learn
knightly manners but he is above all else the potential leader being
trained in the bitter school of experience to distinguish between chiv-

alric and Christian opposition to forces bent on his country's subjugation and the practical realistic opposition needed to prevent its
destruction. Loyal to Sten Sture, he learns quickly, not the code of
honor the regent follows but the practical lessons needed in dealing
with evil:

STEN STURE: A knight doesn't murder a defenseless man who hasn't
any weapon in his hand.

GUSTAV VASA: You, knight, the last of the knights! Would you cross
swords with an infamous traitor? The snake has bitten you three times.
Throw 'im in the fire!

STEN STURE: Lord Gustav Trolle, if I now spare your life, don't mis-
use God's gift; and, if I do good to you, do not avenge my good deed.

GUSTAV VASA: Yes, Sten Sture, if you're too good for this world, don't
forfeit heaven by an evil deed when you set free the dragon no St.
George can slay.

STEN STURE: Take the prisoner away and have him kept at Västerås
Castle. Go!

GUSTAV VASA: You'll regret this, and will pay for it. Sture! Sture!

And a moment later:

STEN STURE: Are you trying to make me change? When I do what's
right?

GUSTAV VASA: The greatest right in the greatest wrong. I thank God
I'm not a knight.

It is Strindberg's very young Gustav Vasa who does not succumb to
the blandishments of either friend or foe but who remains steadfast
to his realistic ideal of securing his country's freedom.

Besides these two highly important secondary characters (Heming
Gad and Gustav Vasa), there is an intensely interesting lot of other
secondary characters who in various ways affect Sten Sture in his
struggle against the archbishop and his allies: Kristina Sture, the
loving and faithful wife of the regent and his feminine counterpart;
Lady Mätta, his stepmother, hated by most of the Swedes for evil
that she has allegedly committed but the person above all others who
has protected Sten from a saving knowledge about human nature

and human society; the almost sentimentally conceived lovers, the unfortunate Johan Natt-och-Dag and Anna Bielke, both faithful to the Swedish cause and portrayed without Strindberg's usual stringent regard for the realistic facts about human nature; the very young Sparre brothers, the one realistically loyal to Sture and the Swedish cause, the other torn between youthful regard for integrity and egotistic envy of others more likely to receive the rewards; Erik Lejonhuvud, the opportunist who would prefer to be loyal but who feels an urgent need to secure his own interests; and the thoroughly realistic and practical representatives of Lübeck.

Sten Sture's world is a typically Strindbergian environment. It is a world in which the people are very human indeed. In fact, almost all of those who dominate it or try to dominate it are not for a moment likely to regard the chivalric code of honor or the Christian moral ideals as more than convenient devices to use in their relentless pursuit of power when that is possible but are ready to believe that applied chivalry and applied Christianity are quixotic. To be sure, they all pay lip service to both closely related standards, but, in their realistic appraisal of their fellowmen and their world, they refrain from conduct which approaches that of Sten Sture.

The Last of the Knights presents Sten Sture as the unrealistic idealist, with precisely the flaws of gullibility and impulsive self-deception, on a pilgrimage from innocence to knowledge. Ironically Strindberg believed the knight without fear and beyond reproach and the good and faithful son of the church is the one destined not only to be excommunicated but to lose his life itself in his defense of what is good. Ironically, too, it is either the Machiavellian archbishop without idealistic illusions or the practical realist who will inherit the power in this world.

A decidedly effective folk drama, *The Last of the Knights* interprets a period in Swedish history when the destinies of Sweden primarily lay in the acts of very young people. Most of the characters are in fact little more than boys and girls with the impulsiveness, enthusiasm, and fervor of the very young. The play does have flaws

—Lady Mätta's startling prophecies and the cloying interpretation of Johan Natt-och-Dag's and Anna Bielke's love for each other—but as a whole, it is the kind of folk tragedy that in addition to such virtues as excellence of characterization, skillful plotting of action, and illuminating interpretation of an important period in Swedish history has, as we shall see a little later, decided appeal to theater audiences.

Strindberg deliberately composed *The Regent* as a companion to the play about Sten Sture. Observe what he wrote in the little note prefixed to the second play:

The same settings as in *The Last of the Knights,* but in reverse order. This contrapuntal form which I have borrowed from music and used in *To Damascus* I has the effect of awakening in the theatergoer memories of the various places in which earlier actions took place, and thereby the drama has the effect of happening much later in life with a great deal behind it; accumulated impressions arise; there are echoes from better times; the hard reality of maturity dominates; the defeated are counted; crushed hopes are recalled; and the drama *The Last of the Knights* serves as the saga of youth in contrast to the heavy struggle of *The Regent.*

Note, too, the reverse order of the identical settings:

The Last of the Knights	*The Regent*
Act I: The Rathskeller in Stockholm's Town Hall.	Act I: The same room in Stockholm Castle (*The Last of the Knights,* Acts II and V).
Act II: A room in Stockholm Castle; the Lübeck office.	Act II: Outside the Blockhouse.
Act III: The sacristy in Uppsala Cathedral.	Act III: Before Stäke Castle; the sacristy in Uppsala Cathedral.
Act IV: Before Stäke Castle.	Act IV: The Lübeck office.
Act V: Outside the Blockhouse; the same room in Stockholm Castle (Act II, scene 1).	Act V: The room in Stockholm Castle; the Rathskeller in Stockholm's Town Hall.

The companion plays are decidedly studies in contrasts. In both of them the primary antagonist and opponent of the central character is the Machiavellian Archbishop Gustav Trolle, but the difference in the techniques for coping with him is striking. While Sten Sture tried desperately to win his struggle by idealistic application of the codes of chivalry and the church, Gustav Vasa, while pursuing the same goal as Sten Sture, rejects those codes for the very realistic and practical ways of dealing with an opponent who shrinks from no means of achieving his ends. It is, as Strindberg suggests, a contrast between the idealistic, impractical, even playful, pursuit of a great goal by extremely young and inexperienced men and the practical, far less playful pursuit of the same goal by men who, while they are not much older in actual number of years, are immeasurably older in knowledge of the world, of human nature, and of the actual problems involved. The contrast between the frequently unthinking, emotional approach of a Sten Sture and the everthinking, analytical approach of Gustav Vasa is effectively underscored by the use of the reverse order of the same settings.

One may say with justice that all three men are on journeys. While Sten Sture's journey was a pilgrimage from innocence to knowledge (and inevitable defeat as Strindberg saw it), the journey of Gustav Vasa is the almost single-minded progress to real achievement in a world curiously blended of good and evil. The archbishop's journey is, as Strindberg presents it, a journey from self-confident use of men and other means for the attainment of egotistic rewards to the shattering knowledge that isolation and inner defeat are the ultimate reward of uncontrolled egoism. In a very real sense, the three men not only represent possibilities in human behavior and development but they also are not a little related to some of the characters in Strindberg's great expressionistic plays from the Damascus trilogy on. Both Sten Sture and Archbishop Trolle are, for example, sleepwalkers in the Strindbergian sense; once awakened, they are for all practical purposes defeated. Gustav Vasa is, moreover, as aware of evil in a very human world as, for instance, the Stranger, but, unlike the

Stranger, he is not addicted to wasting time on futile speculation about the origins of evil and the niceties of its composition.

Consequently, the struggle between Gustav Vasa and the archbishop is far less uneven than that between the chivalrous Sten Sture and the archbishop. Strindberg's Gustav Vasa is an increasingly confident realist coping with an increasingly unhappy and less confident egoist. While duty, devotion to duty, and honor are very real to Gustav Vasa, they do not lie within the framework of a Utopia but within the hard, cold, and very imperfect society of his time and place. Strindberg does not attempt to reduce the basic conflict to simplicity, however; he not only was aware of the complexities of any serious conflict but makes it emphatically clear that Gustav Vasa's pursuit of his goal of a free Sweden and Gustav Trolle's pursuit of power for himself were both highly complex. Hence, the emphasis in the play on such matters as Göran Sparre's envy of Gustav Vasa, the opportunism of followers of both opponents, and the vacillating loyalties of some of the men. Most important of all in Strindberg's interpretation of Gustav Vasa as the final liberator of Sweden is Vasa's sane, careful, and occasionally impulsive working toward the basically idealistic but realistically attainable goal.

Instead of delaying the appearance of the Archbishop until the third act as in *The Last of the Knights,* Strindberg presents him immediately at the beginning of Act I. It is an archbishop, however, who has behind him the Stockholm bloodbath, the infamous massacre of Swedish loyalists, clerical as well as lay (an episode with which almost all Swedes are as familiar as, say, almost all Americans used to be with the story of Benedict Arnold). Trolle is still pursuing his goal of power and has it tantalizingly almost within his grasp. But the archbishop knows that in Gustav Vasa he has an opponent quite different in quality from the gentle Sten Sture, and the archbishop is now a man at peace with neither himself nor anyone else; he is uneasy and tense as he tries to capitalize on the opportunities his own scheming and chance have given him.

Strindberg presents him in highly revealing interviews with Lady

Cecelia of Eka (Gustav Vasa's mother), whom he uses to bring
pressure on his rival; the latter's little sister, whom he treats in a
friendly and kindly fashion; the late Sten Sture's stepmother, Lady
Mätta, whom he underestimates and, unfortunately for him, misun-
derstands; Bishop Brask, whose life he had unexpectedly seen saved
at the bloodbath; his own father; and young Svante Sture, son of the
late regent. Every one of them reminds him of his sins and crimes;
not one of them lightens the burden of inner conflict; even his Swedish hostages speak softly and gently, his father protestingly, and only
Bishop Brask bluntly. Note the exchange:

GUSTAV TROLLE *(shrinks back in horror, trembles, stammers)*: Hans
Brask?
BRASK: Bishop. Hans. Brask!
TROLLE *(bewildered)*: I don't understand!
BRASK: You don't need to, Gustav! You used to call me "father," so I
took the fatherly liberty of coming in before Erik Trolle. *(Trolle shrinks
back when Hans Brask approaches him.)* Are you shrinking? You
thought I was dead, because you got me sentenced to death! That was in
this room! There that bloodhound Christian stood, and there stood the
executioners. There you stood! As the prosecutor! So I was sentenced.
For twelve hours I suffered the agonies of death! *(Gustav Trolle moves
his lips but can't find any words.)* But then I became so well prepared
for death that I was ready for it every moment, and this gave me courage
to live, courage to speak, courage to meet you! Why did you want the
axe at my throat? Because I slapped you in the face once when you were
a boy. That was a blow that you had coming! My business? —I come
from the graves of your victims, from Bishop Vincentius of Skara and
Bishop Mattias of Strängnäs, from the ninety-eight martyrs you had beheaded, and I come for my own sake to keep a vow I swore on the day
of the bloodbath: that, if I got out of it with my life, I would seek you
out, dead or alive, as you had Sten Sture sought out in his grave, and I
would place the mark of the slave on your face. *(Hans Brask strikes Gustav Trolle, who accepts the blow.)* That burned, eh? Like the execu-
tioner's red-hot iron! Now you are brought to shame! That was all of
my business! *(Stands quiet for a while staring at Gustav Trolle)* Now I
shall go, but not so fast that you can say I have fled. *(Walks slowly and
with dignity to the door at the left; then turns)* Within a year from this

day I shall summon you before the judgment seat of the Almighty God, whether you are struck down by death, sickness, or misfortunes! You, the most evil of men! You son of a revenger, you slave, you thief, you liar! May you be damned! *(Goes)*
(Gustav Trolle, shaken, has retreated backward until he has reached the wall, where he stands like a baited cat at bay.)

It is a strikingly dramatic first act, which not only clarifies the basic struggle for power but also succeeds remarkably well in revealing the archbishop as a pitiful as well as a despicable egotist.

Act II, on the other hand, is devoted to the archbishop's new rival for power, the idealistic realist, the man born with a caul, who cannot bear to have anyone take over the duties he has assigned to himself, and who is still young enough to indulge in practical jokes. After one of the few episodes in Strindberg's historical dramas in which there is actual fighting, the whole act is given over to Gustav Vasa and the young men about him, Gustav Vasa and the distrusted Lady Mätta, Gustav Vasa and the boy Svante Sture, Gustav Vasa and his own mother. It is an attractive young leader Strindberg presents in action, single-minded and firm in pursuit of his idealistic goal, rough and not a little crude on occasion, religious in his own way, self-confident, yet humanly disturbed inwardly when faced with the dilemma of having to choose between his cause and his mother.

In scene 1 of Act III Strindberg quickly provides the information that Gustav Vasa's pursuit of his goal has progressed so far that he has been elected regent in spite of disharmony in his own ranks and other difficulties. Scene 2, set in the sacristy of Uppsala Cathedral, is devoted to two important matters—the disintegration of the archbishop and Gustav Vasa's clear-sighted refusal to waste his time in considering his defeated rival when he has the all-important task of making Bishop Brask, now the primary source of power in the church, consider the desirability and inevitability of making the church give way to the state.

Again Strindberg resorts to the techniques of contrast and com-

parison. The archbishop, defeated and wounded, is driven to fear
and terror by what Gustav Vasa has succeeded in doing to thwart
his acts and intrigues. The caretaker's wife—representative of the
common people—denounces the archbishop and his crimes and
makes him look at himself:

It's the enemy, the evil one, who's fetching you! You took the life of
my youngest son, and you have ruined my daughter! You have butchered
bishops and lords, and you've had the corpses brought to the stake by
the barrel! You had the noble Sture dug up, you grave robber, you
corpse spoiler; half the kingdom is in mourning, in sorrow; children rise
up against parents, and parents against children; I have two sons whom
you made traitors; there isn't one person to rely on; I sleep with my
kitchen axe under my bed for my own husband's sake—listen, how it's
rustling out there in the church—do you know what that is? Look this
way, and you'll see. *(She opens the door at the back; black-clad ladies and
children pass by as if in procession.)* There they go to the graves, the
widows and the fatherless—the Vasas, the Stures, Brahe, the Gyllen-
stjernas, Ryning, Kurck, Lejonhuvud—yes, look for your sword, you
hangman; you'll get rope . . .

Forced at last to examine himself, the archbishop sits in judgment
on himself as he examines his portrait:

TROLLE: Is that I? Is this I? Do I look that horrible? The devil himself
has painted it!
VOICE: In his image!
TROLLE: Is someone here? *(Pause)* It is horrible! I believe it is Alexander VI Borgia; and this is I! A human being, born of woman, nursed
by a woman, and doesn't resemble a human being! *(Shrinks back)* It's
not possible! I have seen my spirit—I have seen myself, I must die! But
it is not I; it is someone else! I am not like that! *(He takes down a mirror
from the wall and observes himself in it.)* Yes, it is! This is still worse
. . . Flee? Oneself? How? Throw oneself on one's own sword, like Saul,
but no one wants to hold it! No one!

A moment later, the archbishop's father enters to lead into flight
his "big, old, lost child," no longer a sinister force for evil but a

broken reed. The healthy, brusque but highly competent Gustav Vasa, who enters just as the archbishop escapes, is startingly rational and sound by way of contrast as he discusses calmly but firmly with Bishop Brask his kind of statesmanship: "Honest words! Honest blows! To the point!"

Gustav Vasa does not appear at all in Act IV, but that brief act deals primarily with Gustav Vasa, his election as king, and two of the major problems he will face as king—the twofold debt of money and gratitude to Lübeck, which had helped him set his country free, and the church, whose cooperation or reformation is needed to carry his program to fulfillment. Bishop Brask and Herman Israel, two of the ablest and shrewdest men of the time as Swedish history testifies, talk at cross purposes but in so doing clarify Strindberg's characterization of the young king. It is the foreigner who makes the most cogent analysis:

Lord Bishop, the regent is a very wise man, very wise, because in his younger years he had to learn the difficult art of living in a hard school, and Gustav Vasa knows that the ships and the goods weren't what they should have been—there weren't any others—and he knows that the money is defective; but instead of looking a gift horse in the mouth, and wasting time by complaining, he went ahead on rotten ships and with false money, straight to his objective . . . in a straight line—

The crushed bishop concedes: "I have nothing to add—my time is over. My broom is worn out—toss it on the fire!"

In scene 1 of Act V, the archbishop makes his last appearance; beside himself, he asks Lady Mätta, whom he had dismissed as a crazy fool, "Where shall I flee?" She answers, "It doesn't matter where you flee; you'll never be freed from yourself." A few minutes later, Stockholm Castle falls to Gustav Vasa.

The last scene, set in the rathskeller of the town hall of Stockholm, ties up loose ends of the plot, presents the self-confident young king just after he has made his triumphal entry into his capital, and throws light on factors leading to his victory; on Herman Israel, who will present his duns in the years ahead; on representative Dalesmen who helped Gustav Vasa gain independence for his people but who are already questioning the wisdom of giving him that help; and on Master Olof, "the curry comb" who will reform the church and give the king difficulties in so doing. In his own typical fashion, Strindberg does not make it an unqualified victory or an entirely happy occasion. Gustav Vasa's personal losses, such as the deaths of his mother and his sisters as captives in the Blue Tower of Copenhagen, and the inevitable problems of a world in which everything repeats itself blunt the joy but not the king's gratitude for having reached his goal.

Some of the elements in *The Regent* are distressingly reminiscent of the pre-Strindbergian Swedish historical drama—Lady Mätta's startlingly clear-cut conversion, the rather vapid treatment of love (Kristina Sture–Norrby, Gustav Vasa–Anna Bielke), and some of the boy Svante Sture's strangely unnatural speeches. It may be, of course, that Strindberg included these matters to give the play the flavor of the historic period or made in them concessions to popular taste. Such elements are fortunately uncommon in Strindberg's major historical plays.

The merits of this realistic folk drama are many, however. It tells an old familiar story and tells it well; it succeeds remarkably well in bringing alive for Swedish audiences important episodes and fascinating personalities out of their rich and colorful historic past and does so imaginatively and on occasion impressionistically. It capitalizes on Strindberg's characteristic gift for making well-known and remembered controversies vivid through the sharp and telling exchanges between the archbishop and the women, young Svante Sture, and Bishop Brask; between Herman Israel and Bishop Brask and Erik Trolle; between Gustav Vasa and Bishop Brask; and between Olaus Petri and Israel. Effective characterization, realistic exposition, and the lively tempo add much. Perhaps equally interesting for most readers is the decidedly convincing treatment of ideas about human nature and human conduct.

The companion plays have never gained positions comparable to those of *Master Olof, Gustav Vasa, Erik XIV, The Saga of the Folkungs, Charles XII, Queen Christina,* and *Gustav III,* but the receptions of their production shortly after their completion and of their later tours of the provinces by traveling companies provide sufficient evidence as to their suitability for the theater.

One of the most illuminating sets of Strindberg letters consists of his letters to various theater people and particularly to actors who had either been considered for roles or been assigned roles in the first production of *The Last of the Knights,* starting at the Dramatic Theater on January 22, 1909. Strindberg's anxiety about a just and adequate interpretation of his play as a whole and of his Sten Sture in particular is illustrated in this excerpt from his October 21, 1908, letter to Ivar Nilsson, the actor selected to play the last of the knights:

The role as such is not strong; good people do not really come across on the stage; the evil in the world is so great that people gladly smile at the unsuspicious person who considers it a duty to let himself be fooled; the unsuspicious person easily seems naïve. Fortunately, Sture's lack of suspicion is for the most part a matter of principle, based on the Christian knight's ideally religious view of things, and it is emphasized by "the others" that he is not simple and not a fool. "Firm and fearless, but patient and gentle." Why, he walks like a good child in the midst of evil and deceit, and does not understand how people can be so low: and as a Christian he believes that evil can be conquered by good. (But the evil Gustav Trolle for his part cannot understand how anyone can be so "stupid!") If you are going to get strength, bearing, and authority in this character, you will have to make imaginatively his whole personality part of your own; the born ruler must be seen, not so much through gestures and stiff bearing, but is to be sensed in his whole nature. You must help the author create the character anew, and you must make him stronger than I have. Use your powerful voice but with a humane timbre, kind, well-intentioned but strong. Strong but not hard, and never cruel. Sympathetic, but not sentimentally silly, not so "foolishly noble" that it sounds like a pose. It is his nature that you must conceive and make your own so your presentation will seem natural.[4]

Ivar Nilsson did not play Sten Sture, however, but was ultimately assigned the role of Gustav Vasa.

The first production received a varied reception from the critics and a warm one from the audiences. The reviews ranged from high praise from René (Anna Branting) in *Stockholms Tidningen*[5] to the usual pointing out of anachronisms and unfavorable comparisons with earlier plays. Only nineteen performances were given. An examination of the reviews of presentations of the play by touring companies in the provinces later confirms the conclusion that the play is good theater and good literature. The critic of a Selander Company production, writing in *Skånska Aftonbladet* on February 2, 1910, for example, hits at the Stockholm critics, points out that the Selander performance he had seen was a performance of a very good play, and adds, "It is impossible not to be gripped by this play with its clarity, power, and nobility, its superb dialogue—its thoroughly Swedish quality."[6]

The Regent has had no more impressive a record on the Swedish stage than its companion play. Its *première* production, which opened on January 31, 1911, at the Dramatic Theater, had a run of only thirteen performances. In more or less straightforward terms, the critics testified to the enthusiasm of the audiences. On February 2, 1911, *Aftontidningen* said among other things:

The play as a whole was very effective on the stage and the dramatic interest was kept alive from beginning to end. Strindberg's extraordinary insight into what is theatrically effective and his mastery at dramatically composed, detailed scenes to make his characters live and his dialogue firm and sound did not deny itself here either. Because of all this the performance became interesting and entertaining. . . . The theater was filled to capacity and the applause lively.[7]

Since that initial production, performances of *The Regent* have been largely restricted to performances by touring companies in the provinces.

17

Earl Birger of Bjälbo

The Father's Eye

THE LAST of Strindberg's historical plays is fittingly a study of the founder of the great Folkung dynasty, the earl who in the thirteenth century set out to make Sweden a strong and unified country much as Gustav Vasa was to do almost three centuries later. In fact, *Earl Birger of Bjälbo* (1909) is reminiscent of *Gustav Vasa* (1899) in both substance and form, but at the same time the two plays are decidedly different because of the very natures of the two founders and the circumstances of their far different periods of historical time.

Each play interprets an environment dominated primarily by one man, a strong man with definite goals, a man of ideas and action. Both men have similar human problems to contend with in the pursuit of what is basically the same idealistic goal—the unification of Sweden through the strengthening of the central government and the enforcement of law and order. The human problems include family difficulties as well as troubles with the church, potential rivals and other enemies at home, and powerful but not friendly neighbors abroad. There is, moreover, the decidedly strong inner conviction of each man that he is the one who can achieve the goal and govern the kingdom as it should be governed.

But as Strindberg saw the two founders of great dynasties, Earl Birger, unlike Gustav Vasa, did not have the benefit of generations of traditions and precedents to build on, the measure of inner tranquillity that comes from having a basically honest technique of statesmanship ("Honest words! Honest blows! To the point!"), or a religious conviction to permit him to pursue his goal with the inner assurance that he was an instrument of the Lord. He was burdened with the embarrassing presence of a contemporary in a position to thwart him at crucial points, and he was denied the relatively straightforward progress toward the goal granted the sixteenth-century instrument of the Lord. Strindberg's Earl Birger is forced almost always to act in devious, indirect ways; since he is not king but merely an earl, he has to stoop to hypocritical pretense of conformity to the demands of the church, which he has used on occasion, which has become too powerful to control, and which is in the process of making the people its adherents. A barbarian and pagan posing as a Christian, Earl Birger is affected by the crippling effects of superstition (as interpreted by Dr. Wilibald, the astrologer). He has to stoop to intrigue not only in dealing with neighboring countries but in his egotistic pursuit of his idealistic domestic goal and the power that he desired. Hence, as Strindberg interpreted the historical facts, his arranging for his second marriage; his using others, particularly his own children, as pawns for the achievement of his great goal; and his playing off one son against another, or trying to do so, to guarantee that he himself would have the real power.

As Bishop Kol tells him:

In gambling there are no friends, and you've played for scepters; I believe Valdemar is a better human being than you two [the earl and his second son, Magnus] are, because he has a sense of shame and a sense of right and wrong . . . Ivar Blå is a rascal who has lured you into the swamp, and the magician Wilibald is a French bandit who has pulled the wool over your eyes. But that's how it goes when your ways are crooked, and the one who won't follow good advice generally gets bad; the one who wants to rule over everyone often is conquered. That is your case.

Like all the other major historical plays, *Earl Birger of Bjälbo* concerns a struggle for power, but that struggle is applied to an instrument of the Conscious Will who was in the habit of achieving great things but who was not to be given the ultimate symbol of power as his reward. Unlike Gustav Vasa almost three centuries later, Earl Birger was forced to work through and about his oldest son and, as Strindberg conceived the earl, was not content with the substance of power but tried to grasp the crown, the outward symbol of power, for himself.

In his pursuit of his goal, with his motives a Strindbergian blend of the idealistic and the selfish, Earl Birger did accomplish a certain amount of good but was thwarted at points where his selfishness and arrogance dominated his program and, Strindberg thought, failed in achieving the crown because of such factors as his not daring to oppose the church openly, his reliance on a false adviser, his fear of coming to grips with his personal nemesis Ivar Blå, his stooping to thoroughly dishonest means, and, perhaps above all, his pride and arrogance.

It is interesting that in *Earl Birger of Bjälbo* Strindberg not only has presented an instrument of the Lord somewhat similar to Gustav Vasa (although strikingly different from him, too) but has made a subtly varied use of a technical device already successfully used in *Gustav Vasa.* Just as he had delayed the appearance of King Gustav until the opening of the third act and made it decidedly clear in the preceding acts that everyone else is intensely aware of the king, he delays the appearance of Earl Birger with a strikingly similar effect. From the beginning everyone is aware of the earl; the light gleams from his window in his castle; the "father's eye" is on every one and everything. When the earl appears, in the first scene of Act II, he appears only on the bastion, saying nothing, but watching. Then, in scene 2 when he appears it is as the strong man of action, for whom the preceding scenes have prepared the reader or audience.

Act I is as usual devoted to providing the setting and its atmosphere, an exposition of the background, the introduction of the basic conflicts, and the direct or indirect introduction of the important characters. It is a fascinating setting of a new capital—Earl Birger is usually considered the founder of Stockholm—dominated by its new palace with light gleaming from the earl's window on, what is symbolically highly appropriate, a dull gloomy November day. Easily and naturally comes the exposition of the background— the earl's liquidation of his rivals at Herrevad's Bridge, his perjury, and his years of apparent penance and pretense of penance; the gradual ascendancy of the church and its finally daring to impose celibacy on its Swedish priests; the earl's achievement of peace for the country but not for himself; the family troubles at the palace. The characters that will matter have been introduced, and the conflicts, major and minor, have been suggested.

Scene 1 of Act II immediately makes it clear that the earl has succeeded in making Sweden a country to be reckoned with; the foreign guests and ambassadors are there to illustrate the point. But the scene makes it just as clear that the earl has not succeeded in establishing law and order in his own family. Against the background of recently introduced chivalry, Strindberg presents the attractive but frivolous young King Valdemar, his beautiful Queen Sophia, her Danish sister Princess Jutta (already involved in too intimate a relationship with her brother-in-law), and the dark but extremely able second son, Prince Magnus. Ivar Blå, moreover, returns to interfere once more with Earl Birger's life.

Scene 2 is basically devoted to a characterization of Earl Birger, to an analysis of what he has done, and to preparation for what he plans to do. The scene takes the form of two conversations—the earl's conference with Ivar Blå and the earl's immediately following talk with his astrologer. Ivar Blå says significantly: "The country is everywhere at peace; anybody can travel safely on any of our roads; we can sleep in bed without being burned alive; but, while you manage the kingdom, you mismanage your own house. . . ." Ivar Blå encourages the earl to marry Mechtild of Denmark ostensibly to increase the earl's power and to bring the family into good order but actually to thwart the earl's ambition, which Dr. Wilibald shortly afterward puts into words: "At fifty you face the real goal of your life; an unkind destiny denied you, the worthiest of all, the crown, but now, since you have atoned for your crimes, fortune will turn to your advantage, and your old age will reap what your long years of labor have sown." A moment later the earl is ready to go to work to gain the crown.

Scene 3 shows the earl, released from the threat of condemnation by the church, going to work. Rejuvenated, he starts by attempting to use his youngest son.

Scene 1 of Act III is devoted almost completely to the earl and his sons: Prince Bengt's rejection of his father's devious attempts to use him, the earl's attempt at "buying" Prince Magnus, as he thinks, through flattery and the gift of a duke's title and crown, the earl's use of his oldest son's incest to dispose of Valdemar, the earl's stooping to lying about Valdemar in order to control Magnus. In other words, Earl Birger sows the seeds of dissension and believes that he has prepared Magnus to be willing to *succeed* him. In a revealing episode, Strindberg makes it clear that the earl is startled and amazed by his Folkung rival Lord Karl's decision to sacrifice his claim to the throne in order to serve Christ.

Scene 2 presents highly dramatic matters: Magnus busily at work to gain the crown for himself while his father has gone south to marry Mechtild of Denmark; Princess Judith on the verge of delivering the child conceived in incest; Valdemar's trial and punishment; Ivar Blå's interference to make Magnus take over the royal power and to assure his willing pupil about the earl: "He's done for. Worked out. Needs to rest and to age in peace. . . ."

In Act IV, Earl Birger reaps unexpected results from his conniving and intriguing: By marrying a woman too closely related to his son's wife he has made himself guilty of incest, he has lost his hold on Norway through his son-in-law's death, and Magnus as regent has dared to do what Birger did not—to secure the release of secular priests from celibacy. But the earl is not yet ready to give up his dream of the crown.

In Act V, Earl Birger is still conniving, has his Saracen execute his false adviser, confers at length with Ivar Blå, who analyzes the earl's past, present, and future, as he sees it but without convincing him that "he is done for." The earl tries in vain to use Bengt again. But Magnus takes over by abolishing the position of earl, executing the Saracen, and canceling Mechtild's entry into the capital, and, in a dramatically moving scene, makes the earl realize that in Magnus he has met his match. The earl bows to the inevitable: a son as strong as himself and one who does not need to depend primarily on devious methods to achieve his ends.

As anyone who knows Swedish history will quickly see, Strindberg took exceptionally great liberties with the historical facts in composing his *Earl Birger of Bjälbo*. That fact undoubtedly accounts for his devoting his essay "The Historical Drama" ("Det historiska dramat") to an explanation and a justification of his procedure in composing his last historical play:

About ten years ago when I began to plan and consider Earl Birger as a subject, I immediately discovered that the material was hard to manage. His long life with crusades, miscalculations, penitence, two marriages, children that caused him difficulties, was suited for an epic and not for a drama, unless I selected a portion with dramatic power. I had at first thought of taking the whole story and, following Shakespeare's model of adopting the chronicle form: beginning with the earl's relationship to Erik XI, called the Lisper and Lame, whose decease could certainly be ascribed to the earl's lack of prejudice, which was demonstrated later when he eliminated contestants for the throne in the manner of Richard III. But the murder story did not interest me, and I did not want to charge the earl with an act which was not suggested in the chronicles. Then I thought of starting with Herrevad's Bridge, but that meant I would have to consider the Finnish crusade, which was not appealing. Then I went on and noticed that the strongest motifs lay at the end of his career, and that the Jutta and Mechtild motifs extended beyond the earl's lifetime to the other side of his grave. People generally remember that the earl died in 1266, but they have not learned the date of the Jutta story by heart; so I took the liberty of moving this motif back and combining it with Valdemar's journey of penance to Rome and Magnus' regency. . . . So I knew what liberties I was taking and I knew what I gained for the drama; and since the Jutta motif strictly speaking does not belong to history but to memoirs or family traditions no harm has been done to "The Royal Swedish History" (as Geijer called his history of the nation).

The essay as a whole is Strindberg's frankest and clearest statement of his understanding of the distinction between history and the historical drama. He admits that not only has he taken liberties but that he has had to:

I have never unnecessarily violated historic truth where it has been a matter of generally known facts, because I do not approve this manner of creating historical data and facts. But following the practice of the great models, I have always allowed myself to compress historical events in a remote period, and still do, because the historical drama is an art form through which I must give illusion and in which everything is illusory, language, costume, time above all.

The most important statement of all is undoubtedly the following one: "Even in the historical drama the purely human is of major interest, and history the background; souls' inner struggles awaken more sympathy than the combat of soldiers or the storming of walls; love and hate, torn family ties more than treaties and speeches from the throne." [1]

Strindberg's major interest in his dramas was always people. His historical dramas have vitality largely because Strindberg considered the historic dead as human beings just as complex and dynamic as himself and his contemporaries. What the historical sources failed to give by way of illuminating detail about the historic dead Strindberg supplied from his own experience and imagination.

As he says, "I made the major characters live by taking blood and nerves out of my own life." As I have pointed out elsewhere, elements from his own experience used in this play are the loneliness and frustration of the individual, the unsatisfactory marriages, and the imperfections of the parent-child relationship.[2]

The result of Strindberg's imaginative re-creation of Earl Birger and his time and place in Swedish history and his unusually extensive rearrangement of historical detail is a highly impressive realistic folk drama about one of Sweden's greatest men. It is an intensely dramatic study of an aging family man who at the height of his power sets out to gain the symbol of power—the crown.

The play has the merits of a skillfully conceived plot that assures unflagging interest and suspense; a dialogue stripped of all archaic elements and thoroughly Strindbergian in its colloquial bluntness and variation; a fascinating interpretation of early Stockholm and the period when chivalry and the church were making paganism give way to a gentler kind of civilization or at least the appearance of it. But above all these matters is the remarkable interpretation of the characters.

It is as usual an astonishingly interesting group of "people" that Strindberg has succeeded in creating in his last play: the incidental ones, such as the watchman and the fisherman with their family and other personal troubles and joys, the stableman seen only as a stableman, the silent, obedient, and terrifying Saracen, the deaf-and-dumb page, Ivar Blå's unfortunate but far from stupid Peter; the more highly individualized ones, such as Dean Lars of Oppunda with his frantic response to the enforcement of the edict of celibacy, the chivalrous Lord Karl, in whom the ideals of both knighthood and the church have taken firm hold, the attractive young King Valdemar, who has never had the chance to develop his capacities but has drifted into frivolity and loose conduct, the beautiful young queen who is queen in name only, her sister, Princess Jutta, for whom morality is something to be discovered through bitter experience, the very young Prince Bengt with his loyalty to his mother's memory and his keen desire to serve the church, the wise Bishop Kol, who takes his vows seriously, and the wily French astrologer, who seizes every opportunity to benefit personally from the superstitious fears and hopes of the great earl. All these minor characters not only throw a great deal of light on a semibarbaric young Stockholm and an old Sweden emerging from paganism into the Christian era, and help to interpret the central character and his problems, but also are alive in their own right.

Even more important than these are Ivar Blå, the lord who served Earl Birger as his personal nemesis; Hans, Prince Magnus' court fool; and Prince Magnus, the only one of Earl Birger's sons capable of matching wits and deeds with his father.

In his essay on the historical drama, Strindberg calls particular attention to Hans, Prince Magnus' court fool, who has a special function to perform: "The fool is the voluntary slave who glorifies the earl's achievement in establishing humane laws; but he is also the *raisonneur* as in Shakespeare, where he sings out what all the others think; he is the voice of the people or the Greek chorus, which comments on the action of the drama, warns, and exhorts." [3] But, as Strindberg says, Hans, unlike most fools or clowns in historical dramas, does develop as a character. Strindberg supplies the details about his family background, his individualizing qualities, his progress at court, and his development as a human being. He is indeed made to come alive.

It is the characterization of Earl Birger that engaged Strindberg's major interest, however. The very core of that characterization is the following confession of faith and frank statement of his concept of life:

EARL: I'll throw my mask away, Wilibald; now I know life and people, and I want to use my dearly purchased wisdom. Human beings? Say scoundrels! Friends? Accomplices in crime—they're friends! Love? Say hate! All people hate each other! My children hate me as I hate them! Every morning they come to ask about my health in the hope that I'm ill. If I ask about something, they lie to me! If I didn't have spies, I'd be deceived every time. On my latest birthday they brought me flowers and filled me with lies! If I ask Magnus how his brother Valdemar is getting along with his wife, he says they're happy, so devilishly happy, though Valdemar is living in open adultery! And these foreign ambassadors, who came to wish me luck—what they wish me is misfortune! But I played the fox with them! The art of governing! Write falsely, promise in order not to keep, fool them into making promises. Business and commerce, deceit! I sat down with Hamburg's and Lübeck's pickpockets today! Bishops? Swine! The pope . . .

ASTROLOGER: People don't say things like that!

EARL *(removes outer garments and takes off his hair shirt)*: Yes, in the darkness of the night when the lights are out and people are asleep! Then a person takes off everything and shows himself in all his nakedness. You know, Wilibald, I believe I'm a heathen, and have always been, though I haven't known it! What do I believe in? This! My fist! *(Strikes the table)* But this, my hair shirt, I don't believe in, and never have! Now I'll throw it in the fire!

ASTROLOGER: Earl Birger!

EARL: And, if there are more troublemakers still, they may meet me at Herrevad's Bridge or in hell, and I'll have their heads! With or without safe-conduct . . .

Strindberg's interpretation of Earl Birger is that of a heroic barbarian, a Viking placed as it were in the transition between paganism and the ascendancy of Christianity. A highly intelligent human being, Strindberg's Earl Birger not only has confidence in himself and his basically idealistic goal but has thought through the implications of man and human society. Since he despises human beings even while he pities them, he does not believe that they are capable of either unselfish or decent conduct. He does believe that the exceptional man of ideas and action can keep subjects orderly with a clearly defined legal system and that he as that exceptional man should have the ultimate earthly rewards, actual and symbolic.

Strindberg traces with great care the development of the heroic barbarian who has no faith in the gods, pagan or Christian, but who is to a degree superstitiously aware that there may be powers beyond human understanding. Proud and arrogant about himself and his capacities, Earl Birger is willing to use anyone and any fairly safe means to achieve his own ends. He is willing to submit and to resign himself to loss of power only when he meets his match in his second son, who, a believing Christian, receives both power and crown and can carry on the program Earl Birger has achieved:

> EARL *(after a long pause)*: Are you a Christian, Magnus? I mean, in your very heart!
>
> MAGNUS: I am a Christian, and so I feel justified!
>
> EARL: Karl Folkung is dead. Herrevad's Bridge is atoned for! My saga is over! *(Pause)* Magnus, take the inheritance of the first born; be master and ruler. My son, I forgive what you have done to your father this hour. My king, I hail thee! *(Bows)*
>
> MAGNUS *(rises, uneasy; gives his father his hand)*: Father, Earl Birger, you have never spoken like that, and you must not . . . Are you tired? . . .
>
> EARL: I am tired, of everything, and now I'll go—I'll go to Visingö. I'll walk in the forest, look at the lake, think about what I have lived through, try to be reconciled with the past and to prepare myself for what is ahead.

But, in keeping with his conviction that human beings develop but do not suddenly and finally experience permanent change of temperament, Strindberg shows the earl submitting to his son only because he must and because he has the feeling that he has fathered a real king; he decides to go to exile on Vising Island to try to resign himself and to try to find inner peace. The characterization of Earl Birger is without question one of Strindberg's greatest.

Earl Birger of Bjälbo has not received the attention it deserves from either Swedish scholars or Swedish critics. When the play was produced at the Swedish Theater in March and April, 1909—sixteen performances in all—the audiences, according to the testimony of the critics, liked the play very much, and the critics themselves were kind. The reviewer in *Dagens Nyheter* called the play far better than either *The Last of the Knights* or *The Regent*. Anna Branting (René) in *Stockholm Tidningen* wrote: "There is spirit, life, and vitality in the scenes, a wealth of imagination and variety . . . which does not however disturb the dramatic intensity and suspense. The dialogue has the brilliance—as almost always—of a superb art of dialogue."[4] John Landquist in *Svenska Dagbladet* went so far as to assert: "The future of *Earl Birger of Bjälbo* seems fully secure, it seems to me. The drama is not in any way a loose collection of historical tableaux; it has . . . a completely dominant central character, about whose inner development at the turning point of life there is a sure unity."[5] But *Earl Birger of Bjälbo* has undoubtedly suffered from scholarly and critical concentration of attention on earlier plays and, as theater, from the fact that it has had to compete with other earlier and tried historical plays by Strindberg.

18

Evaluation

If the impression has been left that Strindberg's achievement as a historical dramatist is uneven, that is quite correct. As great theater and as great literature, every one of the historical plays written before the Inferno period, with the exception of the prose *Master Olof* and the so-called verse *Master Olof,* can safely be disregarded. Even though all of them from the first experiment in the genre through the two plays written for Siri bear the impress of a master, they do not have the sustained qualities of good drama or good theater that will make them indispensable reading for the general reader or likely successes on any stage except perhaps as curiosities to be considered on very special occasions. All these early plays will, of course, remain the objects of close scrutiny for the Strindberg scholar.

Twelve—roughly half of his historical dramas—do, however, have the literary qualities that should assure them a permanent place in the reading of the person who wants to know what is best in literature and, with certain qualifications, the potentials of good theater that should assure them a permanent place in the repertoire of the stage. Six of them—here listed in chronological order of the periods represented, not in the order of time of composition or of comparative merit—are Strindbergian tragedies: *The Saga of the Folkungs,*

Engelbrekt, The Last of the Knights, Erik XIV, Gustav Adolf, and *Charles XII;* and six are serious dramas with more than a trace of the tragic experience: *Earl Birger of Bjälbo, The Regent, Master Olof, Gustav Vasa, Queen Christina,* and *Gustav III.* (The plays can, of course, be classified in other ways. *Engelbrekt, The Last of the Knights, The Regent,* and even *Earl Birger of Bjälbo* are folk dramas, too.)

Through these plays Strindberg has given the Swedish people a dramatization of their history from the middle of the thirteenth century to the beginning of the nineteenth—a unique achievement in terms of spread of time and of modern literary quality. The whole pattern of Swedish culture through five centuries is there presented by a literary artist who, while he was not an academic or scholarly historian, was a remarkably widely read and well-informed intellectual. His almost constant delving into Swedish and general history had convinced him that Swedish history is indeed the history of its people and, a fact that had on occasion been given improper emphasis, that Swedish rulers had been exceedingly important members of the Swedish populace. Two matters stood out among his general conclusions from the scrutiny of his nation's history: the never-ending struggle for power and the never-ending search for internal order and harmony. Those two conclusions are the ideas that give unity to the whole sequence of plays. In not a single one of the twelve is either idea missing, even though, as in *Erik XIV,* it may be obscured at times because of the very nature of one or more characters. The treatment of both ideas is, moreover, given depth and meaning, for Strindberg was fascinated by all phases of the cultural pattern evolving down through the ages—economic, political, social, artistic, religious, ethical. Only rarely, as in *Gustav Adolf,* do these matters obtrude; they are almost always part and parcel of the whole fabric of the play.

While centering his attention on Sweden and the Swedes, Strindberg did not limit himself to events that could be considered merely narrowly national but set them within the frames of reference of international events and, what is more important from a literary point of view, within the frames of reference of the timeless and the universal struggle for order and harmony. It is particularly important to emphasize, I think, that Strindberg had a theory of history based on reading, observation, thinking, and feeling, and that theory included a firm faith in deity (or, as he put it on various occasions, God, the Eternal One, the Powers, Providence, or the Conscious Will) and a genuine conviction that the individual human being has at least a measure of freedom of the will. That faith and that conviction gave meaning and significance to his historical characters; they are at no point mere puppets or automatons in a deterministic world. (Significantly enough, in the late 1880's and early 1890's when he toyed with naturalism and tried to accept determinism, he composed no historical plays.)

Interesting and informative as his interpretation of Swedish and world history may be, his twelve plays about Swedish history would not merit classification as great theater and great literature on that basis alone. The element which above all others warrants such a classification is Strindberg's central interest—human beings. But that interest is no simple matter. It is a matter neither of mere sympathy with his fellow human beings nor of intellectual curiosity about the more or less haphazard human results of the evolutionary process. It is instead an exceedingly complicated matter which involves human beings as they are individually, the society in which they must have their existence, the very nature of existence, the force or forces that can and do affect human beings, and the possible significance of human experience.

Strindberg regularly accepted as a fact the belief that human beings are products of their heredity and even more of their environment. That assumption, based on the very ideas dominating much of the intellectual life of his time, led to the conclusions so clearly stated in the preface to *Lady Julie,* conclusions that made it imperative for him to consider people as complex and dynamic beings, no two of them exactly identical but everyone of them proof of the infinite variety within mankind. Never too far removed from the Biblical context of his early training, he saw people as mixtures of good and evil, fascinating compounds of strength and weakness. It is such a concept that permitted Strindberg to bring alive in his historical dramas not only the great figures of the Swedish past but also an amazing number of the near-greats, the average, and the less fortunate people surrounding them. One of the many rewarding aspects of doing research within the area of his historical dramas has been to run across bits of confirming evidence, one after another, of Strindberg's gift for understanding people. No two of his royal figures, for example, are identical, all of them are complex and dynamic, and Swedish actors and actresses have admitted frankly and on occasion with amazement the overwhelming possibilities in a Strindberg characterization. Consider *Gustav III*, for example. Until one of Sweden's greatest actors of all time—Lars Hansson—created the role of the eighteenth-century king in 1916, it had been generally assumed that the play was a monstrosity and the characterizations feeble. In general, that sort of experience seems to have been common in the early days. Too little close and imaginative scrutiny of the play itself and too much attention to what "leading critics" had said kept Sweden from enjoying dramatizations of its great heroes and the people about them, the like of which England alone could pretend to have.

While in every one of these plays Strindberg successfully suggests and represents the time and the cultural setting of the particular central character and his fellows, the world in which these human beings had their existence is remarkably similar to that in which we have ours. For Strindberg has avoided romanticizing the past and, in addition to those external matters and ways of thinking and behavior peculiar to a specific period, has concentrated his attention on the human condition, i.e., the human condition that was essentially the same in Earl Birger's thirteenth century as it is today.

Strindberg was always keenly aware of the fact that human beings are finite creatures in a bewildering, confusing world, very little of which even the most gifted among them understand though they may grope uncertainly yet hopefully toward such an understanding. The very limitations placed on man—inadequate senses, the inability to adjust more than relatively slightly to their fellows by curbing their own egos, their drives that are both social and antisocial, their being almost constantly at the mercy of forces outside themselves and stronger than themselves, and their tendency toward optimism and hope in spite of experience and the obviously short span of years granted the individual—are all part of Strindberg's concept of the human condition. Implicit is an attitude toward his fellows of all time that is well expressed in *"Det är synd om människan"* ("Man is to be pitied"), the leitmotiv of his *Dream Play* and Indra's Daughter's statement in that drama: "All these are my children. Each one by himself is good but all that you have to do to turn them into demons is to bring them together."

The most important thing that Strindberg does with his characters in the historical plays is to bring them together—in almost every conceivable sort of situation and always with the conviction that people are never identical but always different from one another, and even the individual is not simply and statically always the same. His theory of the characterless character, based as it was on his observation of himself and others as well as on his reading of psychologists and to a degree on his predecessors, primarily Shakespeare, and modified subtly in Charles XII and Magnus the Good, is basic to an understanding of how Strindberg could manage in his historical dramas to create such a great number of characters, all of whom not only come alive for the sensitive reader but most of whom also have come alive unforgettably for Swedish audiences as Sweden's actors and actresses have re-created them on the stage.

His techniques in the twelve major plays are, of course, primarily realistic-naturalistic, shifting to the expressionistic when necessary, of course, to convey aspects of the human experience that a purely realistic technique of characterization could not suggest. On the whole, however, his technique of characterization is to present his

central characters from as many points of view and in as many sorts
of situations as his intentions and his plot permit; to a remarkable
degree, the same procedure applies to his secondary and minor
characters. We "see" the central characters as men and women
limited by the human condition, involved in numerous roles besides
that of king, queen, regent, or leader struggling for power to carry
through a program. The Strindbergian king, for example, is at once
an individual, a professional man, a husband or a lover, a son, a
father, a friend, an enemy, a religious man, in fact many things. He
is, moreover, not glorified or transfigured into a flawless hero; it is
significant, I think, that the only apotheosis Strindberg ever indulged
in in these plays, the remarkable final scene in *Gustav Adolf,* is
clearly not Strindberg's own evaluation of the king but a summary
of others' opinions through the ages; it is significant, too, that when
Strindberg cut *Gustav Adolf* for the stage, he promptly eliminated
the apotheosis. But what does emerge from Strindbergian characterizations of central characters, whom he considered exceptionally
gifted human beings, is that they are not flawless paragons but
flesh and blood human beings in both their greatness and their little-
ness, in other words, perfectly believable people, who shared with the
rest of humanity the limitations of the human condition.

Strindberg knew the theories of tragedy well, but he adopted none
of them—classical, Shakespearean, Christian, Hegelian, or modern—
to the exclusion of the rest. Nor did he mechanically apply any one
of them in the major plays. Instead, his concept of tragedy apparently is based on his own knowledge of, and interpretation of,
man and the human condition. For Strindberg, the world was
basically moral; evil and good were terms with genuine significance
even if nature as such was essentially hostile to man. Man has his
measure of freedom of the will, Strindberg believed; and men have
in varying degrees the capacity to distinguish between what is right
and what is wrong. Above man, to be sure, are the divine forces who
not only can and do interfere in everyman's life but have placed him
in a natural environment that is far from friendly. Even if man is

subject to all the limitations imposed on him by the very facts of existence and subject, too, to interference at any time, he has, nevertheless, the dignity implicit in choice and in responsibility.

Finite though he may be, the Strindbergian hero finds his life meaningful because human life is meaningful. Ultimately, the struggle of the great Swedes of the past for power resolves itself into a struggle for order and peace for Sweden against the forces of evil, even though the motivations of an Earl Birger, a Gustav Vasa, a Gustav Adolf, a Charles XII, and a Gustav III are not wholly unselfish. Even Engelbrekt, Magnus the Good, and Sten Sture, with purer motives, have their share of selfishness and egotism, and Queen Christina, when awakened from her sleepwalking, is aware of the purpose (twisted though it may be) behind her actions. Erik XIV, tortured as he is by his inner disharmonies and external difficulties, struggles in his rational moments for what is good for the Swedish commons and hands authority to his procurator for that purpose, among others. With the partial exception of Erik XIV, these Strindbergian heroes are keenly aware of themselves as individuals, they have values, they are fundamentally alone, they assume responsibility for what they do, they can and do make choices, and they struggle to master life.

As we have seen, Strindberg classified some of his historical tragedies. *The Saga of the Folkungs* he considered a tragedy of which the basic idea rested on classical and Christian foundations in that King Magnus was sacrificed because of others' guilt. (Strindberg could have added that the play is, in its way, an application of the Hegelian concept that tragedy is brought about through the king's inability to obey two contradictory imperatives.) *Engelbrekt,* Strindberg implied, was also classically conceived and executed, although as he added, in *Samlade skrifter* (L, 246), "[The] final scene is tragic and could be called Swedenborgian." It is this well nigh constant attention to the Biblical or Christian idea that he also emphasized in *The Last of the Knights* and in *Gustav Adolf,* the play that ends in death for the hero and in glorious victory for his cause. Charles XII he labeled a classical drama of character and catastrophe, while *Erik XIV,* which he did not label, is a tragedy that in spite of its concentration on a royal character (and his adviser) is as modern in conception as any tragedy of recent decades could be. The truth about Strindberg's concept of tragedy as applied in his historical dramas seems to lie in his acceptance of the models of his great predecessors on the one hand and in an extension, on the other hand, of the tragic experiences far beyond the narrow limits set by most of them.

For it is not only King Magnus, Engelbrekt, Sten Sture, Erik XIV, Gustav Adolf, and Charles XII, and the heroes of Strindberg's lesser historical tragedies, that share the tragic experience, but Master Olof, Earl Birger of Bjälbo, Gustav Vasa, Queen Christina, Gustav III, and a large number of characters of lower rank and of secondary status partake of it as well. They share both the misery of the human condition and the struggle for victory over the very implications of that misery.

It is in keeping with that fact and his conviction that men and women are highly individualistic that Strindberg also constructed his plots and built his plays. The historical records and other accounts determined, of course, the essential and broad outlines of all the plots, but the innumerable plans, sketches, and notes for the plays in the manuscript division of the Royal Library reveal that every one of them was planned and replanned until Strindberg had reached a solution that, while it did not essentially depart from the broad outline of history, fitted very subtly indeed his concept of the particular central character whose story he was dramatizing. Hence, the remarkable variety of plots as well as the variety in the characterizations. It is true, of course, that he was guilty of anachronisms on occasion, that he deliberately compressed history and concealed the fact by rarely mentioning dates, and that now and then—particularly in *Earl Birger of Bjälbo*—he rearranged historical facts. But he did these things largely because he wanted to give his historical plays forms that would be dramatic and would not, as was true of the works of most of his Swedish predecessors, dramatize a series of episodes in the manner of the chronicle play. He did these things, too, because of his conviction that even in the historical drama the most important matter is the individual human being whose story is being told.

How varied the plots are will be clear to anyone who contemplates them in terms of Strindberg's concepts of the central characters. *Queen Christina* and *Gustav III* are Strindbergian adaptations of the French well-made play, to be sure; they have plots that have been deliberately constructed to give the effects of artificiality and theatricality. But that the plays themselves have much more than the artificial and the theatrical, than moves and countermoves, is clear to any reader: Strindberg knew that both Queen Christina and Gustav III were far more complex than the term "crowned actress" or "crowned actor" implies. Engelbrekt, Sten Sture, the young Gustav Vasa, and even Earl Birger are folk heroes. Strindberg constructed the plots of those plays to strike audiences as in keeping with the traditional plots of the folk drama but injected into *Engelbrekt, The Last of the Knights, The Regent,* and *Earl Birger of Bjälbo* the life-giving Strindbergian characterization and other techniques that raise them above all other Swedish folk dramas.

For the original prose version of *Master Olof* he adapted the sort of plot Shakespeare used frequently: the blend of major episodes and minor ones designed to tell the reformer's story in terms of his evolving goal, his external and inner conflicts, his time and place, and his immediate environment. His choice of a relatively loose structure to carry a far from simple and straightforward story was happy indeed. All one needs to do to be convinced of that is to compare the prose play with the so-called verse *Master Olof,* in which Strindberg compromised his sense for the thoroughly effective dramatic by converting his plot (and more) to fit the contemporary preference for the traditionally artificial structure of a historical drama. The prose *Master Olof* makes the reformer come alive; moreover, it has proved eminently successful on the stage. Or, compare the prose *Master Olof* with *Gustav Vasa,* which is a model of the concentrated plot and tightness of structure. Such a plot and such a structure are peculiarly suitable to a play about a central character who is always the center of attention and who is not, like Strindberg's Master Olof, one of several men striving to guide and direct events in a community virtually without order and harmony. The one great illustrative episode of *Gustav Vasa,* skillfully, naturally, and almost imperceptibly divided into its component parts and exploited with the sure art of a master dramatist, conveys unforgettably the story of a miracle man of God with one undeviating basic goal and contrasts beautifully with the necessarily less direct, frequently fluctuating, often deviating story of the young reformer.

Then there is *Erik XIV,* in which Strindberg happily had the audacity to use a plot involving two central characters in defiance of previously accepted practice but in keeping with the historical accounts and with his own sense for what is correct dramatically—in terms of his own concept of the strangely rational and irrational king and his decidedly rational procurator. "Without Göran, no Erik!" The productions of *Erik XIV* have confirmed without question the effectiveness of Strindberg's departure from a principle of dramatic structure which is usually valid and desirable.

For *Gustav Adolf,* Strindberg selected a monumental and episodic plot designed to tell the story of a king who had played a far greater and more substantial role in world history than any other Swedish ruler. As a result, the play presents challenges of production that have not yet been met; it is even possible that the theaters of our time are not yet such, either in equipment or stage capacity, that any one of them could conceivably undertake the production of the monumental, sprawling drama which for the reader conveys superbly Strindberg's interpretation of the heroic king. Of all the forms available to drama, the film alone could begin to do justice to *Gustav Adolf* with its epic and panoramic proportions. Judicious cutting— and Strindberg himself tried it and was not opposed to it—could most likely bring the play with its involved plot within the limitations of the contemporary stage.

Imaginative and gifted Swedish producers have over the past thirty years and more demonstrated that the poetically conceived and composed *The Saga of the Folkungs* has the sort of plot and dramatic structure that lend themselves well to the modern stage. In keeping with Strindberg's concept of Magnus the Good, the play is a blend of realistic structure and highly poetic expressionistic elements that permits everyone from the director to the humblest super to participate in an unsurpassable dramatic experience and that also is just right for telling the story of a man Strindberg considered one of Sweden's most admirable kings and through his story the story of one of Sweden's great dynasties. Even the final act, with its quiet narration of the family's past, is amazingly effective in conveying Strindberg's concept and intention.

Remarkable as all the eleven other plays are in their variety of structure and characterization, none of them is as decidedly different from all other historical dramas as *Charles XII*. Selecting the final years of the king's life as the basis of his interpretation, Strindberg constructed a plot that on a superficial level resembles the plots of his realistic plays in so far as care of selecting events and relating them go. But the infusion of a predominantly expressionistic technique into all the acts but one subtly underscores what Strindberg here tried to do. The elements of plot, the external events, give way again and again to the inner state of the king and to the inner states of the people about him. In *The Saga of the Folkungs* he on occasion definitely and overwhelmingly subordinated the external events to the inner states and moods; only in *Charles XII* has he made realism give way to expressionism. The result is a remarkably good play, loosely constructed as it may seem to the reader who insists on the observation of the criteria of realism but amazingly rewarding to the reader or to the actors and director who surrender themselves to Strindberg's intention and expressionistic technique.

What can be said about Strindberg's plots by way of summary is that they are exceedingly carefully planned and constructed to serve as effective vehicles for conveying his understanding of the central characters involved. Since he saw no two of these as identical, the plots in turn usually obviously and frequently subtly differ from each other.

What may make some readers who consider Strindberg's historical dramas for the first time feel that his plays are very much like one another is his consistent use of a mass of dramatic techniques designed to give dramatic effectiveness to his plays. In all of the twelve major historical plays, even *Charles XII,* Strindberg, ever keenly aware of the fact that his characters were the re-creation of actual human beings who in their day had been flesh and blood people like himself or his contemporaries, proceeded from the assumption that their stories involved cause and effect, fairly logical patterns of development, and the factors of chance and change. Consequently, he has made exceedingly painstaking use of such devices as natural exposition and foreshadowing or preparation of the kind he employed in his great realistic-naturalistic plays of the second half of the 1880's, but he has refrained from carrying the techniques through to the point where they become merely artificial and distressingly obvious. His exposition is that of life itself, almost always carefully but naturally interwoven into the dialogue.

There are, moreover, a host of other devices such as parallel actions, effective use of comparison and contrast, folk scenes (in some of the plays such as *Master Olof, The Saga of the Folkungs* and the folk dramas), poetic use of symbolism, occasional telling use of the flashback, and, as important as any, the use of Strindbergian dialogue.

That dialogue does not have a poetic verbal magic like Shakespeare's, but it does have a magic all its own, consisting ultimately of the magic of actual conversation between genuinely alive and alert people. Colloquial language adapted to each particular character and ranging from the sharp cutting give-and-take of blunt exchange (for example, in the scenes between Queen Blanche and her royal mother-in-law) to the gentle accents of the queen in the presence of her dying son and daughter-in-law, is, in general, the major characteristic of Strindbergian dialogue: colloquial speech adapted with care to the particular speaker and his particular mood or purpose. On occasion, the dialogue can become poetic prose, as in Gert's moving appeal for freedom or the Madwoman's prophetic revelations. It is, in general, the kind of dialogue eminently suited for the stage; with its manifold nuances of potent meaning it is a dialogue that not only challenges the actor to make full use of his gifts but also permits him to participate in the process of creating verbal magic of a kind highly suited to the modern theater and to modern man.

These twelve major plays are, I believe, a unique gift to a nation in our time; not only do they dramatize effectively Strindberg's understanding of the history of Sweden from the thirteenth century to the nineteenth, but all of them are such dramatic masterpieces that they deserve not only to be read but—with the single exception of *Gustav Adolf* in its uncut form—to be produced. Such a statement should not imply insuperable difficulties in a country as fortunately endowed as Sweden is with theaters, audiences, producers, and actors.

For the international theater the folk dramas and *Gustav Adolf* will possibly not have the appeal that the other seven—the prose *Master Olof, The Saga of the Folkungs, Gustav Vasa, Erik XIV, Queen Christina, Charles XII,* and *Gustav III*—could have as excellent drama and excellent theater. Every one of the seven has been so well written with an eye to the stage that the mere fact that Swedish history is not well known abroad need not deter either producer or actor. While it may still be true that older generations of American theater audiences are fairly well acquainted with the broad outlines of English history and so can appreciate Shakespeare's historical dramas, it is also true that younger generations who do not know much about early English kings and queens enjoy the Shakespearean plays nevertheless. If *Erik XIV* could become a sensational success in Moscow, as it did in 1921, there is no good reason why it or any of the other six could not do as well in New York or in any other large American city.

Hermione (and its earlier version, *Det sjunkande Hellas, Greece in Its Decline*), *In Rome, The Outlaw, The Secret of the Guild, Lord Bengt's Wife,* and *The Nightingale of Wittenberg* will, I suspect, have little interest for anyone but the Strindberg scholar and the literary historian, largely because they do not have sufficient literary merit and theatrical finish to compete with Strindberg's twelve major historical plays or with historical dramas written by others. The *Moses-Socrates-Christ* trilogy may conceivably serve effectively within a decidedly minor area of dramatic art but surely will do no more than that.

It is the cycle about Swedish rulers that stamps Strindberg as the major modern contributor to the genre, and no objective reader who examines these plays with care is likely to fail to recognize them as a unique contribution, not only to Swedish literature and the Swedish stage but also to world literature and, with certain qualifications I have indicated, to world theater. Seven of the plays have already, as I have said, stood the test of successful production on the stage; four of them—*Earl Birger of Bjälbo, Engelbrekt, The Last of the Knights,* and *The Regent*—deserve, because of their dramatic and theatrical merits, that sort of test at least on the Swedish stage. It is even conceivable that *Gustav Adolf,* in spite of its length and unwieldy structure, can eventually get the sort of production needed in a Sweden where brilliant producers have not hesitated to produce O'Neill plays that equal it in challenge. In the meanwhile, even *Gustav Adolf* will remain one of the finest literary interpretations of one of Sweden's great kings and leaders who is at the same time one of the great men in world history.

Bibliographic and Other Notes

THE standard but far from definitive Swedish edition of Strindberg's works is John Landquist's *Strindbergs Samlade skrifter* (55 vols.; Stockholm: Bonnier, 1912-20). All of the historical dramas except *Moses-Socrates-Christ* and *Det sjunkande Hellas* appear in the Landquist edition.

The trilogy about world history was printed in G. Carlheim-Gyllensköld's *Samlade otryckta skrifter* (2 vols.; Stockholm: Bonnier, 1918-19), and *Det sjunkande Hellas,* the first version of *Hermione,* was published by Bokgillet (Uppsala, 1960).

Not all the historical dramas have been translated into English. Specific information about translations is included in the notes on each play below.

The best available brief English treatment of Strindberg's work in general is Alrik Gustafson's in *A History of Swedish Literature* (Minneapolis: University of Minnesota Press, 1961), pp. 243-75; unfortunately, he says relatively little about most of the historical plays. In Swedish, the best considerations of Strindberg's general contributions are Sven Rinman's "Strindberg," in *Ny illustrerad svensk litteraturhistoria* (Stockholm: Bonnier, 1957), IV, 31-145, and E. N. Tigerstedt's *Svensk litteraturhistoria* (Stockholm: Bonnier, 1948), pp. 383-97. Each of these three histories of literature also contains excellent bibliographies, all of them with critical commentaries.

For English readers, the annual bibliographies published in *Scandinavian Studies (SS)* and *Publications of the Modern Language Association (PMLA)* are useful. The bibliographies published in *Samlaren* are indispensable for the Strindberg scholar. Elizabeth Sprigge's *The Strange Life of August Strindberg* (London: Macmillan & Co., 1949) is useful as an introduction to Strindberg biography.

In 1959, Professor Walter Berendsohn—partly as a result of examining my five-volume American edition of the major historical plays—published a series of three highly interesting articles on Strindberg's historical plays in *Värld och Vetande* IX, 268-74; X, 303-10; XI, 340-48; XII, 377-82 (a continuation of the article in Vol. XI). His approach is largely stylistic.

Special studies are listed in the notes on the various chapters.

In the notes I have given the original of all quotations from newspapers and other sources not likely to be easily available to readers in English-speaking countries.

Strindberg's spelling, as Swedish scholars know, was not always consistent either before or after 1906.

Chapter 1

1. Letter to Schering, Dec. 12, 1902. The correspondence between Strindberg and his principal German translator, Emil Schering, is preserved in the archives of Bonniers Bokförlag, Stockholm. The original reads: "Efter Fagervik insåg jag att en paus måste inträda i mitt författeri, och som tidsfördrif läste jag midt igenom världshistorien. Denna underliga Geschichte som alltid förefallit mig som en Röfvarroman, uppenbarade sig nu som diktad af En medveten Vilja, och jag fann Logik i dess Antinomier, En Resultant af dess stridiga komposanter. Sålunda fann jag straxt i början att verldsanden uppenbarade sig samtidigt på flera ställen af jordklotet utan att dessa ställen stodo i förbindelse med hvarandra. Exempel: Samtidigt med Mose Lag på Sinai (1300 B.C.) fick Indien Rigveda, Grekland Orfeus . . . Kina Schi-King. Detta är icke slump! —Undersökningarne fortsattes synkronistiskt och 'Den medvetna Viljan' i historien var konstaterad."

2. All quotations from the Landquist edition (John Landquist, *Strindbergs Samlade skrifter,* 55 vols.; Stockholm: Bonnier, 1912-20) are presented only in translated form, since that edition is readily available. All the quotations in this chapter are from Vol. LIV; the page numbers are given at the end of each quotation.

3. Although relatively brief treatments or comments on Strindberg's

ideas about history exist, the only book-length treatment is Harry V. E. Palmblad's *Strindberg's Conception of History* (New York: Columbia University Press, 1927), a useful but far from definitive treatment of the subject.

Chapter 2

In *Handskriftsavdelningen* (the manuscript division) of the Royal Library are preserved extensive collections of Strindberg's notes, sketches, outlines, and incomplete fragments of plays. A substantial number of these come from *Gröna säcken* (the green bag), the valise in which Strindberg carried with him materials that he either was working on or that he thought might be useful in the future. The "green bag" apparently proved inadequate in time and spilled over into a second bag. While most of the material is unpublished, some of the fragments were published in G. Carlheim-Gyllensköld's *Samlade otryckta skrifter* (2 vols.; Stockholm: Bonnier, 1918-19).

Chapter 3

While the histories of literature and the biographies all deal in some detail with Strindberg's early effort at dramatic composition, the fullest treatments are those in Martin Lamm's *Strindbergs dramer* (2 vols.; Stockholm: Bonnier, 1924-26).

Edith and Warner Oland's translation of *Den fredlöse* appeared as *The Outlaw* (Boston: Luce, 1912).

1. Gerda Rydell's *Adertonhundratalets historiska skådespel i Sverige före Strindberg* (Stockholm: Bonnier, 1928) and Nils Molin's *Shakespeare och Sverige intill 1800-talets mitt. En oversikt av hans inflytande* (Göteborg: Elander, 1931) are useful accounts both of the historical drama in Sweden before Strindberg's day and of the influence on Swedish writers of historical dramas. For the influence of Shakespeare on Strindberg's historical dramas, see Joan Bulman's *Strindberg and Shakespeare: Shakespeare's Influence on Strindberg's Historical Drama* (London: Jonathan Cape, 1933), and Lamm's *Strindbergs dramer*. No definitive study of the relationship between Strindberg and his predecessors in the genre has yet appeared.

2. See Alrik Gustafson's *A History of Swedish Literature* (Minneapolis: University of Minnesota Press, 1961) for an account of Rydberg's

Den siste athenaren; this was translated by William W. Thomas as *The Last of the Athenians* (Philadelphia: J. B. Lippincott Co., 1869, 1879).

3. *August Strindbergs brev* (Stockholm: Bonnier, 1948———), I, 49: "Hermione är nu hos de aderton vise männen—Gud vare med henne! En kritik kan jag dock vänta mig i hvad fall som helst!'

4. Henrik Schück's *Svenska Akademiens historia,* VII, 204-5: ". . . ett studium ur antikens värld . . . företeende goda enskilda tavlor samt en levande uppfattning av tidsförhållandena."

5. *Strindbergs brev,* I, 58.

6. *Ibid.,* I, 102: "Det förundrar mig högeligen om ingen skulle komma att nämna Bjørnsson som förebild—så bed honom kyssa mig i röfven [*sic*] o. läsa Fornmannasagor så får han se att vi—Björnsson och *Jag* (!) . . . öst ur samma källa."

7. *Ibid.,* I, 80: "Känner Du Hansson—ta honom då mellan fyra ögon— ruska honom; sparka honom (vi högakta honom ändå) föreställ honom hvad det vill säga att vara den siste vikingen—bed honom läsa Geijers 'Den sista kämpen'—men bed honom också besinna att författaren vill se mer än en rutten, envis, hårdnackad gubbe som blir stukad af qvinfolk— säg att jag vill en sjelftillräcklig menniska som tvingas erkänna ett högsta väsende en Titan en Prometheus som slåss mot gudarne eller en Kung Fjalar som utmanar ödet—ja säg honom allt hvad Du kan—bed honom leta i sitt minne efter någon djup sorg—riktigt djup, om han haft lyckan att ega en sådan—bed honom ställa den för sig när han säger detta enda 'Gunlöd!'—då hon vägrar att dricka."

8. *Ibid.,* I, 84: "När jag i går läste om den Fredlöse fann jag tyvärr honom så olik sig mot hvad han var i sitt ursprungliga skick att bättre varit han tillika med sina föregångare blifvit bränder än af hvar man känder! Alla gubbarna ha blifvit så eländigt sentimentala—den der iskylan har försvunnit—den nordiska stoicismen är weg och stycket har en helt annan färg—allt det der kommer man väl att kasta i ansigtet på mig —må gå! lycka är att jag är så upptagen att föga tid är mig öfrig att skänka åt deras—recensenternas lärdomar—hvilka jag dock med tacksamhet motser—då man ej kan märka sina egna fel."

9. "Men i den 20-åriga Strindbergs koncentrerade skildring av kristendomens brottning med hedendomen, personifierad i den självgode Torfinn, som till slut blir knäckt och osäker, finns det gnistor af kraft och

originalitet, som gjorde att man följde stycket med en viss spänning, hur skematiska figurerna än äro."

Chapter 4

Translations of the prose *Master Olof*: Edwin Björkman's, with an introduction (New York: The American-Scandinavian Foundation, 1915); C. D. Locock's and Joan Bulman's (London: The Anglo-Swedish Literary Foundation, 1931); and Walter Johnson's, with an introduction, *The Vasa Trilogy: Master Olof, Gustav Vasa, Erik XIV* (Seattle: University of Washington Press, 1959). All quotations from the play are from my translation. The few quotations from the so-called verse form of *Master Olof* are my own translations.

Aside from Martin Lamm's *Strindbergs dramer* (2 vols.; Stockholm: Bonnier, 1924-26), Vol. I, the most important of the extensive scholarly treatments of *Master Olof* are Per Lindberg's *Tillkomsten av Strindbergs "Mäster Olof"* (Stockholm: Bonnier, 1915) and E. Lindström's *Strindbergs Mäster Olof-dramer* (Göteborg: Elander, 1921), detailed considerations of the evolution of the various versions of the play; Hanna Rydh's *De historiska källorna till Strindbergs "Mäster Olof"* (Stockholm: Bonnier, 1915), a fairly satisfactory introduction to Strindberg's use of sources for historical details; Joan Bulman's *Strindberg and Shakespeare: Shakespeare's Influence on Strindberg's Historical Drama* (London: Jonathan Cape, 1933) and Hans Andersson's *Strindberg's Mäster Olof and Shakespeare* (Uppsala: Lundequist, 1952); A. Hagsten's *Den unge Strindberg: Studier kring Tjänstekvinnans son och ungdomsverken* (2 vols.; Stockholm: Bonnier, 1951); and Carl Reinhold Smedmark's *Mäster Olof och Röda rummet* (Stockholm: Almqvist & Wiksell, 1952).

The definitive edition of *Mäster Olof* is Smedmark's *Mäster Olof* in *Svenska författare utgivna av Svenska vitterhetssamfundet*, Vol. XIX.

There is no thoroughly complete study of *Master Olof* (or any other major Strindberg play) on the Swedish or foreign stage. Yngve Hedvall's *Strindberg på Stockholmsscenen 1870-1922* (Stockholm: Lundstrom, 1923) is useful but incomplete and at times, unfortunately, inaccurate.

1. *August Strindbergs brev* (Stockholm: Bonnier, 1948——), I, 109: "Jag håller på med 4de akten på mitt femaktstycke, i en spritt ny tidsenlig stil."

2. All the quotations from *Öppna brev till Intima teatern* are from

Vol. L of John Landquist's *Strindbergs Samlade skrifter* (55 vols.; Stockholm: Bonnier, 1912-20).

3. *Ibid.*, XIX, 37.

4. *Strindbergs brev*, IV, 306: "Det hela är en otjenst K.T. gör mig! Ville det göra mig en tjenst, så spelade den M. Olof i 4e upplagan, som är ett väl arbetadt stycke, och vore Ni raska karlar, så tog Ni och uppförde Mysteriet också! Der hade du en rol för resten! Stycket i 4e kan af mig få uppföras i Sthlm, ty N.T. har bara köpt det 'i den form det i mina Samlade ungdomsarbeten' förekommer!' "

5. *Ibid.*, I, 166: "Theaterstycket Olaus Petri har jag genomläst och tar mig nu friheten säga Er mina tankar om detsamma. Det börjar med en högst intressant dialog som spänner förväntningar—hvilka icke motsvaras; de stora verldsbekanta namnen tyckas mig icke uppburna som sig bör; man ser icke de trådar, får icke veta de orsaker som föranleda händelserna. Med fullt erkännande af styckets vackra tendens kan jag, på grund af ofvanstående, icke uppföra detsamma, hvarföre jag härmed har äran återsända det."

6. *Ibid.*, I, 165: "Om jag vore förmögen skulle jag rätteligen förstöra föregående manuskript och göra om saken från början. Detta är omöjligt. Att göra något annat kan jag icke och ändock måste jag, ty den dramatiska konsten är ju så svår och fordrar öfning. Jag har fyllt 26 år och har nu icke öfvat mig på länge. Min pjes hade urartat till en fix idé, för hvilken jag under två års tid försakade allt och ruinerade min ekonomiska ställning. För att reparera denna är jag nu privatlärare, tjenstgörande i Biblioteket, öfversättare och skötare af följetong i en daglig tidning. På de lediga stunderna skola temaböcker rättas och lexor prepareras. Under sådana förhållanden kan jag icke företaga något nytt och begär det icke heller. Jag ger mig på nåd och onåd och vill göra om mitt stycke om jag har nagon utsigt att kunna få det fram."

7. *Ibid.*, I, 169: "Mäster Olof har gått åt helvete också!"

8. "Den historiske M. Olof är i få ord: 'En het och framfusig man' som hvarken litade på Furstar eller underklass, anarkist i ungdomen, anklagad för medvetenhet om mordanslag mot konungen. Sedan, längre fram skref han sin krönika som misshagade Gustaf Vasa, emedan M. Olof skildrat de Katolska biskoparne alltför sympatiskt, hvaraf konungen slöt att M. Olof var ångerköpt på reformationen och nu återfått ett 'papistiskt conscience.' . . . Och de svaga ögonblicken hos M.O.

är bara tillfällig trötthet, och hör icke till karakteren. Har ni fått andra instruktioner, så slunga dem. Endast jag är kompetent att tolka rolen!"

9. "Det är ingen elegisk Hamlet, utan en 'arg karl.' 'Den bleke kaniken,' hvass i logiken; tänker mycket etc. Att slås med en sådan, det må sjelfver saten. . . . en man af stångjern, med en oerhördsjelfkänsla som icke är sympatisk och icke bryr sig om att vara det. De flesta framställare ha felat deri att de spelat med värme, i stället för med eld, och att de icke brytt sig om författarens karakteristik, utan velat vara sympatiska eller kokettera för publiken, visat sig söndersliten och rörande. Detta sätt att förtolka en rol subjecktivt, medför den olägenheten att det hela blir falskt. Ty när framställningen af figuren icke stämmer med den karakteristik som afges af de andra medspelande, så svär ju rolen mot skildringen af densamma (butter, stursk, kung etc.). Hela hans tal är öfvermodigt, hvem han än må tala med, biskop, kung eller dräng. . . . Kraft nästan brutalitet: eld, men icke s.k. värme; äfven vid modrens död är han hård, men öfvermannas af sömn och trötthet som han sjelf säger. . . . Dramat är skrifvet för 40 år sedan: många ha spelat Er rol, de flesta som Hamlet. . . . Låt oss nu, i nya Hvita Huset, se min M. Olof, vår Luther! 'för första gången?' "

The letter is also quoted in the article, "Aug. Strindbergs egna direktiv för 'Mäster Olof' (August Strindberg's Own Directions for *Master Olof"*) in *Stockholms Tidningen* of August 27, 1920.

10. *Knittelvers* consists usually of rhymed couplets with four to seven feet per verse. Both rhyme and rhythm are treated with great freedom. The quoted passages may be freely translated: "Sleep, oh sleep, I shall not/ disturb your dreams! Take, oh take,/ holy sleep, peace on your wings/ you, who relieve everything and conquer pain./ Blessed morning, if thou art already awake/ come in and receive my God's peace!/ See the smoke already rising over the roofs/ like sacrificial fires, lighted for the work of day/ by the children of toil on the dark hearths."

11. *Strindbergs brev*, II, 17: "Stjernström förklarade att han ej hade råd att göra nya dekorationer. Alltså fem mina bästa år strukna ur mitt lif!"

12. *Ibid.*, II, 230: "För den händelse Herr Josephson ännu har några tankar på uppförandet af mitt stycke Mäster Olof, skickar jag härmed det första manuskriptet (tryckt) sådant det skrefs 1872 och sådant det då refuserades af K. Teatern. Det är nog dåligt, det tror jag, men der

finnes, i prosaversionen, folkscener, hvilka skulle kunna göra sig förträffligt på scenen, i synnerhet om Herr Josephson tog hand om dem."

13. *Ibid.,* II, 231: "Jag skyndar mig, efter genomläsningen af 'Mäster Olof' i styckets ursprungliga form, förklara att jag på många år ej läst ett drama som på mig gjort ett så öfverväldigande intryck. Jag förklarar rent ut, att det skall ha varit den kortsyntaste, okonstnärligaste, lataste och mest osvenska teaterstyrelse som refuserat att antaga detta stycke till spelning."

14. *Ibid.,* II, 353: ". . . jeg har haft Grund til at fryde mig derover, thi 'Mester Oluf' har paa Nya Teatern haft en glimrende Sukces."

15. In *Post-och Inrikes Tidningar* on January 11, 1882.

16. In *Dagens Nyheter* on February 3, 1920, under the heading " 'Mäster Olof' på Det kongelige" (*Master Olof* at the Royal Theater [of Copenhagen]), Söderberg wrote: "*Hamlet, Kameliadamen* (ursäkta!), *Vildanden* . . . Och även *Mäster Olof* hör till dem. . . . Han har fångat stämningen, fläkten och suset av den tid han ville måla, emedan det alltsammans brusade genom honom själv. Och dramats växlande scenbilder etsa sig in i ögat och minnet, emedan de äro fyllda till brädden av ett dramatiskt liv, som stundom spränger ramen, men aldrig låter den vara till för sin egen skull."

17. "Det var konventionalismkulturens hela stupiditet, representerad främst av Svenska akademien—naturligtvis—och teaterintendenten Frans Hedberg, som Strindbergs ungdomsverk förgäves sökte bryta igenom. Den tidens tongivande litteraturkritik var knappt intelligentare än våra dagars, även om den uppträdde under mera polerade former."

Chapter 5

English translations of the two plays have not yet been published.

The most illuminating accounts of these plays are Strindberg's own— in *The Son of a Servant* and in the preface to *Giftas.* The fullest Swedish account is Martin Lamm's in *Strindbergs dramer* (2 vols.; Stockholm: Bonnier, 1924-26), Vol. I.

1. *August Strindbergs brev* (Stockholm: Bonnier, 1948———), I, 386: "Något nytt stycke har jag ej färdigt, men tänker till hösten komma med en qvinnopjes—allt för min hustrus skull!"

2. John Landquist, *Strindbergs Samlade skrifter* (55 vols.; Stockholm: Bonnier, 1912-20), XIX, 171.

3. *Ibid.*

4. The translations of quoted excerpts from the plays are mine.

5. Landquist, *Samlade skrifter,* XXIII, 104.

6. *Ibid.,* XIV, 34-35.

Chapter 6

Translations: C. D. Locock's and Joan Bulman's (London: Anglo-Swedish Literary Foundation, 1931) and Walter Johnson's *The Saga of the Folkungs; Engelbrekt* (Seattle: University of Washington Press, 1959).

All quotations from the play are from my translation.

The major treatments of *The Saga of the Folkungs* are in Martin Lamm's *Strindbergs dramer* (2 vols.; Stockholm: Bonnier, 1924-26), Vol. II; Joan Bulman, *Strindberg and Shakespeare: Shakespeare's Influence on Strindberg's Historical Drama* (London: Jonathan Cape, Ltd., 1933); and the standard Swedish histories of Swedish literature. For an analysis of the play and for the historical background, see the introduction and the notes in my translation.

Yngve Hedvall, in *Strindberg på Stockholmsscenen 1870-1922* (Stockholm: Lundstrom, 1923), gives incomplete information about *The Saga of the Folkungs* on the Stockholm stage up until 1922. The drama has had highly successful production over the years. See for a brief account Gunnar Ollén's *Strindbergs dramatik* (Stockholm: Radiotjänst, 1948, 1961).

1. The best account of the Inferno crisis is Gunnar Brandell's *Strindbergs Infernokris* (Stockholm: Bonnier, 1950). Elizabeth Sprigge's *The Strange Life of August Strindberg* (London: Macmillan & Co., 1949) contains a fairly good summary based on Strindberg's autobiographical volumes, two of which are available in English (Claude Field's translation of *The Inferno,* London: Rider, 1912; and *Legends: Autobiographical Sketches,* London: Rider, 1912).

2. See particularly Johan Mortensen's *Från Röda rummet till sekelskiftet,* Vols. I and II (Stockholm: Bonnier, 1918, 1919); Hedvall, *Strindberg på Stockholmsscenen 1870-1922;* and Ingvar Andersson's *A History of Sweden* (London: Weidenfeld and Nicolson, 1956).

3. Plan A:

Akt I: *Stockholms Slottsgård.* Fogden. Man ser fönstret till fängelset der prins Magnus sutit. Knektar breda ut en röd matta. En kubbe; en bila. Det spökar./ Tornering.

Akt II: Modern uppdagas.

Akt III: *Stockholms Slottsgård.* Fogden./ Sonens uppror./ Fadren Hertig Erik afslöjas. Birger hade rätt; men var Syndabocken. Skilnad från Blanche.

Akt IV: Digerdöden./ Eriks död. Menniskoffret som fordrades för pestens upphörande.

Akt V: *Stockholms Slottsgård.* Fogden./ Vadstena Kloster.

Plan B:

Akt I: Sal i Stockholms Slott. Porträtten. Birgitta profeterar./ Torget. Intåg.

Akt II: Begrafningsbjudning på slottet./ Stämplingar.

Akt III: Eriks uppror.

Akt IV: Digerdöden bebådades af gräshoppor, jordbäfvningar. Flagellanter hungersnöd. Mennisko offring.

Akt V: Magnus bannlyst./ Vadstena Kloster.

4. John Landquist, *Strindbergs Samlade skrifter* (55 vols.; Stockholm: Bonnier, 1912-20), L, 245.

5. Carton 1, Number 4: "Konung Magnus. Försoningsoffret som skall vara rent. Blod i kronan. Allt hvad han gör förvränges—besmutsas"; "K. Magnus vill undvika faran af hertigar och gör konungar i stället."

6. *Ibid.*: "Magnus: God, hänsynsfull, rättänkande; kristen. Tänker godt, talar af princip väl om alla: Blir derför nedtrampad och föraktad af alla parter, sedan först varit allmänt omtyckt. Han får pligta för andras grymheter, dumheter och öfvermod. Är så van få skulden att han aldrig kommer sig för utröna om han har skulden eller ej. *Skyll på mig.* Upplyst despot. Qväser herrarne: Störtas af folket. Straffar ingen; flott man utan småaktigheter; kallas slapp. Allt hvad han gör häcklas. Alla hans dygder tolkas som laster: Är han nedlåtande anses han slusk; är han gifmild kallas han slösare; är han sparsam = girig; är han mild = svag; är han sträng = grymm."

7. Landquist, *Samlade skrifter,* L, 240, 241.

8. Martin Lamm, *Strindbergs dramer* (2 vols.; Stockholm: Bonnier, 1924-26), II, 106-8, for example.

9. Landquist, *Samlade skrifter,* L, 240.

10. *Lycko-Pers resa* has been translated as *Lucky Peter's Travels* (Lon-

don: Anglo-Swedish Literary Foundation, 1930). An allegorical children's play, it presents a youngster's journey through life to the knowledge of what is important in life. In many ways it foreshadows Strindberg's brilliant use of his pilgrimage and symbolic technique in *To Damascus* and other expressionistic plays.

11. "Dramats verkan stegrades från akt till akt, för att vinna sin kulmen i fjärde aktens våldsamma och upprörda torgscener och i slutaktens därmed kontrasterande stilla och veka scener, vilka tillhöra det vackraste som Strindberg någonsin diktat. . . . Personligen ställer jag det främst av alla Strindbergs historiska dramer. Det är en frändskap, en inre samhörighet mellan stoffet och den fantasi, som ombildat detsamma, vilka jag stundom saknar i de andra dramerna. Med vilken länge uppspard kraft, med vilken säkerhet i språnget, vilken njutning över att åter igen känna sin egen styrka griper icke fantasien sitt ämne och fasthåller det sedan i en vild och stormande brottning! . . . Och vad jag i främsta rummet beundrar, det är Strindbergs sätt att behandla massorna, hans förmåga att gjuta liv i detta 'folk,' vars uppgift på scenen annars vanligen inskränker sig till att fylla den och med unison karaktärslöshet ropa ja eller nej till dramats hjältar."

Poet Lore (Vol. XXXII, 1921) published Helga Colquist's translations of two of Tor Hedberg's plays, *Borga Gård, A Play in Four Acts* (pp. 317-74) and *Johan Ulfstjerna, A Drama in Five Acts* (pp. 1-63). Tor Hedberg (1862-1931), dramatist and novelist, made his primary contribution to literature as a critic, however.

Chapter 7

Translations: Edwin Björkman's *Gustavus Vasa* (New York: Charles Scribner's Sons, 1916), also in *Eight Famous Plays by Strindberg*, 1949; C. D. Locock's and Joan Bulman's *Gustav Vasa* (London: Anglo-Swedish Literary Foundation, 1931); and Walter Johnson's *Gustav Vasa* in *The Vasa Trilogy* (Seattle: University of Washington Press, 1959).

All quotations from the play are from my translation.

For an analysis of *Gustav Vasa* and its historical background, see the introduction and the notes in my translation. For Swedish discussions of the play, see the standard histories of literature and particularly Martin Lamm's *Strindbergs dramer* (2 vols.; Stockholm: Bonnier, 1924-26).

For information about *Gustav Vasa* on the stage, see Yngve Hedvall,

Strindberg på Stockholmsscenen 1870-1922 (Stockholm: Lundstrom, 1923), and Gunnar Ollén, *Strindbergs dramatik* (Stockholm: Radiotjänst, 1948, 1961).

1. *Vasa-sagan.* Akt I. Slottsterassen./ Konung Gustaf I's födelsedag firas med tablåer föreställande de vigtigaste händelser ur hans lif./ Akt II./ Akt III./ Akt IV./ Akt V./
Gustaf I.
Akt I. Slotts-terassen. Tablåerna klicka, så att af misstag en skräckta-blå kommer fram som ett varsel. Födelsedag = Prisar sin lycka: Paus: Nemesis hör./ Han talar väl om någon: straxt nederlagd. Olyckorna följa. *Hansa-Kontoret:* Israel = spinner. Daljunker. Dacke. Köpmans-moral.

Akt II. Konungens arbetsrum = Johan. Erik. Ömsesidiga ingifvelser. Eskils gemak = Israel = klockorna: kyrksilfver.

Akt III. Gemak. Magnus och Cecilia = Leka med kronan. Hos Johan = astrologi. Katolik.

Akt IV. Slottssal = slaganfall = möte med Måns Nilsson och Anders Persson. Daljunkaren stödes af Lübeck=Israel. Hos Erik.

Akt V. Sängkammare. Styfmodrens magt är slut.

2. John Landquist, *Strindbergs Samlade skrifter* (55 vols.; Stockholm: Bonnier, 1912-20), L, 347.

3. The barbs were directed even more against *Erik XIV*. See the quotation toward the end of the chapter on that play.

4. Page 633: ". . . outsläckligt dolskt Strindbergshat à la C.D.W. eller af småaktiga kotterivyer och betänkligheter."

5. Page 638: "När dagens ästetkotteriers skrala domar länge sedan äro glömda, skall *Gustaf Vasa* med sina syskonarbeten ha sin obestridda plats bland det svenska dramats klassiska verk."

6. "Om Vasa-sagan, Aug. Strindbergs mäktiga dramatiska trilogi, skola akademiska esteter en gång i framtiden bemöda sig, under glad förvåning över, att de samtida litteraturdocenterna inskränkt sig till att skälla i en mänsklig ilska över det, de inte orkat följa. Inte så, som om de framtida snillena på området skulle få mera förståelse av naturen, men de skola tvingas erkänna mästaren efter hans död. Döda genier måste nämligen t.o.m. akademidocenter erkänna."

7. "I det Strindbergska dramat pulserar livet alljämt lika starkt. Intet teaterdamm i världen kommer någonsin att fördunkla den centrala ges-

taltens monumentalitet. Det beror på . . . diktarens geniala grepp på det mänskliga hos riksuppbyggaren."

8. "Det är helt enkelt vårt klassiska nationella skådespel."

Chapter 8

Translations: C. D. Locock's and Joan Bulman's (London: Anglo-Swedish Literary Foundation, 1931) and Walter Johnson's *The Vasa Trilogy* (Seattle: University of Washington Press, 1959). All quotations from the play are from my translation.

For an analysis of *Erik XIV* and the historical background, see the introduction and the notes in my translation. Martin Lamm in *Strindbergs dramer* (2 vols.; Stockholm: Bonnier, 1924-26), Joan Bulman, in *Strindberg and Shakespeare: Shakespeare's Influence on Strindberg's Historical Drama* (London: Jonathan Cape, Ltd., 1933), and the standard Swedish histories of Swedish literature consider the play.

No adequate account of the stage history of *Erik XIV* exists. See Yngve Hedvall, *Strindberg på Stockholmsscenen 1876-1922* (Stockholm: Lundström, 1923), and Gunnar Ollén, *Strindbergs dramatik* (Stockholm: Radiotjänst, 1948, 1961), however.

1. John Landquist, *Strindbergs Samlade skrifter* (55 vols.; Stockholm: Bonnier, 1912-20), L, 75-76.

2. *Ibid.*, pp. 80-81.

3. *Ibid.*, p. 248.

4. Erik XIV. Half Tysk, Styfbarn, Nero.

Akt I. Nils Stures hemkomst med Renatas nej. (Renata Kristian II's dotterdotter, arfsrätt till Norge och Danmark)./ Sture skymfas. Karin och folket försvara honom. Johan ålägges gifta sig med Katarina Jagellonica. Göran P. ställer sig in hos Karin. Försonas med Erik. Nils Gyllenstjerna från England. 10,000 daler för Leicesters lif.

Akt II. Karins fästman upptäckes och dränkes. Maximilian fänrik. Erik bränner och härjar i Blekinge. Nils Sture vägrar nedhugga Danskar i Vester Götland. Johan fängslas. Erik hatar och afvundas Johan som gjort bättre parti än han.

Akt III. Alkemi, svart magi/ Sturemorden/ Johan släppes. Göran fängslas. Erik tror sig afsatt och fången.

Act IV. Bröllopet med Karin. Inga gäster komma; endast svärfadren och slägten. Erik snobbar demokrat, passar upp gästerna. Blir sedan full

och sparkar ut dem. Erik och Görans nachspiel. Karin får gå och lägga
sig: sedan Erik upptäckt att Karin varnat hertigarna.

Akt V. Erik fängslas. Göran pinas. Hertigarna komma. Göran P: Har
ingen ett godt ord om honom: Agda svarar.

5. Erik XIV.

Akt I. Eriks frierier afslås./ Akt II. Johan fängslas. Akt III. Sture-
morden. Akt IV. Giftermålet. Akt V. Fängslingen.

6. "Föreställningen, som bevistades af prins Eugen, slutade kl. nära
elfva och följdes af en nästan oräknelig rad af framkallanden. Hrr De
Wahl och Svennberg framträdde gång på gång och mottogos af starka
handklappningar. Då ropen på författaren länge fortforo, tillkännagaf
direktör Ranft, att hr Strindberg ej vore på scenen närvarande. Slutligen
framropades äfven hr Molander och blef föremål för publikens hyllning."

7. "Måhända skulle i denna anmälning skådespelets fel mindre ut-
förligt framhållits, därest ej det fanatiska jubelsorl, hvarmed oförstån-
diga beundrare nu i likt och olikt upphöja hr Strindberg, gjorde det till
en pligt att anställa en liten sofring. De, som med verklig eftertanke
genomläsa hr Strindbergs 'Erik XIV,' skola ej kunna undgå att med-
gifva riktigheten af de anmärkningar, som här ofvan uttalats. Det må
vara en annan af denna tidnings medarbetare förbehållet att, när stycket
gått öfver scenen, uttala sig om spelet. Intet spelsätt, vore det än aldrig
så öfverlägset, skulle kunna förändra det omdöme, som i denna uppsats
—efter gång på gång förnyad genomläsning—fälts öfver själva arbetet."

Chapter 9

Translation: Walter Johnson's (Seattle: University of Washington
Press, 1957, and New York: The American-Scandinavian Foundation,
1957). All quotations from the play are from this translation.

For the historical background and an analysis of the play, see the introduction and the notes for my translation as published in 1957. Nils
Ahnlund's *Gustaf Adolf the Great* (New York: American-Scandinavian
Foundation, 1940) and Michael Roberts' *Gustavus Adolphus, A History
of Sweden, 1611-1632* (New York: Longmans, Green & Co., 1953, 1958)
are scholarly biographies useful for comparison with Strindberg's interpretation and for full treatments of both Gustav Adolf and his period.
See also Martin Lamm's *Strindbergs dramer* (2 vols.; Stockholm: Bon-

nier, 1924-26), and Gunnar Ollén's *Strindbergs dramatik* (Stockholm: Radiotjänst, 1948, 1961).

1. John Landquist, *Strindbergs Samlade skrifter* (55 vols.; Stockholm: Bonnier, 1912-20), L, 249-50.

2. See my article, "Strindberg's *Gustav Adolf* and Lessing," *SS*, XXVIII, No. 1, 1-8.

3. See page 27 of the introduction to my translation.

4. See the preface to *Lady Julie*.

5. Page 569: "Läst är Strindbergs Gustaf Adolf ett mästerverk med många fel. På scenen blir den säkerligen enbart ett mästerverk." P. 568: "Ett af hans förnämsta konstmedel är det enkla att oupphörligt säga om samma sak. Så i hans underligt gripande Advent, så, fast naturligtvis mindre, här. Det är också på detta sätt han lyckas skapa den stämning af krigets fasa, af medlidande med allt, allt, af bäfvan för Herrens underliga vägar, som fyller och bär hela stycket. Han har skickligt förhöjt den genom några enskildheter af egendomlig mystisk glans, som hägringen öfver Östersjön och korsen vid Lützen. Han har också höjt den genom sitt sätt att forma replikerna: högtidligt och enkelt, mystiskt och naivt."

6. ". . . ett mäktigt tänkt och, frånser man författarens vanliga, som det tyckes obotliga, nycker och okonstnärligheter, även brett och stort utfört skådespel. . . . Men frånser man sambandet med verkligheten och betraktar Strindbergs Gustaf Adolf som en drömfigur i och för sig är skildringen av stor skönhet och ett vemodigt djup. En sådan innerlighet och nobel älskvärdhet har Strindberg icke skänkt många av sina gestalter, och de scener mot slutet, i vilka man ser hjälten bjuda sig själv som offer till ödet, hava en grandios melankoli. . . ."

7. "Hvad nu min karaktärsskildring af Gustav Adolf beträffar, så är den så trogen alla svenska traditioner att den äcklar tyskarne. Ljus, gladlynt, galant, men med detta tragedidrag, blodskulden från fädernet; hvarmed jag äfven motiverar hans intimitet med generalerna, hvilka ju äfven äro hans släktingar."

8. "Hans personliga tapperhet har jag i flera scener framhållit. Att han däremot var upprörd och nervös natten och morgonen före Lützen, det berättas detaljeradt i häfdaböckerna, och är alldeles i sin ordning. Han gick till och med före slaget omkring såsom utom sig, sjungande psalmer. Nu skulle jag fråga de svenske, som beskyllt mig att ha 'dragit ner' Gustaf

Adolf, hvarutinnan denna neddragning består. Vore de uppriktiga, skulle de svara, 'emedan ni icke gjort honom till helgon.' '—Men I tron ju icke på helgon. Et cetera, i evighet, Amen!' "

9. "Gustaf Adolf har nu varit ute och blifvit bedömd. Jag känner såsom om ett orimligt hat urladdade sig emot mig, och såsom om detta hat hotade mig med faror och ändå har jag skrifvit min dram på god tro att jag skulle bilägga gamla stridigheter."

10. "I dag läste jag om Gustaf Adolf som jag ej sett på tre år—och jag återfick min ljusa glada tro på verket, som man beröfvade mig för tre år sen. Nu är jag besluten—att, i Samlade Dram. Arb. hvilkas tryckning pågår—stryka Apotheosen. Den är öfverflödig! Och är Svenskt skryt! Denna apotheos förnedrar stycket till festspel eller Tillfällighetsstycke! Nu är det ett karaktersdrama med utveckling, och en tragedi med skuld."

11. "I exemplaret har Strindberg gjort strykningar och ändringar för att förkorta pjäsen. Detta är antagligen det exemplar, som Landquist omnämner på sid. 282 i vol. 32 av Strindbergs Samlade skrifter."

12. "Dramat är förkortat till hälften, halva personalen är struken, roller äro hopslagna, och den farliga Vasaborg borttagen, ehuru Vasaborgska gravkoret står kvar, på baksidan af Riddarholmskyrkan."

13. "Icke vill du fördärfva oss, vi äro ju människor. Wennersten har riskerat kapital, och jag har återigen nedlagt fåfängt arbete på omarbetning och uppsättning, och dock gratis! Säg nu ja till min kanske sista begäran."

14. "På teatern försiggår det mesta af talscenerna och på arenan de stumma scenerna som än utgöras af flyktingar, marodörer, hungrande hopar, likbärare med fyllda bårar, symboliserande krigets fasor, än af krigiska scener, inmarscherande af trupper till häst och fot, järnklädda ryttare, hakesskyttar, landsknektar med hillebarder, än deras feberhetsade uttåg till strid vid trumpeters smatter och trummors dån."

15. ". . . en stor seger både för dramat och dess entusiastiska iscensättare. . . . föreställningen i går ådagalade till fullo dess [styckets] utomordentliga sceniska möjligheter. Gustaf Adolf är utan tvivel Strindbergs praktfullaste, teatraliskt mest storslagna drama, och aldrig har hans sceniska fantasi utvecklat sig ståtligare än i detta skådespels glansfulla och poetiskt suggestiva uppträden och processioner. . . . Gustaf Adolf är framförallt ett drama om kriget, om segerns storhet, om brottets,

lasternas, sjukdomarnas och dödens fasor, som följa i dess spår. . . . Det blev en minnesvärd afton."

Chapter 10

Translation: Walter Johnson's *Strindberg's Queen Christina, Charles XII, Gustav III* (Seattle: University of Washington Press, 1955, and New York: The American-Scandinavian Foundation, 1955). All quotations from the play are from this translation.

For the historical background, see the introduction and notes to my translation. See also Frans G. Bengtsson's *The Life of Charles XII, King of Sweden 1697-1718* (Stockholm: Norstedt, 1960); Bengtsson's *The Sword Does Not Jest* (New York: St. Martin's Press, Inc., 1960); Martin Lamm's *Strindbergs dramer* (2 vols.; Stockholm: Bonnier, 1924-26); and Gunnar Ollén's *Strindbergs dramatik* (Stockholm: Radiotjänst, 1948, 1961).

1. For an account of the celebration of Charles XII by Swedish writers of poetry, drama, and prose fiction, see Olov Westerlund's *Karl XII i svensk litteratur från Dahlstierna till Tegnér* (Lund: Gleerup, 1951). Undoubtedly the most universally known and admired treatments at least until recently were Esaias Tegnér's and Erik Gustaf Geijer's lyrics, "Karl XII" and "Ord till Karl XII:s marsch vid Narva." A few years before Strindberg wrote his play, the neoromantic Verner von Heidenstam— once Strindberg's friend but by 1901 his enemy—wrote *Karolinerna* (1897-98; translated by C. W. Stork as *The Charles Men*, [New York: American-Scandinavian Foundation, 1920]), a "novel" in which Charles is interpreted as a noble and tragic hero.

2. Voltaire's *L'Histoire de Charles XII* (1731) is available in English translation in Everyman's Library (New York: E. P. Dutton & Co.). See Samuel Johnson's *The Vanity of Human Wishes* for his treatment of Charles.

3. John Landquist, *Strindbergs Samlade skrifter* (55 vols.; Stockholm: Bonnier, 1912-20), L, 251.

4. *Ibid.,* pp. 251-53.

5. See my translation of *Strindberg's Queen Christina, Charles XII, Gustav III,* p. 101.

6. See Carl E. W. L. Dahlström's *Strindberg's Dramatic Expressionism* (Ann Arbor: University of Michigan Press, 1930).

7. "Konungen ställes i ett högst sympatiskt ljus i Strindbergs drama. Där skildras människan, som af händelser och förhållanden alltså ödet, föres sin väg framåt, och icke blott en historisk personlighet, som numera har mest intresse för biografer och historieskrifvare. Det är det stora i Strindbergs senaste diktning, att han öfvergått till att skildra människor, för alla tider gällande människokaraktärer. . . . Är det förmätet att spå —slutar korrespondenten—att 'Karl den tolfte,' som nu refuserats, i en framtid kommer att blifva en af de allra mest omtyckta af Strindbergs svenskhistoriska dramer?"

8. ". . . den vankelmodige, den svage, som ledes af 'makterna,' ej af sin egen stålsatta vilja och karaktär, despot i botten mellan utbrotten af detta lynne böjlig för både personer och omständigheter. Och så gör hr Strindberg honom *feg!!*"

9. ". . . given i några korta antydande drag."

10. "Ett drama som detta får inte spelas med bortseende ifrån allt det lösa, impressionistiska i sättet, varpå det är gjort, ej med försök att så gott sig göra låter skilja över dessa 'brister.' Det skulle spelas så som det är med tillvaratagande av den särskilda stämning, som denna lösighet, kantighet, improvisation ger åt scener och figurer. . . . Genom den stämning av ovisshet, som därmed skapas, har Strindberg säkerligen avsett att åt hela stycket ge något spökligt osammanhängande och overkligt."

11. Landquist, *Samlade skrifter*, L, 251.

Chapter 11

Translation: Walter Johnson's *The Saga of the Folkungs, Engelbrekt* (Seattle: University of Washington Press, 1959). All quotations from the play are from this translation.

For the historical background, see my introduction and notes in the above volume. See also Ingvar Andersson's *A History of Sweden* (London: Weidenfeld and Nicolson, 1956), Martin Lamm's *Strindbergs dramer* (2 vols.; Stockholm: Bonnier, 1924-26), and Gunnar Ollén's *Strindbergs dramatik* (Stockholm: Radiotjänst, 1948, 1961).

1. John Landquist, *Strindbergs Samlade skrifter* (55 vols.; Stockholm: Bonnier, 1912-20), L, 245.

2. "ENGELBRECHT. Karakters-Drama. Idé-drama. Miniatyr-målningar,

intimt. Engelbrechts enskilda lif skildras såsom detta påverkas af de stora historiska händelserna."

3. Akt I. I skogen vid Kolmilorna: lördagsafton. Margarethadagen. Bergsmän stiga upp ur grufhålet med lyktor. Bönder med lior och räfsor. En minnestötte af gravris med de tre Rikenas vapen./ I Engelbrechts hem. [Note variations in Strindberg's spelling of Engelbrekt.] Akt II. Hos Konung Erik. Akt III. På Herredagen./ Engelbrecht får göra om alltsammans. Akt IV. Engelbrecht förbigången. Akt V. Engelbrecht mördas.

4. Scen III. I Dalarne. Hemma hos Engelbrecht; Hustrun går sin väg./ Dotterns kärleksförhållande till Måns Bengtssons son uppdagas. Sonen är redan borta. Huset öde. Scen IV. Herremötet. Engelbrechts tvivel./ Konungen bryter tro och lofven. Engelbrecht måste göra om allt. Scen V. Karl Knutsson väljes. Scen VI. Engelbrekt mördas./ Barnen måste skiljas./ Göksholms Slott brinner.

5. Akt I. Engelbrekt har tagit Måns Bengtssons Brud. *Milstolpen på en landsväg i Dalarne.* Engelbrechts son Karl och Dotter. Man ser pålar vid hvilka bönder varit bundna. Intresset går blind. *Hemma hos Engelbrekt.* Biskop Styrbjörn. Barnen berätta om fremmande land. Måns Bengtssons son Harald och Engelbrechts dotter.

Akt II. Hos Jösse Eriksson. Elgjagt—Björn. Orgie: Biskopen förgår sig. Man hör bönder skrika. Biskop Arnold Clementson, Måns Bengtsson Natt och Dag, Karl Knutsson, Erik Puke, Kristiern Nilsson Vase på besök. Engelbrekt med barn och hustru komma. Gårdsrätten. Margarethas mot Magnus Eriksons. Jens Erikson anställer Karl Engelbrekt i sin svit. Brytning mellan Engelbrekt och Måns Bengtsson. Järtecknet: Mannen som bröt benet. Sammansvärjning. Gullhjelmarne. Biskop Styrbjörn.

Akt III. Riksråden. Engelbrekt har underhandlat med Erik XIII; då blir folket misstänksamt. Engelbrekt vald Rikshöfvitsman. Tror sig vara framme. Hybris. De Fyra Stånden. *Hemma hos Engelbrekt.* Alla öfverge honom.

Akt IV. Riksföreståndarvalet. Engelbrekt förbigås. Får börja om igen. Akt V. *Engelbrekt mördas.* Ensam på bryggan.

6. Landquist, *Samlade skrifter*, L, 245-47.

7. "Jag har läst om Engelbrekt; den är bara 66 sidor: behöfver icke

strykas, ty den är redan Intim. Men Du får icke imitera stor teater. Spela med kolonner och fonder. Engelbrekts rum får vi förvandla till stenhus: ta Dödsdansens tornrum, som stämmer med kolonnerna. Och bygg icke. Inga pålar och inga brovakterstuga i Ia akten. Inga grip och ingen syn på gästabudet. Låtsas i kulissen. Inga folkscener: bara *en* bågskytt. Inga smeder, bara *en* smed. Ingen sång, bara recitering af en smed. Ungdoms-skaran representeras af *en,* som syns i kulissen, låtsande att de andra stå bakom. Försök icke det omöjliga, och misslyckas! Bryt icke programmet: Intimt."

8. ". . . den lösliga och virriga kompositionen."

9. "Där var det en tragisk storhet över Engelbrekts figuren. Denne är för övrigt i sina stora omfattande drag väl tänkt. Det är den lugne, still-samme, rättrådige mannen, som sent och nästan mot sin vilja drives till stor och ingripande handling, som då ser sin personliga lycka krossas och i stället griper efter ärans och maktens fantom, som han icke själv tror på och som äfven glider ur hans händer och förflyktigas."

Chapter 12

Translation: Walter Johnson's *Strindberg's Queen Christina, Charles XII, Gustav III* (Seattle: University of Washington Press, 1955, and New York: The American-Scandinavian Foundation, 1955). All quotations from the play are from this translation. See the introduction and notes to this translation for the historical background. See also Ingvar Andersson's *A History of Sweden* (London: Weidenfeld and Nicolson, 1956), Martin Lamm's *Strindbergs dramer* (2 vols.; Stockholm: Bonnier, 1924-26), and Gunnar Ollén's *Strindbergs dramatik* (Stockholm: Radiotjänst, 1948, 1961).

1. John Landquist, *Strindbergs Samlade skrifter* (55 vols.; Stockholm: Bonnier, 1912-20), L, 241-43.

2. *Ibid.,* p. 250.

3. See, for example, Ellie Schleussner's translation of *En dåres försvars-tal* (*The Confession of a Fool* [Boston: Small, Maynard and Co., 1913]) and Arvid Paulson's translation of many of Strindberg's letters to Harriet Bosse (*Letters of Strindberg to Harriet Bosse,* ed. and trans. Arvid Paul-son [New York: Thomas Nelson & Sons, 1959]), both of which give illuminating treatments of his marriages to the two actresses.

4. "Kristina får icke försumma stora scenen i Räknekammaren, der

hvarje ord är en knif; och hon skall se efter om den hugger. . . . Oxenstjerna och De la Gardie vexla blickar hela scenen."

5. He wrote to Falck: "Mitt finaste arbete med fulländad teknik, karaktärer genomförda i detalj, den största kvinnoroll på svenska, de vackraste kärleksförklaringar som finnas . . . spelat som fulla verkligheten."

6. Per-Axel Branner's *Vår lilla teater* (Stockholm: Bonnier, 1944), pp. 81-91.

Chapter 13

Translation: Walter Johnson's *Strindberg's Queen Christina, Charles XII, Gustav III* (Seattle: University of Washington Press, 1955, and New York: The American-Scandinavian Foundation, 1955). All quotations from the play are from this translation. For the historical background, see the introduction and notes. See also Martin Lamm's *Strindbergs dramer* (2 vols.; Stockholm: Bonnier, 1924-26), Gunnar Ollén's *Strindbergs dramatik* (Stockholm: Radiotjänst, 1948, 1961), Ingvar Andersson's *A History of Sweden* (London: Weidenfeld and Nicolson, 1956); and R. N. Bain's *Gustavus III and His Contemporaries, 1746-1792* (London: K. Paul, Trench, Trübner & Co., 1894).

1. John Landquist, *Strindbergs Samlade skrifter* (55 vols.; Stockholm: Bonnier, 1912-20), L, 250.

2. *Strindberg's Queen Christina, Charles XII, Gustav III*, p. 179.

3. "I dag ges Strindbergs historiska skådespel *Gustaf III*, för hundrade gången på Intima teatern. Regien är berömvärd, uppsättningen god, aktörerna utan vank och lyte. Hr Hanssons teckning af tjusarkonungen är i många fall intressant, en personligt egenartad skapelse, som väl förtjänar att lofordas, äfven om man ej i allo delar publikens och kritikens förtjusning. Men pjäsen—och Gustaf III? . . . Mången, som i afton applåderar August Strindbergs underliga missfoster, hade kanske godt af at minnas, hur den verklige Gustaf såg ut!"

4. "En del av den stockholmska kritiken har inte kunnat förlåta Strindberg den lysande succesen med 'Gustaf III.' . . . Den breda publiken har med oförvillad känsla fällt sin dom. Men detta Strindbergska drama har, som månget annat av hans hand, en för stark omedelbarhet, en för våldsam rikedom av liv för att inte bringa i uppror klena sinnen, liksom de ovan nämnda herrarnas, som är ut och är in fylla tålmodiga

spalter med sina floskler, men aldrig skådat en skön verklighet i ögat."

5. ". . . trots den sura kritiken."

6. Pp. 149-50: "Tanken att ge Strindbergs aldrig spelade Gustaf III växte sig allt starkare hos mig. Jag visste ju vad man ansåg om stycket, men jag trodde på att det skulle visa sig äga den underbara Strindbergska egenskapen att vid själva framförandet få ett oanat sceniskt liv. Det fanns i Strindbergs Gustaf III enligt min mening så mycket som först då skulle komma till sin rätt."

Chapter 14

No English translation is at present available. All quotations from the play are my own translations.

1. John Landquist, *Strindbergs Samlade skrifter* (55 vols.; Stockholm: Bonnier, 1912-20), LIV, 364-65.

2. "Jag älskar stycket och sätter det bland mina bästa."

3. "Jag har varnat Er for Gustaf Adolf; den är obegriplig och måste vara osympatisk för Preussaren. Hvad vet Tysken om Gustaf Adolfs blodskuld från Carl IXe och Linköpingsherrarne? Det är mitt tragiska motiv! dock! Derför skref jag: Tag Luther i stället! Den känner I! Jag läste i går om Luther! Den gaf mig kraft och ljus! Den är det starkaste och yngsta jag skrifvit! Inga tvifvel som Mäster Olof, inga skrupler, inga qvinnor om halsen, inga föräldrar i vägen, inga kompromisser med vänner. Och sådan är den historiske traditionelle Luther."

4. "Strindbergs Lutherpjäs, som spelats med ganska stor publikframgång i Tyskland, har nu genom Svenska teatern införlivats med svensk repertoar. Det är intet dramatiskt verk Strindberg har åstadkommit, veterligen har han heller aldrig gjort anspråk på att det skall betraktas som ett arbete med scenisk spänning. Det saknar alldeles rummets, tidens, handlingens enhet. Det hela är en serie tablåer, hela fjorton stycken, där Luther och flera av hans bemärkta samtida spela sina mer eller mindre karakteristiska roller. Den enda mera dramatiska figuren i pjäsen är doktor Johannes Faust, men han uppträder som ett slags deus ex machina."

Chapter 15

Translation: Only *Moses* is available at present in English. Edwin Björkman's translation appeared in 1916 in *Plays by August Strindberg*

(5th series; New York: Charles Scribner's Sons). Quotations from the trilogy are my own translations.

1. "Frågan blir sedan om jag i en serie dramer af värde kan få in min synoptiska synpunkt, och om jag kan få tillräckligt många lefvande karakterer utan att upprepa mig—hvilket jag betviflar. Min upptäckt är ju 'Den medvetna viljan' som uppenbarar sig på flera ställen af jorden samtidigt, och i skönlitteratur får man icke servera upptäckter utan endast operera med och referera till kända saker."

2. "Nu kommer Serien! 20 stycken, *fristående,* men med den osynliga tråden, som gör perlbandet!"

3. G. Carlheim-Gyllensköld, *Samlade otryckta skrifter* (2 vols.; Stockholm: Bonnier, 1918-19), I, 6: "Denna Trilogi, som äfven kallats Moses-Sokrates-Kristus, utgör de tre första delarna af en större oafslutad cykel 'Verldshistoriska Dramer,' hvaruti Näktergalen i Wittenberg ingår som den elfte. —En affattning af samma ämnen i novellistisk form finnes i Historiska Miniatyrer, i följande berättelser: Egyptiska träldomen; Hemicykeln i Athen, Alkibiades, Sokrates: Leontopolis, Lammet, Vilddjuret. Förevarande tre stycken skrefvos 1905 och påtänktes till uppförande 1908 på den förenklade teatern eller draperibanan, med rörliga fonder och barrièreemblemer på scenen. För att ännu mer förenkla kunna flera af fonderna till de 55 tablåerna repeteras, så att inalles blott 15 olika fonder behöfva användas. Se dispositionen af fonder som meddelas som bihang i det följande."

4. *Ibid.,* p. 197:

Moses.	*Sokrates.*	*Kristus.*
Bågen: Palmer och Sfinxer	Kolonner och Statyer med Cypresser	A. Oliver och en Brunn B. Kolonner, Statyer, Rostra, Pinier
Fonder:	Fonder:	Fonder:
1. Tempel	1. Parthenon	A
2. Pyramider	2. Gardin	
3. Sinai	3. Gardin	1. Betlehem
4. Se N:o 1	4. Se n:o 1	2. Samma
5. Öknen	5. Se n:o 1	3. N:o 1 från Moses Soltempel
6. Se N:o 5	6. Gardin	
7. D:o	7. Gardin	4. Gardin

8. D:o	8. N:o 1	5. N:o 15 från Moses
9. Se n:o 3	9. Gardin	För-gården
10. D:o	10. N:o 1	6. Templet i Jerusalem
11. D:o	11. Gardin	7. Samma
12. D:o	12. Gardin	8. Samma
13. Se n:o 3	13. N:o 1	9. Gardin
14. Tabernaklet	14. D:o	10. Golgatha
15. Dess För-gård	15. Gardin	B
16. Se n:o 5	16. N:o 6	11. Gardin
17. D:o	17. Gardin	12. Gardin
18. D:o	18. Tempel	13. Gardin
19. D:o	19. Fängelse	14. Katakomberna
20. D:o		Gardin
21. Nebo och Kanan		15. Rom och Förgrund
7 Fonder	3 Fonder	5 Fonder

S:a 15 Fonder

5. Martin Lamm, *Strindbergs dramer* (2 vols.; Stockholm: Bonnier, 1924-26) II, 355: "Han har aldrig åstadkommit något jämmerligare än denna trilogi. Det första dramat, *Från öknar till arvland,* är en dramatisering av Moses' historia från födelsen med en trofast och träaktig anslutning till bibeln, som närmast kommer verket att erinra om vår reformationstids naiva bibeldramer. I det andra stycket, *Hellas,* möta vi alla de stora männen från Hellas' blomstringstid, talande med varandra i de platonska dialogernas manér. Intresset koncentreras snart på Sokrates' äktenskapliga lidanden, vilka Strindberg framställer med mycken medkänsla. I det tredje dramat, *Lammet och Vilddjuret,* råder fullkomlig Offenbachsstämning."

6. *Det moderna dramat* (Stockholm: Bonnier, 1948): "Strindberg är det moderna dramats djärvaste och poetiskt störste experimentator," i.e., "Strindberg is modern drama's most daring and poetically greatest experimenter." The American translation of *Det moderna dramat* was published in 1953 as *The Modern Drama* (New York: The Philosophical Library).

Chapter 16

Translations: Walter Johnson's *The Last of the Knights, The Regent, Earl Birger of Bjälbo* (Seattle: University of Washington Press, 1956). All quotations from the plays are from these translations. See the introduction and the notes for the historical background.

1. Anders Fryxell's *Berättelser ur svenska historien* (Stockholm: Norstedt, 1900), II, 182-84: "Herr Sten Sture den yngre var, liksom hans far, en mycket förnämlig och utmärkt man i många ting. Rättskaffens men ödmjuk inför Gud, redlig och trofast mot människor, klok och skarpsinnig i rådslag, tapper och oförskräckt i strid; allt detta var han, liksom fadern, men därtill var han mycket mera mild, vänlig och godhjärtad än herr Svante. Ofta såg man honom som ung gosse med tårar knäböja för att blidka sin fader, då dennes häftiga sinne uppbrusade mot fega, falska eller försumliga tjänare; och han räddade sålunda mången från de hårdaste straff. Samma milda, försonliga sinnelag bibehöll han äfven, sedan han växt upp, och var därför af folket älskad. Men hans bästa vänner, som just för denna egenskap så mycket älskade honom, klagade öfver att samma mildhet förledde honom till lättrogenhet och alltför stor efterlåtenhet mot fiender. . . . Han reste beständigt kring landet för att lära känna folkets tillstånd, och både hans öra och hjärta voro då öppna för de klagomål, som af menigheten anfördes; ty han ville beskydda alla, så lärd som lekman, så hög som ringa, att ingen skulle lida någon orättvisa under hans regering. Han betraktade sig utan skrymteri som sina undersåtars fader; han sökte icke sina nöjen och sin fördel utan uppoffrade för folkets väl sin tid och sina krafter, ja, slutligen sitt lif."

2. C. George Starbäck och P. O. Bäckström's *Berättelser ur svenska historien* (Stockholm: Beijer, 1885), II, 640: "Han kom alldeles icke åter såsom Sten Stures vän, utan som hans fiende. Hatet bodde i hans hjerta och andra förbindelser bestämde hans handlingssätt. För öfrigt var han till sitt sinnelag alldeles densamme, hvilken vi sågo såsom gosse drifva sin vilja igenom mot sin moder. Det mål, han en gång gjort till sitt, afvek han aldrig ifrån; för det offrade han allt. Och detta mål var nu hämnd, äfven om dess utkräfvande skulle leda till fosterlandets undergång."

3. *The Last of the Knights, The Regent, Earl Birger of Bjälbo*, pp. 4-5.

4. "Rolen som sådan är icke stark; goda menniskor ta sig icke ut på

scenen; verldens ondska är så stor att man gerna ler åt den godtrogne som anser vara en pligt att låta lura sig; den godtrogne förefaller lätt enfaldig. Lyckligtvis är Sturens godtrogenhet i stor skala, principiel, byggd på den kristne Riddarens ideelt religiösa syn på tingen, och det accentueras ju af 'de andra' att han icke är enfaldig, och icke mes: 'Fast och frimodig, men tålmodig och saktmodig.' Han går ju som ett godt barn midt i ondskan och sveket, och förstår inte hur menskor kunna vara så gemena: och han tror som kristen att det onda kan öfvervinnas med det goda. (Men den onde Gustaf Trolle förstår å sin sida icke hur man kan vara så 'dum!') Att få stadga, hållning och auktoritet i denna figur fordrar att Du diktar in hela personen i din person; den födde herrskaren skall synas, men icke så mycket i åtbörd och stram hållning, utan kännas i hela hans väsen. Du får hjelpa diktaren att dikta figuren ånyo, och Du får göra starkare än jag gjort. Begagna din kraftiga röst men med en human timbre, välvillig, godsinnad men stark. Stark men icke hård, och aldrig grymm. Medlidande, men icke pjåsk, ädel men icke så der 'S-t ädel' så det verkar pose. Det är hans natur, som Du skall sätta Dig in i, så att din framställning verkar natur."

5. Yngve Hedvall's *Strindberg på Stockholmsscenen 1870-1922* (Stockholm: Lundström, 1923), p. 173.

6. "Det är omöjligt att ej gripas af detta verk med dess klarhet, kraft och nobless, dess härliga repliker—dess svenskhet."

7. "Det hela gör sig mycket förträffligt från scenen och det dramatiska intresset hållas levande från början till slut. Strindbergs utomordentliga blick för vad som gör sig på scenen, och hans mästerskap att dramatiskt forma ut detaljscener, göra personer levande och replikerna kärnfasta, förnekar sig ej heller här. Därigenom blev ock föreställningen intressant och underhållande. . . . Salongen var fullsatt och bifallet livligt."

Chapter 17

Translation: Walter Johnson's *The Last of the Knights, The Regent, Earl Birger of Bjälbo* (Seattle: University of Washington Press, 1956). All quotations from the play are from this translation. For the historical background, see the introduction and notes to the translation.

1. John Landquist, *Strindbergs Samlade skrifter* (55 vols.; Stockholm: Bonnier, 1912-20), L, 254-58.

2. The introduction to my translation, p. 174.

3. Landquist, *Samlade skrifter*, L, 257.

4. "Det är humör, lif och fart öfver scenerna, en uppfinningsrikedom och en omväxling . . . som dock icke stör den dramatiska koncentration och spänningen, replikerna glänsa—som ju nästan alltid—af en mästerlig språkkonst."—March 26-27, 1909.

5. "Bjälbojarlens framtid synes mig fullt betryggad. Dramat är ingalunda en lös samling historiska tablåer, det äger . . . en allt dominerande hufvudfigur, kring hvars själshistoria på lifvets vändpunkt det bildar en säker enhet." —March 27, 1909.

Index